TONY HORWITZ'S

ONE
FOR THE
ROAD

"Pull over and stop for Tony Horwitz. He is that rare traveler who does not disappoint." —Ted Conover, author of *Coyotes*

"Ironical, perceptive and subtle . . . will have readers getting out their maps and itching to follow Horwitz's tracks . . . The internal journey is his finest achievement; he allows the reader into his heart, to go travelling with him there, sharing his adventures of the spirit."
—*Times on Sunday*

"*One for the Road* is a delight. . . . Tony Horwitz is a fine, witty, perceptive and occasionally even elegant writer who, I'd say, acquired in the span of a year or so more knowledge about Australia than most Australians will ever have. . . . A true and loving portrait painted from the outside." —*The Newcastle Herald*

"A fascinating insight into what we're all about on the highways and byways along the outback track." —*The Telegraph* (Sydney)

"Three cheers for Tony Horwitz. . . . Perhaps it takes a foreigner to properly show us our own land. . . . Horwitz brings a new eye to an old landscape." —*The Sydney Morning Herald*

VINTAGE DEPARTURES

TONY HORWITZ

ONE
FOR THE
ROAD

HITCHHIKING THROUGH THE
AUSTRALIAN OUTBACK

VINTAGE BOOKS

A Division of Random House New York

To all the people who gave me rides.
And to Geraldine, who picked me up for good.

First Vintage Departures Edition, June 1988

Copyright © 1987 by Tony Horwitz

Library of Congress Cataloging-in-Publication Data
Horwitz, Tony, 1958–
One for the road.
(Vintage departures)
Reprint. Originally published: Sydney;
New York:
Harper & Row, 1987.
1. Australia—Description and travel—1981–   .
2. Hitchhiking—Australia.
3. Horwitz, Tony, 1958–   .
I. Title.
DU105.2.H67   1988   919.4'0463   87-40476
ISBN 0-394-75817-X (pbk.)

Book design by Debbie Glasserman

Manufactured in the United States of America
10 9 8 7 6 5 4 3 2 1

CONTENTS

Let any man lay the map of Australia before him, and regard the blank upon its surface, and then let me ask him if it would not be an honourable achievement to be the first to place foot in its centre.
(*Explorer Charles Sturt in an address to the South Australian colonists*)

Good Heavens, did ever man see such country!
(*Explorer Charles Sturt, in his journal, after trying, and failing, to reach the center in 1845*)

ONE FOR THE ROAD

If a hitchhiker falls in the outback and no one hears him, does he make a sound?

Nothing moves in this landscape, not even the sun. It has been in the same spot for hours, poking a hot skewer into my skull and all the way down to my heels.

The air smells burnt, like a bushfire. But there is nothing to burn out here, just a flat plain of dust and stone. The road cuts across it, a line on blank paper: paper without edges, line without end. And I am the only coordinate, pinned by the sun, waiting for a ride to carry me farther along.

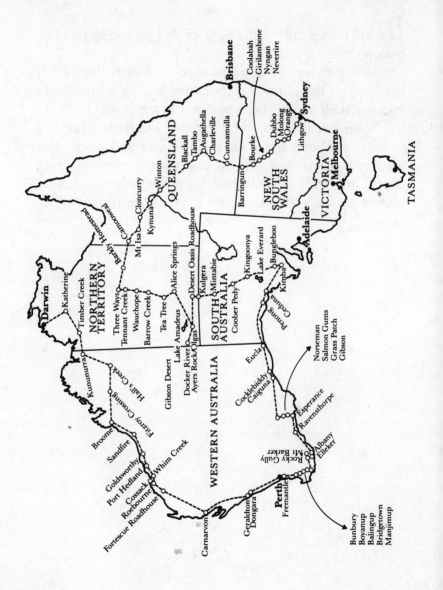

1
GO BUSH, YOUNG MAN

Even aimless journeys have a purpose, I suppose. The seed for an outback ramble was planted a year before the trip actually began, when I awoke in the final hours of a daylong flight to Sydney. The moment seemed important—a desert dawn, a new year, a new country—so I unstuck my kidneys from the armrest, opened a virgin journal, and recorded my first impression of the continent on which I was soon to land.

Jan 1. Australian airspace

It looks like a massive vacant lot down there. Ridge upon ridge of sand and stone, splashed with saltpans, stretching to a thin strip of red on the horizon. If an alien probe landed here it would say 'no life' and go home.

For a few dreamy months I was that alien probe, albeit in Sydney. I bolted awake at dawn to the sound of kookaburras laughing like madwomen outside my window. I went to the pub and ordered beer—"Tooth's Old" or "schooner of New"—just to hear the strange silly words spill from my lips. I listed like a 12-meter yacht under the weight of Australian coins.

And I wrote endless letters to America about the curious customs of my adopted land. "Lawn care is very big here," my parents learned a few days after my arrival in Sydney. "On weekends all the 'blokes' are out in the yard with hoses and 'tinnies' of beer. They dress like little boys in shorts called stubbles (?)."

Before long, I too wore stubbies and lolled in the sun, acquiring the native color. I found a newspaper job my first week in Sydney and that made the conversion even quicker. "Dogs shit on footpaths, not sidewalks!" the editor yelled when I filed my first story, a back-page item on filthy Sydney streets. "And 'trash' is an Americanism, mate. We toss out rubbish."

The next week a press release from the town of Wagga Wagga landed on my desk. I thought it was a misprint; one Wagga seemed improbable enough. "Check the map next time," the copy editor suggested rather coolly. Sure enough, there was Wagga Wagga, not to mention Bong Bong and Woy Woy, or the one-word names that sounded like the fanciful inventions of a four-year-old: Mullumbimby, Bibbenluke, Woolloomooloo.

Those first few months at the newspaper were like my inaugural plunge in the rough Sydney surf: sink or swim. Before long I'd mastered a passable Australian crawl, in and out of the water.

But I was just stroking the surface of things; urban landscapes bear a family resemblance, whatever the hemisphere. And part of me was disappointed. "I wish I could show you a younger people and an older land." Geraldine had written me on a postcard from Australia, three years before. It arrived a few weeks after our first embrace on a grimy sidewalk beside Broadway in New York. The next day we finished graduate school and she flew home to Sydney. I read and reread the card, studied the strange red desert on the other side, and wondered how I'd fallen in love with a woman who lived a hemisphere away.

Then she returned to work in America, and for eighteen months I showed her my land instead—or a frozen, industrial corner of it where we both found jobs, known in those recession days as "the rust bowl." In fact, you couldn't see the rust for all the snow. "Cleveland," a friend wrote to her in the midst of a blizzard, "is a place I have visited only in jokes."

Moving together to Sydney was like a beach party after that.

But 6,000 miles from home, I felt as though I'd entered a mirror image of America. If the words were often different, the world to which they referred was much the same. TV was "telly" but the show was still *Dallas*. The eucalyptus-shaded sprawl of suburban Sydney could have been lifted from Los Angeles. There were even the familiar neon monoliths of McDonald's, or Pizza Hut, or Kentucky Fried Chicken.

The outback I'd glimpsed from the airplane window was foreign enough, but it seemed impossibly remote from urban Australia; my friends in Sydney traveled more readily to Bali than to Alice Springs. They'd titillate me with snatches about the weird outback life: farms as big as European countries, Aborigines on walkabouts, dingoes eating babies, pubs that never closed. But as a journalist I could sniff out hearsay information. I wanted to see the real thing. I wanted to see it firsthand.

The plan itself wafted in with the westerly winds, almost a year after my arrival in Sydney. It was a December day, the first real stinker of summer. Inside the office it was cool, but unnaturally cool, like the vegetable drawer of a refrigerator.

I hit the "kill" button on my keyboard and turned to the reporter at the next desk. I feel like hitchhiking off, I told him, with no route and no timetable, toward the hot red center of the continent. The rides would decide where I went and how long I took to get there.

"In summer? Mate, your brains will fry." His voice was flat and his eyes didn't budge from the computer screen. "That's if you're lucky. Dying of thirst is worse."

The maps I stared at were even less encouraging. I'd imagined a spiderweb of highways through the outback: instead, I found a spindly thread connecting one coast to the other. The literature from the motorists' association was bleaker still. Not only was an "extra spare wheel" required for outback driving, but also "a fan-belt, top and bottom radiator hoses, coil, condenser, spare fuse, light bulbs, puncture repair outfit, tin of brake fluid, roll of plastic insulation tape, 6.35 mm. plastic tubing and a troublelight or torch."

That was just for mechanical emergencies.

"A well-equipped first-aid kit and fire-extinguisher could also be invaluable, while a reserve drum of petrol, food, and 4.55 litres of drinking water per person are necessities." Remembering, of course, that "radiator water, although containing impurities, is a valuable emergency water supply."

With all that gear, how would anyone have room to pick me up? And with that kind of warning, what sort of maniac would venture out there in the first place?

"In addition," the motorists' association cautioned, just in case you hadn't got the point, "your proposed itinerary should be made known in case of mechanical breakdown or even becoming lost, so that a search for you can be more easily and quickly instituted."

Not even mad dogs and Englishmen went out in the desert sun. Certainly not sensible Australians.

But there was still a margin of madness for a road-stricken Yankee. I slipped out of the office one restless afternoon and drove my car toward the hills, just to feel the rubber reaching out for open road. Broadway, the congested street outside my office, eventually becomes the Great Western Highway, shooting straight across the Great Dividing Range.

Romantic names, I thought; Australia's answer to Route 66 and the Appalachians. Instead I found myself crawling along a scar of used-car lots—Petrol Wowser! Low Kilo! Priced to Sell!—connecting one smoggy suburb to another. The mountains were an elusive blur in the distance. I crept back through rush-hour traffic, wondering if it was worth all the bother. I could hitchhike for days and never penetrate the brick veneer skin of suburban Sydney.

This time I sought advice from a workmate who had actually hitchhiked in the bush.

"I was stuck for three days and finally took a Greyhound bus," he told me. Then his eyes narrowed. "Anyway, I was nineteen. Aren't you a little old for this game?"

My ticket was paid for, so to speak, before he finished speaking. I *was* too old. Not physically, though sleeping in roadside ditches didn't hold the romance for me at twenty-seven that it once had at seventeen. It was the outward shape of things that seemed prematurely aged: marriage, mortgage, a bank manager who knew me on a first-name basis. Sometimes I felt like a teenager who gets a jacket with "growing space" then waits and waits for his shoulders to broaden, his chest to expand. Mine hadn't. Surely there was still room for boyish adventures. And if not now, then when?

At least that's how I explained myself to Geraldine one hot night in early January. It was an uncomfortable proposition. She was a journalist too; we were used to separation. But this was different. Three years before, she'd promised to show me an older land. Now I was heading off to see it without her.

"We could drive out there together," she said.

"We could." More pacing. "But there'd be no unplanned adventures."

"We could hitch together, then."

"We could."

We couldn't really. This thing I had for hitchhiking was an extramarital affair—premarital, rather. I wanted to meet up with it alone, in a dark bar someplace, where old memories could be relived and put to rest in private.

For a long time the two of us just sat there at the kitchen table, waiting for a breeze to pass through the house.

"I saw a curious message printed on a T-shirt yesterday," she said with a crooked grin.

"What'd it say?"

"If you love something, set it free. If it doesn't come back to you, hunt it down and kill it."

In the morning I packed my rucksack and caught a ride with Geraldine to the end of my known Australian world: a patch of grass at the fringe of Sydney's red-brick western suburbs.

2
MY FIRST KANGAROO

The wing-tipped Ford swoops across two lanes of traffic and skids to a halt at my feet. A door swings open and I lunge inside as the car weaves back on the road out of Sydney.

"I'm Skip. She's Trish," the driver says, thrusting an oil-stained palm in my direction. I shake with one hand and flail with the other for the passenger door, which is swinging open onto blurry space.

"Tony. Thanks for stopping."

Or slowing at least. Skip says he's headed to a drag race in Lithgow, on the other side of the Blue Mountains. He seems to be doing his warm-up laps en route. The city skyline dips behind a hill and suburbia stops sprawling. Then, as we plunge into rolling farmland, a chorus of carnivorous voices starts wailing from beside the road.

"Fresh Dressed Chickens!" squawks one sign.

"Country Killed Meat!" cries another.

"Pig 4 Sale. Corn and Mash Fed. Good Size 4 the Spit!"

Skip shoves a cassette in the tape deck and the car begins throbbing to the beat of heavy metal. Apparently, this is the cue for further conversation.

"Where ya headed?" he shouts.

"Alice Springs, I guess."

"Yer joking."

"No, really. I'm going to hitch through the outback, maybe write something about it."

"Could be a very long book, mate."

Not if I stay in Skip's Ford: a short story, say, or a tombstone epitaph (Fresh Dressed! Country Killed!). We hit mach I at the base of the Blue Mountains; mach II on the windy ascent.

"I work as a carpenter all week," Skip says. "Pay's okay but anyone can bang a bloody nail. Racing's different. It's dangerous business and not every bloke makes it."

He jerks the Ford across double yellow lines to pass a truck on a blind mountain curve. Trish digs her fingernails into Skip's bare thigh. I close my eyes and hear the dull thud of rubber hitting rabbit flesh. And I decide that Skip isn't going to be one of the blokes that make it.

I abandon ship at the first pit stop, a thirty-second pause for gas about 60 miles west of Sydney. "You staying or what, mate?" Skip yells as I scurry across the highway. Before I can answer, he climbs back in the cockpit and plummets down the mountain.

I drop my pack to the ground and catch my breath. In one great leap, I've pole vaulted out of the city and onto the western slope of the Blue Mountains. From where I stand the foreground is green, but the more distant furrows of the Great Dividing Range are washed in a hazy aquamarine. And they share the gentle beauty of their American cousins, the Blue Ridge Mountains: old and soft and familiar, like well-worn denim jeans.

Very nice. I find a well-shaded spot, suck in the clear mountain air, and inhale a dozen flies. Another dozen divebomb my eyes. And a phalanx of mosquitoes start gnawing at my ears and neck. I grope inside my pack for the tube of insect repellent that I purchased yesterday after a long, technical conversation with a camping goods salesman. I locate it near the bottom of the pack, bleeding onto my clothes and leaving acid burns on my fingers. "An insect killer that doesn't sting is like good-tasting toothpaste," the salesman assured me. "It can't have any guts."

The flies aren't so stupid. They swarm on twice as strong now that the flesh has been basted (Corn and Mash Fed! Good Size 4 the Spit!). I am blind and wretched, wondering which way to run, when a dilapidated Holden putters to a halt.

"Just going a little way up the road," the driver says through the passenger window. I would have settled for a ride in a parked car.

We have traveled only ten minutes when my host, an amiable teenager named Trevor, pulls up at a roadside picnic ground. "Picnic stop," he announces. "I'm shouting." Inside the car's boot is a pile of jagged metal that looks like leftover hardware from the Spanish Inquisition. Trevor walks about 50 yards into the trees, digs a shallow trench, then drops in one of the irons and covers it with dirt.

"Toss my cigarette on that," he says. I do. The trap leaps from its grave like a missile from an underground silo. The cigarette is shredded between metal teeth.

"Bloody ripper, eh?" Trevor says proudly, resetting the trap. "Rabbit's a good feed, except for the head. Want to stick around for supper?"

I decline, and pick my way carefully back to the road. Just two rides and already it's coming back to me—the helpless feeling of climbing into cars with total strangers.

Two rides and already I've crossed a mountain range that the colonists spent twenty-five years struggling to conquer. Charles Wentworth, who was only twenty when he joined the successful expedition in 1813, wrote a poem about how the party "gain'd with toilsome step the topmost heath," to behold the western lands, opening before them like "boundless champagne."

Apparently, this vision led to an immediate hangover. Gregory Blaxland, who was no poet, recorded that the party beat a hasty retreat to Sydney, "their clothes and shoes in particular worn out and all of them ill with Bowel Complaints."

No mention of flies. I make my eyes and nostrils into narrow slits, hold out my finger and stand perfectly still until I finally snag a car. The driver is a farmer, clad in shorts and singlet, with a faint whiff of manure drifting up from his workboots.

"I only take her out for church, and trips to the city," he says, patting the dashboard of the shiny sedan. This is a city trip, to pick up seeds in Orange. "Been to a real city once," he adds, apparently referring to Sydney. "Didn't like it."

He doesn't say a word for the rest of the hour-long drive. I stare out the window at a weed called Patterson's Curse heaving its purple breath across the orchards and paddocks. Occasionally there is a town, but only of the blink-and-you'll-miss-it variety: a pub, a grocery store, a few houses. Blink. Orchards and paddocks again.

Orange is a major metropolis by comparison. And it has the broad main street I've seen in a hundred news photos of country towns: false-front shops, angle parking, and a wide awning shading the footpath. What the photos don't show is that the grand façade of Main Street, New South Wales, is designed like an Old West movie set to mask the nothingness behind. Even in a town with 30,000 people, the side streets fade quickly into a thin layer of housing before dwindling back into the bush.

The shops are silent on Sunday, but there's plenty of traffic. Unfortunately, none of it is moving. Parking on the main street with the radio on is what passes for a Sunday outing in Orange.

I lean my pack against a ten-cent parking meter and watch a thermometer creep toward 85 degrees Fahrenheit. Much worse lies ahead, I know, so I face the sun, purposefully. When I was a child, I used to take off my shoes in early summer and sprint back and forth across the stony driveway, hoping to toughen up my soles for the barefoot months ahead. Maybe I can do the same now and train for the withering heat of the outback.

My first workout lasts ten minutes. I retreat into the shade and take a swig from my waterbag to clear my head. An hour later, a car finally unglues itself from the curb and swings around to pick me up. It's one of those souped-up dragsters with the back wheels raised so high that the grillework is pushed down in front, as if to inhale any loose gravel. The driver, a sullen-looking teenager in black jeans and a black sleeveless vest, moves his arm like a minesweeper across the passenger seat, sending three dozen Coke cans clattering to the floor.

"Hop in, mate. I can get you as far as Molong."

"Thanks for the ride!" I tell him, threading my legs between the can heap and a tangle of fuse wires. It is the one and only obligation of the hitchhiker to seem eternally grateful—and to keep up the chat. Hitchhiking is a big leap of faith for both parties. The driver has no way of knowing if you've just climbed the wall of a maximum-security prison. You have no way of knowing if he's a mugger, rapist, or worse. Chat, however mindless, is the best way to break down any lingering suspicions.

I try again: "So what's to do in Orange on a Sunday?"
"Nothing."
"How about Molong?"
"Dead, mate. Laid out like a stiff."
"So what takes you there?"
"Testing my transmission."
Silence. Transmission isn't one of my conversational strong suits.
"Actually," he adds, unprompted, "that's a lie. There was a cricket
match on Channel Two and reruns of *Bonanza* on Nine. And nothing
happening on the street. I reckoned there might be something more
bloody exciting between here and Molong."

Perhaps he means me. Boredom is, after all, the main reason people
pick hitchhikers up; if not boredom, then to stave off sleep. Occasionally, the sight of a hitchhiker actually pricks at someone's conscience,
like one of those African kids staring off the magazine page: "You can
stop for this poor bastard, or look the other way." Usually, they turn
the page.

Anyway, this teenager from Orange is bored, but he's after something
more exciting than my idle chatter. "Look at that," he says, slowing
beside a heap of car-squashed flesh. It is the first kangaroo of my
Australian journey.

I stare hard at the shapeless corpse and try to conjure up the animal
described in the journals of explorer William Dampier, who was the
first white person to record seeing a kangaroo. "The land animals were
only a sort of raccoon," he wrote of his visit to the Australian coast in
1699. Unlike the American raccoons he'd seen, they "have very short
forelegs, but go jumping upon them as the others do, and, like them,
are very good meat."

Good roadside meat too, like raccoons. But not good enough for my
companion.

"I thought it might be a big wombat, or maybe an echidna," he says,
picking up speed again.

I've never seen an echidna, but I've read that they're the only mam-
mals in the world that don't dream. Conscious and subconscious are
rolled together in the wakeful world; just life as it is, experienced through
their snout and spiny body. Until they wander into the road and end
up, like this kangaroo, in a deep echidna sleep.

Molong makes Orange look like Times Square on New Year's Eve. There are two pubs but both of them are closed. Even the parked cars have gone elsewhere for the afternoon. My host decides not to push his luck; he turns around to Orange in time for *High Chaparral* on Channel 7.

The day is still young when he leaves me at the northern edge of town. It creeps through middle age and into retirement as I wait for a car to pass. There is a paranoid clarity that comes to those who stand alone by the road, for hours. In this case, it's directed at a garden statuette of a kangaroo in the yard behind me. I can feel its beady plaster eyes on my neck, hexing me for having ridden with animal killers all day.

I beg forgiveness and pray to the 'roo to bring me a ride. I get another hitchhiker instead.

"How long you been on the road, lad?" A disheveled man with two bloated duffel bags studies me from across the road.

"First day out. How about you?"

"Thirty-three years, lad. And them boots are still not tired of walking."

Phil "Boots" Harris, cook by trade, card shark and con man by preference, kicks his bags into the shape of a chaise longue and stretches out on top. He spotted me from a ditch beside the road where he spent most of the day sleeping off an all-night card game. "Drunk, see."

The boots are high patent-leather pumps—night shoes, not for walking. Mid-shin, the boots give way to a tattered pair of tuxedo pants that must have once belonged to a stouter, shorter man. A massive beer gut droops above his narrow waist, protruding from a T-shirt that reads: "My wife has a drinking problem. Me." Alcoholism is written across his face as well: it is red, lumpy and deflated, like a day-old birthday balloon.

"Landed these threads at a church in Orange," Boots says, hooking his thumbs on an imaginary waistcoat. "Spun a real hard-luck yarn. Lost my job. Started drinking too much plonk. Wife showed me the door. Blah blah, boo hoo hoo."

He opens one of the bags and a few potatoes roll out. "Landed some tucker too. Blankets in the other bag. I'll sell the bloody lot of it in Dubbo."

I ask to hear his story.

"Information costs in the bush," he says, rubbing his thumb and forefinger together. "Have you got a beer?" I haven't, so I toss him a dollar coin instead.

"Anyone can have a home and an honest job," he says, leaning back and putting his hands behind his head. "But if a man lives by his wits, he can get by without all that. And stay free as a bird, like me."

Free to roam the continent, which is what Boots has done since running away from Kalgoorlie as a teenager. The first stop in every town is the pub, where he hustles card tricks for schooners of beer. When the tricks play out, he hustles poker. On a good night he makes enough to walk on down the road a little farther. On a bad night he sleeps off the beer and starts all over the following day. "Fresh as a goose. Only poorer.

"If there aren't any mugs at the pub, there's always one at the church," he says. "Convents are the best. You can tell a nun any bloody nonsense and get everything but a place in her cot."

I interrupt his story as two cars approach, headed north. They pass. A few minutes later, several more drive by.

"Still on city time, lad?" Boots asks, laughing. He hoists a bag over each shoulder and leads me up the road to a signpost that's scratched with the names of hitchhikers who have languished here before us. There are memorials like this all across America, inscribed by legions of stranded travelers. Apparently Australia is the same.

"Don't ask me why, but Molong is bloody hard to get out of," Boots says, locating his initials beside the years 1972, 1978, and 1981. He adds "P.H. in 1-86" for good measure. "Won't be the last scratch, neither. Once I get to Dubbo I'll probably just turn around. I get itchy feet if I stay in one place too long."

Hitchhiking etiquette seems to be universal as well. Since I was first on the road, Boots plants himself out of sight and juggles potatoes until I can coax a ride. There's little traffic, though, and no one is interested in picking me up.

Boots watches for half an hour before returning to the roadside. He sits on one bag and offers me the other. It is almost sunset: the hustling hour.

"Pick a heart, any heart," he says, drawing a well-worn deck of cards from the pocket of his tuxedo pants.

"Six."

He opens the deck to a six.

"Dollar says I can find the ace." I nod. He cuts to the ace.

"King?" The king it is. A two-dollar note trades hands.

I ask for the deck and deal out a round of poker. Another note disappears into his pocket. We try euchre and I lose again. I am ten dollars down when a truck pulls up and offers a ride to Dubbo. There is only room in the back for one.

"You take it, lad," Boots says, folding up the deck. "Them boots are still not tired of walking."

I watch the moon rise from the back of the truck and take stock of my first day on the road. A meal offer, my first kangaroo, and a true Australian swagman, albeit at some cost.

There will be much shared food and more kangaroos than I can count before this journey is done. But the travel is lonely from here on. Boots is the last hitchhiker I will see for 3,000 miles.

3

WOOP WOOP AND OTHER PLACES

It's all Jon Hamilton's fault, this thing I have about hitchhiking. We were best friends at sixteen when Jon thumbed his way across America over a holiday from school. I stayed at home, in Washington, D.C., serving French fries at a Wild West version of McDonald's.

"I'm holed up at this flophouse filled with naked old winos," Jon wrote from New Orleans. "They lie in bed all day with their doors wide open, so I walk down the hall and look at the bottoms of their feet. Too much. Jon."

I studied the card between customers on the fast-food assembly line. "Howdy, partner, want some fries?" I'd ask. They always did. So I'd scoop a pile of spuds between the milkshake and the cheeseburger, point them to a cowgirl at the cash register and cry out, "Happy trails!" I lasted a week.

Jon was halfway across the continent by then. "Hopped a freight train in Shreveport and rode it all the way to Santa Fe," he wrote from New Mexico. A pair of Navajos galloped across an open plain on the other side of the card. It looked like cowboy country, only the real thing, not a French-fried version of it. "Got drunk on Ripple wine with some hobos in a boxcar. The desert out here is unreal. Happy trails, Jon."

Jon showed up at school that September with a beret and an adolescent stubble sprouting across his cheeks. Between classes he'd sit alone under a tree and roll cigarettes, looking shell-shocked, only in a good way; like he'd seen something vast and important out there, in a New Orleans flophouse or a freightyard in Santa Fe.

All through the school year, I studied the pages of the *Rand McNally Road Atlas of America*. I read and reread Jack Kerouac's *On the Road* and pinned a poster from *Easy Rider* over my bed. Wanderlust mingled with other passions in my adolescent dreaming.

And so it was that I found myself the following summer, a month of dishwasher's pay in the pocket of my jeans, standing beside a highway headed west out of Washington. My destination was California, 3,000 miles away. My route was to be as random as the drivers who took me in.

In the two months that followed I found out just how boring the amber waves of grain can be. I threw up my first shot of tequila behind a Mexican bar in South Dakota. I landed in a Nevada jail for riding on a motorcycle without a helmet—behind a biker who was going a hundred miles per hour, with an ounce of grass in the pocket of his leather jacket.

But misadventure was part of the appeal. Hitchhiking was a rite of passage, and a way to slum it across America like so many generations before. Go West, young man. Seek your fortune on the road. Get your kicks on Route 66. At seventeen, there was nothing that compared to sprinting toward an open car door, half in terror and half in exhilaration, to climb in for another ride with a total stranger.

I was hooked, and for several summers I hitchhiked whenever I could. Then full-time work intervened; the aimless rambling ended. But a part of me clung to the seventeen-year-old, holding out his finger by an open road, not knowing where in the world he was headed. It was an image of myself that I liked and trusted.

Now, ten years later, I'm trying the real thing on for size again, and so far it fits. Watching the dawn from a park outside Dubbo, I feel oddly at home. Roll up the sleeping bag. Poke around in the rubbish bin for a piece of cardboard to make a sign saying "Bourke." Amble out to the highway to check the traffic. Who knows what's just around the bend?

A truck stop. It's still early, so I go inside to sip coffee until the sun rises above the black soil plain. A radio over the grill beeps six times and the cook stops rearranging slabs of bacon to turn up the volume.

"Mornin' stock report," he says. Two farmers at a nearby table stop talking. I make a mental note of this town called Dubbo where everyone follows the Dow Jones index. My folks will get a kick out of that.

"In Gunnedah on Friday there was a good display of heavy steers," the radio drones, "with prices starting firm then fetching two to three cents more than the previous week. Woolly lambs were also dearer, as were bullocks and pigs. . . ."

I listen carefully to this garble and realize that I heard similar broadcasts about a dozen times yesterday. Livestock reports and test cricket are the music to which country life is set.

"Any sales on today?" I ask the cook.

"Nyngan, I reckon. Maybe Wee Waa. Ask the cockies."

He gestures at the two men I'd noticed listening to the radio. They are lean and tanned, clad in what seems to be the uniform of New South Wales farmers: stubbies, singlet, and short, pull-on workboots. The brims of their work hats flop like tired lettuce leaves.

I study the map for a moment. Nyngan is north and west, in the direction of Bourke. I can't find Wee Waa anywhere. I hoist my pack over one shoulder and wander over to the cockies, who are counting out change on the laminex table.

"G'day." I smile cheerfully. "This little piggie is headed to market. Anyone got room?"

The two farmers look at each other.

"What'd he say?"

"Dunno. Something about grunters, I think."

The first one turns to me again. "Nosirree, buster," he says, mimicking my accent as badly as I've mimicked his. "No room for a pig. But I might have a spot of room for a goddamn Yank. Where ya headed?"

"Bourke, I guess, then farther. Just touring around."

"I wouldn't tour too long in Bourke if I were you. Too many Abos. But I can get you to Nyngan."

We climb into his truck and head off through the early morning light. Like the farmer I rode with yesterday, this one's not the talkative sort, so I stare out the window as the stunted skyline of Dubbo falls away behind us. From here on, I know, civilization dwindles rapidly.

I imagine that in the typical bush settlement, the grain silo will be the biggest building in town.

But in my mind's map it is Bourke, not Dubbo, that marks the true beginning of an outback journey. All before is known and fertile ground: orchards, hobby farms, paddocks thick with sheep. But "back o' Bourke," as everyone calls the serious bush, there lie plains of nothing stretching all the way to Alice.

Ten miles out of Dubbo, I realize it may be hard to tell back of Bourke from front. There's a Kansas-like expanse of cotton and wheat, a few silos, then endless tracts of blank and untilled space. A telephone line and the occasional eucalyptus are all that rise above the dirt and scrub.

"One seems to ride forever and to come to nothing," Anthony Trollope wrote after touring the New South Wales bush in the 1870s, "and to relinquish at last the very idea of an object."

A century later, this landscape is still the scenic equivalent of Valium.

I stir awake as the truck pulls off the road at a town called Nevertire. Not a town really—just fifty or so homes, a rail spur, a pub, and a store. Nevertire wasn't always so inconsequential. If I had come this way a century ago, I might have been stampeded by livestock from remote grazing stations. There were only 134 people living here in 1891. But no fewer than 295,708 sheep, 6,998 cattle, and 710 pigs loaded on at the rail spur. That works out to about 2,300 hooved creatures for every head of human.

A cyclone blew away two of the town's three pubs in 1890. But the one that remains does a brisk trade in overheated cockies, and motorists thirsty for a beer and a yarn before plunging on to Bourke.

Most of the blow-throughs want to know, as I do, how Nevertire acquired its stoic-sounding name.

"There's a few theories, all of 'em probably bull," the publican says. He is polishing bottles behind the bar while the cockie and I cool off over lemon squash. One theory says a bullock driver was the first to plod across the muddy plain. He bogged down, yelled "Never tire! Never tire!" at his chattel and so gave the town its name.

Another theory tells of a white settler who asked his Aboriginal guide to build a fire at the end of a long day's slog. When the native refused, his companion said, "But I'm not tired." To which the Aborigine replied: "White man never tired."

A revisionist version holds that it is the Aborigine who is never tired. But visitors to the pub are well advised to ally themselves with the original text.

"You being a Yank, you probably don't know why blacks are called boongs," the cockie tells me. He strikes a match on the bottom of his boot and lights a cigarette for dramatic effect. "*Boong!* That's the sound they make when they bounce off the 'roo bar."

Being a Yank, it takes me a moment to realize that a kangaroo bar is the metal guard I noticed on the front of his truck. I muster a polite smile.

The cockie orders a beer, and then another, before I realize that this may be an extended stop. Other farmers are rolling in for lunch. There are fertilizers, fat lambs, the price of pigs, and other matters to mull over in the heat of the day. So I surrender my stool and scan the pub walls for entertainment. A Technicolor cotton plant blooms on one wall beneath an advertisement for the American company that owns much of the land hereabouts. "Cotton—now it's a whole new boll game!" it cries with Yankee exuberance.

The cockie weaves his way to the toilet. I will have to find my own way to Nyngan, it seems. But first I wander up the road to visit Jim Goatcher, who, the publican tells me, "knows all about this Nevertire stuff."

I find the bespectacled man leaning against a petrol pump in front of his smallgoods store. Goatcher bought the building thirty years ago, when it was still the Nevertire Roman Catholic church. The one-time nave is lined now with lollies, cold drinks, and magazines with names like *The Farm* and *Barbecue Cookbook*. But a certain hymnal air still prevails, thanks to the proprietor's fondness for bush balladeers.

"I like Lawson best and Banjo Paterson second," Goatcher says. He glances out the window to see that there are no customers about, then brings a tattered volume of Henry Lawson poems from underneath the counter. Clearing his throat, he reads in a soft and lilting voice:

> *It chanced upon the very day we'd got the shearing done,*
> *A buggy brought a stranger to the West-o'-Sunday Run;*
> *We chaps were smoking after tea and heard the swell inquire*
> *For one as travelled by the name of Dunn of Nevertire.*

Jack Dunn of Nevertire
Old Dunn of Nevertire;
There wasn't one of us but knew Jack Dunn of Nevertire.

A truck engine rumbles outside. Goatcher glances up, as if to wish the intruder away. "Nice poem, eh?" he says, returning the book to its hiding place and heading out the door. "There's pages more. Too bad it doesn't explain a thing about how the town got its name."

I chat up the driver while Goatcher fills his petrol tank. The man's had a few at the pub and isn't in much better shape than the cockie I abandoned. But there's no other traffic, so I accept the offer of a ride to his sheep station, 18 miles up the road.

It is this journey's first logistical mistake. The driver navigates safely enough, but the turn-off to his station, where he lets me off, is a barren stretch between fields of cotton and fields of nothing. There is no shade from the midday sun, nor the prospect of any shelter farther on.

"If you ever get stuck in a place like this, just follow the cattle patties," the farmer says as I climb out. "They always lead to water." With that, he drives off, leaving me to swelter by the highway.

After ten minutes my head is boiling and my feet have become two pieces of hot, soggy bread. The body in between feels as if it's being basted in sweat and slow-cooked over a backyard barbecue. It must be over 90 degrees out, maybe 100. I make a full circle and see nothing at all, just heat waves rising off the bitumen. No choice but to sweat it out.

I try to distract myself by devising a plausible theory about Nevertire's name. Nevertire . . . Tire never . . . Tire tire. . . . Maybe Nevertire is an imprecise label, like "back o' Bourke," referring not to the town but to the dull plain that stretches endlessly around it, never tired. Maybe it's got something to do with Never Never, and with all the other strange words for the Australian interior. The bush. The scrub. The mulga. Outback. Woop Woop. Buggery. Out to Buggery. Back o' Bourke. Beyond the Black Stump.

The Eskimos, I'm told, have fourteen words for snow. No wonder then that Australians have so many names for the emptiness of their own bleak continent.

This thought occupies five minutes or so. Hoisting my groundsheet as a shield against the heat occupies another five. Then nothing. There's no traffic in sight, and I can see for about 10 miles in either direction. Even the blowflies have more sense than to come out on a day like this.

A slug of water clears my head long enough for me to begin panicking. For the first time I realize that I'm woefully ill-prepared for this journey, despite all the warnings. My waterbag holds enough to wash down a few aspirin; at the moment I could drain an entire radiator and still feel parched. My hat has already gone AWOL, probably back at the Nevertire pub. And the sunscreen is swimming inside the toxic waste dump that is my rucksack's side pocket—the one where I stashed the bug repellent yesterday.

The other contents of my pack are better suited to a week in Bali than to an outback journey of unknown duration. Besides a small supply of clothes and camping gear, there's a camera, a poetry book, two novels, and assorted tourist pamphlets, road maps, magazines, and unread newspapers. I feared boredom by the road when I should have feared frying.

An hour passes. Time to start searching for cattle patties? Not yet, not yet. I reach for the poetry book. *The Waste Land and Other Poems*. Hardly an uplifting bit of verse for a traveler stranded in the bush, but all part of the hitchhiker's plan for self-improvement. On previous hitching trips, I carried a harmonica under the delusion that I would become Bob Dylan during the long waits between rides. This time I will be T. S. Eliot instead.

> *You cannot say, or guess, for you know only*
> *A heap of broken images, where the sun beats,*
> *And the dead tree gives no shelter, the cricket no relief,*
> *And the dry stone no sound of water. Only—*

I have found a new charm. A car engine rumbles in the distance before I reach the third stanza. Staring through the heat waves curling off the bitumen, I can see a speck way off, where the road meets the sky. Then the speck becomes a dot and the dot becomes a car and the car comes slowly up to greet me. Now all I have to do is make sure it doesn't pass me by. I hold out my finger, then think better of it and step partway onto the road, with the authority of a border patrol. The car slows and

I rush to the driver's window, jabbering like the madman I must appear to be.

The driver smiles. "You're the crazy Yank we heard about at Nevertire," he says, stepping out and offering me a swig of his beer. "Mate, what you need is a camel. Anyway, hop in."

It seems my fame precedes me, or trails me, rather, by a few miles. But as a celebrity I am a disappointment. A minute after collapsing in the backseat I am helping myself to a drink from the cooler, or "esky" (short for Eskimo?). A few minutes after that, I'm dozing in beer sweat. This is just as well. Each time I open my eyes, the driver is in the oncoming lane.

"Road's so dull that a bloke's got to do something to keep awake," he explains. Indeed, the road is so straight that with a good alignment, a driver can go from Nyngan to Bourke without ever touching the steering wheel. Except for the wide S-bends at the entrance to each town, designed to jolt drivers from their road-induced trance.

The towns aren't much to wake for. Nyngan could be Coolabah could be Girilambone—a broad main street, a pub, a railroad crossing, then more straight road shooting through blank space. Town is too grand a title for these places, as it is for most of the settlements beyond the Dividing Range. But Australian English has failed its landscape in this respect; there are few linguistic gradations between the "big smoke" of Sydney and the "one horse" villages of the rural plain.

From a distance, Bourke looks as welcoming as a desert oasis. Trees! Water towers! Motels! Up close it's something different. The town was founded in 1835 as a frontier stockade and it still has the feeling of a well-armed garrison. There are iron bars on the shop windows and broken glass in the streets. One storekeeper hasn't bothered to replace the smashed glass, filling in the window with bricks instead.

I've been warned that Bourke is a tense and racially divided town, a kind of bush Johannesburg. Just a week ago, there was a news item about blacks burning down a pub in Bourke because the bartender wouldn't serve them. Once before, I'd read about police beating up Aboriginal prisoners. Apparently, the town is famous for such incidents.

But I didn't expect shutters and iron grilles. That's city battlements, I thought—not the sort of stuff you put in the windows of quiet country stores.

Nor do I anticipate the response of the three Aboriginal girls I ap-

proach for directions to the campground. They stare at me, wide-eyed
and mute, before scattering into the night like small birds. My first
encounter with black Australia is something less than a resounding
success.

The reporter in me wants to know how things could possibly have
got so bad. But the only way to find out is to enter the pub traffic,
which is divided like a two-lane highway: whites streaming into one
hotel and blacks to another. I don't want to join this apartheid, so I
settle for the median strip and hike to a Chinese restaurant instead.

It is the day's second logistical error. The "special soup" is special
for its careful blending: one part soggy noddles, two parts soy sauce,
and twelve parts monosodium glutamate. I ask the waitress if the cook
could hold the MSG on the second course. She looks at me as I've
asked her to take off her blouse.

Half an hour later, I crawl into my sleeping sack, clinging to my
water bag as if to an intravenous drip. I am too tired to mind the day's
collection of dirt and grime. But an alarming thought keeps me awake.
If it is this hot and dry and barren in semisettled New South Wales,
what torment of hell awaits me in the genuine outback?

4
QUEENSLAND IN
BLACK AND WHITE

Thirty miles from the Queensland border, the car I'm riding in skids onto the shoulder, swerves sickeningly, then skids onto the bitumen again. The driver, an off-duty Navy man named Rod, bolts upright in his seat and pulls a small pill from the pocket of his jeans.

"Almost caught a nap back there," he says with a high-pitched laugh. He jerks his hand forward, pops the pill in his mouth, then jerks his hand down for a swig from the tinnie of beer between his legs. "Too many clicks, I reckon, and not enough blue tabs."

Rod traveled four hundred clicks on his mileage gauge and popped about as many uppers before stopping for me outside Bourke in the early morning. "Had to go bush to get my head together," he said, offering me a wake-up pill soon after I climbed aboard. "Someplace quieter than Sydney. Like someplace where there's no static, nothing to cloud things up."

The road north of Bourke has about as much static as deep space. It is even bleaker than yesterday's stretch—as dry and dusty and dull as muesli without milk. A strange urge to surrender takes over. Turn off the engine. Burrow into the hot red earth. Go to sleep. Forever . . . That's when a tire catches the shoulder, the steering wheel swerves and the car spins into the scrub.

"That Ford was out there in '78—last time I was up this way," Rod says, pointing at a rusted chassis lying upside down by the road. It is the first bit of scenery for over an hour. "Just think, if we'd run off the road back there, we'd be the same. Like in a time warp, lying out there for drivers to look at, like for years."

Another off-key peal of laughter. Another beer. I scan the horizon for signs of a town, a petrol pump—anything. But all I see is a dusty plain, as flat and featureless as a young girl's chest.

Those who have never hitchhiked imagine roads filled with cutpurses, panderers, and psychopathic killers. My mother once sent me a cautionary news clipping about two hitchhikers who were actually killed and eaten by the driver who picked them up. I've never caught a ride with a thief or a cannibal, but I've ridden with enough drunk or drug-crazed drivers to fill the average city rehab center.

Usually you don't know they're high until you're inside the car. And even when you suspect something, the urge to take a ride usually wins out. If things get weird, well, you can always hop out at the next stoplight or crossroads.

That's in America. In the Australian bush there's no place to jump ship, except into empty scrub. So I keep searching the horizon for signs of civilization while Rod downs another beer, another blue tab.

A clump of trees and the outline of a rickety wooden building form on the horizon. It is the beginning of my love affair with the bush pub. For the traveler thirsty for drink, diversion, or in my case, escape, the backwoods hotel leaps off the horizon like a St. Bernard pounding across the snowfields. Salvation, liquid and otherwise, is only an S-bend away.

So is my first taste of the odd society of these remote watering holes. It is 11 A.M. on Tuesday when I follow Rod into the Tattersall's Hotel at Barringun, just shy of the Queensland border. It might as well be Friday night. The bar is crowded with pool sharks, drinkers, dart throwers; your average country pub, you might say—except that the darts are two-dollar notes, skewered on tacks. The dart board is the wooden ceiling above the bar. A tapestry of bills already hangs from the rafters.

"Once a month I take the pins out and send the money to a spastic society in Melbourne," the publican explains. I wonder what the charity makes of these pricked and beer-stained contributions. I leave Rod hurling paper missiles at the ceiling and laughing as the dollars float to earth again.

Outside, I hitch a ride with two boar shooters from Bankstown. "Only headed to the next pub, mate," the driver tells me, emptying a carton of beers into an ice-filled esky. I squeeze between the cooler and the window as the utility truck weaves onto the highway. The driver opens a beer and foam spurts onto his shirt and face. The ute swerves into the right-hand lane. It seems that alcoholism is an occupational hazard of outback driving.

The driver's companion is an enormous factory worker with a T-shirt that reads "I Only Sleep with the Best." He passes the time by loading, unloading, and reloading his shotgun. I reach for a beer and stare the other way, at the "scenery." Soon after leaving the pub, we pass a bullet-ridden sign marking the border of Queensland. The factory worker aims his rifle across my chest and out the window but doesn't fire.

"Set your watch back an hour—and then another twenty-five years," he mumbles over the gun's muzzle. Other than the time zone, the only change is that the stock grids rise up in the road instead of dipping down, as they do in New South Wales. You notice these sort of things when there's nothing else to look at.

The pig shooters plan to settle in at another pub until dark, when the boars will be running and the hunters will be drunk enough to fire high-powered rifles at anything that moves. But there isn't another settlement, much less a pub, for over an hour.

When we do reach civilization, it is a grazing and shearing town called Cunnamulla, whose 1,800 inhabitants somehow support seven hotels. This should make for a reasonable pub crawl before the shooting of pigs. I buy the two men a round of beer but decline their invitation to "kick on" to the next pub; the tyranny of the Australian "shout"—everyone must buy a round before the drinking's done—will doom me to midday collapse if I accept.

I opt for indigestion instead. The counter lunch sounds harmless enough. For three dollars or so, I will be served a meat pie, some chips, gravy, vegetables, and salad. No MSG. The meal that arrives has three veg (cooked to perfection, then left on the stove for another hour). Also a pie the size of my head, floating across a gray-brown sea of gravy. And a salad that has more spuds than greens. Then bread and butter, just in case. Just in case I never want to eat again. And beer of course, measured now, Queensland-style, in middie-sized "pots" and tiny glasses called "ponies."

In any other setting, the five-ounce pony would seem unmanly. But in the semitropical heat of a Queensland's summer day, it is a good way to get down a swallow before the beer turns to molten lava.

"With this cuisine the appetite dies quickly," a Frenchman, Oscar Commettant, wrote of Australian hotel food in 1888. "The shilling meal consists of one of those soups that are neither soup nor sauce, a plate of tasteless meat accompanied by even more tasteless vegetables boiled in saltless water, and a pudding that you swallow while reminding yourself that you must eat to live, not live to eat."

Bloated and belching, I walk slowly through the blinding midday heat. I am beginning to understand the low blood pressure of the bush. Slow down. Go troppo. It's too hot to take a siesta and too early in the day to pack it in for good. So I head for the OTB parlor, where, I am told, the best "egg nishner" in town can be found.

It is under the cooling wind of a Kelvinator that the slow transit of the day takes an unexpected twist. I have just dropped my pack on the floor, and my body on top of it, when an oddly accented voice beckons from beneath the air-conditioner.

"Come over here where it's nice and cold."

I look up to find a potato-shaped, potato-colored Aboriginal woman of about sixty years of age. The sight startles me. After my awkward debut in Bourke, I don't expect any black person to approach me, much less ask me to come closer.

The woman senses my discomfort. "I won't bite," she says, smiling. "Promise." She shifts her bare feet and yellow cotton frock to make room by the air-conditioner. I look at her ample breasts and dark eyes, magnified by thick lenses like a fairy-tale grandmother's, and feel a momentary urge to put my head in her lap. Instead, I slump down beside her and tell of my experience in Bourke the evening before.

"Cunnamulla is a friendlier town," she says. Indeed, there is a small circle of women in the cool corner of the OTB parlor, half of them black and half of them white. Apparently, this is quite the social spot on a hot summer's day in Cunnamulla.

"Have you seen the sights?" my new friend asks.

"I've been to the pub, if that's what you mean."

She laughs. "There's more to it than that. Cummon, if you've got a few hours I'll show you around."

I look at her a bit incredulously.

"Cummon," she says, and I follow her out the door.

The tour that follows isn't the sort that makes it into travel commission brochures. The first stop is the home of my guide, Hazel McKellar: a weatherboard cottage that she shares with four goats, twelve hens, three geese, and almost as many relations. Hazel feeds a few of the animals, then herds a half-dozen children onto the backseat of a battered sedan, introducing each one as they pile in. "This is Jackie and this is Little Man," she says, patting a young girl and boy on the head. "They're my grandchildren." Then Kylie and Polly. "They're Jackie and Little Man's cousins." Then a few little kids who just wandered in from a neighboring house. I climb onto the front seat with a small child squirming in my lap.

Hazel drives down a dusty stock route for a few miles and parks beside an unkempt lot littered with rusting cars and broken glass. It looks much like the harsh and forbidding landscape I've traveled through since Bourke. But to Hazel it is "yumba"—home—the place where she was raised among the Kooma people.

Like many of the Aboriginal clans in this part of the country, the Kooma once ranged across the bush, following the supply of game and water. When living off the land became difficult, they'd settle at the fringes of white civilization, taking jobs as drovers and housemaids, or collecting food and blankets distributed by the government. By the 1930s, this camp outside Cunnamulla had become a permanent home to a few hundred of Hazel's people.

Ever since, the Kooma have had one foot in their traditional culture and one foot in the white man's world.

"See that cedar tree over there?" Hazel says. "That's where I was raised. We had a hut made out of posts and calico." It is the first time I have ever seen someone point to a stand of timber and call it home. A little farther on, Hazel shows me a "scarred tree" that has a cavity in its soft mulga trunk where wood was cut out and carved into a clublike weapon, called a "nulla nulla." There are bits of flake and flint on the ground, and grooves in the rock where axes were honed. It all has the feel of an archaeological site, except that the cultural remains are still aboveground.

Hazel, like many Aborigines, went to work as a housemaid at a white station when she was twelve. At sixteen, she married an Aboriginal drover, by arrangement, and began raising eight children while her husband followed herds of stock through the bush of southern Queensland. They would be away for four or five months at a time, building huts like the one in Cunnamulla, or as Hazel puts it, "living from tree to tree."

If the life-style was traditional, the schooling was not. Hazel taught her kids by correspondence, sending away for books and lessons from the Queensland government. She'd help the children study, then send the books in to be graded.

And between droving trips, the family returned to the camp outside Cunnamulla, where the lean-to by the cedar tree was always there waiting for them.

"If you caught an emu, the neighbor got a leg," Hazel says. "Then maybe there'd be some mulga apples or kangaroo. That was a big night then, a real party. No one worried about going uptown in them days."

Uptown was Cunnamulla, the white fellas' place, where the Kooma kept to the fringes. Blacks could go to the pictures, but they had to enter through a side alley and sit in front, cordoned off by a rope barrier. Otherwise, the two societies kept to themselves.

Then, in the 1960s, the government began moving the Kooma into fibro houses in town as part of the grander scheme of assimilating Aborigines. In 1975 the government bulldozed the camp and turned it into the town dump. After an initial period of unease, Cunnamulla's blacks now live peaceably beside their white neighbors, in identikit houses with identikit lawns. The shops and workplaces have all been integrated, though an informal separation survives at the local pubs.

Hazel isn't sure how to feel about the change. On the one hand, her children have prospered in the white man's world, as schoolteachers, public servants, and wool classers. They don't have to worry about educating their children by correspondence, or wonder if the white fella will suddenly bulldoze their home.

But Hazel fears that the Kooma's communal life-style has been lost. "People still help each other," she says, "but it's not automatic, like in the old days." The move into town has also severed the Kooma's link to the land and traditional belief. Only the elders remember. For years after the camp was bulldozed, old men took their tucker boxes and hiked from town to picnic amidst the broken metal and twisted glass. It was still yumba to them.

Hazel has also held on. She talks to the old people and writes down what they know of the "Matya-Mundu," the time long ago. Sometimes the stories are legend, telling of the rainbow serpent, the mundugatta, who made waterholes along the Warrego River and filled them with yellowbelly, catfish and cod. At other times it is day-to-day practices that she records; how to gather the sweet fruit of the wilga tree, known as "snorty gobble," or the best way to get emu eggs and hunt goannas.

Often, though, the memory is bitter, telling of the brutal ways of the white man. One curious tale concerns a German doctor who came to study a small group of hairless Kooma men in the 1880s. He wanted to take skin samples back to Germany, but the Aborigines refused. Later, a Kooma corpse was mysteriously shipped to Berlin. Hazel thinks it had something to do with the scientist's research.

Hazel also clings to the rituals of her people. Traditionally, a death among the Kooma was followed by the "smoking" of the relatives' homes. Hazel continues the custom by walking through the house with a bucketful of burning dogwood leaves. She says it clears away the bad spirits and calms the young ones.

"We can't go back to what we were," she says, "but if we keep running after the wayibald—that's the white fella—we will belong to him, not to us."

Hazel seems to have found a way to do more than just preserve her people's past. When she walks me through the "Bottom Camp," where the Kooma once hunted echidnas and fished in summer, it is with the simple ease of a woman showing a friend the nooks and crannies of her rambling home. The past is still present for her.

For the children, who have grown up in the white man's world, identity is more muddled. Little Man tells me how he won the lizard race in town; apparently, the white fellas can't compete at that. And one of the little girls teaches me a few Aboriginal words; bread is "muntha" and mouse sounds something like "mangumangu."

But when Hazel finishes telling how Kooma men tapped on the ground to chase out goannas, Little Man and another boy tug at my sleeve and quiz me about *The A-Team* and *Sesame Street*. One of the little girls asks me for the names of Americans she can adopt as pen pals. And all of them want to know about black people in the United States. "If I went there, could I be in movies too?" asks a girl of about eleven. "Or would they know I was not really a Negro?" Just a generation removed from the bush, they are as eager to embrace my culture as I am to embrace theirs.

After a swim in the Warrego, after goat's milk and tea, Hazel offers me her home as resting place for the night. But I am still impatient to put some distance behind me; after three days, I am not yet 600 miles from Sydney. So I thank her and promise to stop in if I come this way again.

In the sharp, shadowed light of late afternoon, I go uptown, through the white fellas' land, and then out to the wilderness beyond. If I don't get a ride before dark I'll camp somewhere out here, beneath a cedar tree perhaps.

I see the landscape differently now. For the past few days, I've kept my eye trained on the distant horizon, hoping for something more interesting than the bleak, monotonous foreground. Hazel has shown me that there's often a gem, full of history and even beauty, right there out the passenger window. All you need is someone to show you how to turn it to catch the light.

5
THE SHEEP'S BACK

It is in the nature of epiphanies that they go "piph" and disappear. The magic glow that embraced me at dusk evaporates in a paddock at dawn with a nudge from a policeman's boot. "Private property, mate," the trooper says. I have gone to sleep in Hazel's yumba and awakened back in the white fellas' Queensland.

The officer checks my driver's license while I pull on pants and shoes. "Carrying any of that funny stuff, mate?"

I assume he means marijuana. "No sir, Officer. No sir." This is Queensland after all, Australia's answer to Alabama. I'll lick his boots if that's what's required. "Mostly just books, Officer." I hand him T. S. Eliot, Patrick White, Woody Allen.

His official face falls away. "I'm headed up the road for a cuppa tea," he says. "Want a ride?"

So much for big bad Queensland.

We pull up beside a truckie who is poking his arms through the wooden siding of a road train, trying to unlock the horns of two butting sheep. I watch him wrestle for a moment, then ask if he's headed north. He nods. I ask if he's got room for a rider. He shrugs. I climb into the cab and we rumble off through the mulga.

There are 160 breeding rams in the two trailers behind us. All must be delivered by day's end. Apparently, it is a job requiring intense concentration. For the 900-mile round trip from his home in New

South Wales, the driver, a part Aboriginal named Paul, carries nothing more than a bedroll, a waterbag, and an Elvis Presley cassette. There is room for me but not for conversation.

"A bloke has to keep moving when he's hauling stock," Paul says after half an hour of silence. It is the last word he utters in the three hours until midday.

The scenery's not too lively either, so I start combing the library stacks crammed inside my pack. This time I pass over T. S. Eliot for a more prosaic text—a tourist commission brochure entitled "Outback Queensland." The first glossy page tells me that Charleville, through which we are about to pass, is home to the Steiger Vortex Gun. Apparently, townspeople became so hot and bothered in 1902 that they fired six homemade cannons to move the air and draw in a raincloud.

Nothing happened. So they retired to the bar instead. Charleville was already a "ten-pub town" by the turn of the century, the brochure says. A rather strange way to measure population; but then, much stranger yardsticks lie ahead.

The tourist guide is less effusive about the next dot on the map. "Augathella," it reports, "is 50 miles north of Charleville." That's all. This obscurity is compounded by a new highway having recently by-passed Augathella, which is 750 miles from Sydney and about 500 from Brisbane. A plaintive sign now beckons from the distant road: "Do not pass us—call in!"

We go one better, depositing ten stud rams in the town's empty main street. The sheep are earmarked—literally, with red and pink ear tags—for a man named Tony Wearing, who owns a property out of town. He and his son, Clint, are to meet us in Augathella at midday.

I assume the Wearings will be dressed like New South Wales cockies, in shorts and singlets and elastic-side workboots. Instead I find myself at high noon, face-to-face with Marlboro Man and Marlboro Boy. Lean and ruggedly handsome, the two cowboys saunter toward me in stiff jeans, riding boots, and wide-brimmed hats. I'm not sure whether to say "G'day," "Howdy partner," or "Draw!"

It seems that silence is the appropriate response; sheep herding, like sheep delivering, breeds a certain reserve. Tony tips his Akubra hat at Paul. Paul nods. Clint, who appears to be about twelve, stands slightly behind his father, kicking gravel and staring at his feet. He looks as if he began mustering stock in the stroller and has done little else since.

The three go about their business so quietly that I begin wondering if there's something illicit about the whole operation. Then Tony breaks the silence with a flat-toned one-liner.

"The girls are gonna love these big stud rams." His wink is so big it lifts one whole side of his face. "And if they don't, we'll just have to give 'em a kick in the you-know-where." Then he and Clint load their bleating cargo inside a truck and disappear into the bush. I suspect Clint won't see another stranger before the next load of rams.

My own horizons are about to broaden. Ever since Dubbo, the automobile has been a cocoon against the bleak and arid landscape beyond the windscreen. And north of Charleville, the road becomes so narrow that vehicles drop two wheels onto the dirt shoulder to avoid sideswiping each other as they pass. The travel is as unsettling as it is dull.

But after Augathella the road plunges into a sweeping grassland that resembles the "big sky" country of the American West. Clouds drift lazily toward a distant horizon, broken only by the occasional flat-topped mesa, or "jump-up," as they're called in Queensland. It is the sort of setting that looks naked without a Sioux Indian or two galloping into the middle distance.

I feel my eye and spirit drawn outward across the open plain. Even Paul is stirred to comment. "Plenty of room to move out here," he says, stretching his legs. Then silence for another hour.

The writer Paul Theroux once observed that conversing with strangers is a peculiarly American compulsion. "To get an American talking it is only necessary to be within shouting distance and wearing a smile," he writes. "Your slightest encouragement is enough to provoke a non-stop rehearsal of the most intimate details of your fellow traveler's life."

He's right, of course. Whenever I replay my first hitchhiking trip across America, ten years ago, it comes out like a blurry home movie— Rocky Mountains, Grand Canyon, the wet green Oregon woods—with a voiceover of one Middle American after another reciting his life story. That was one of the things I liked so much about hitching; getting a personalized tour of the continent with people I'd never otherwise meet.

So far on this trip I've been lucky to extract a complete sentence from a driver, much less a life story. As a reporter in Sydney, Australians have sometimes struck me as shy, at least by American standards. But I assumed it was a city-bred reticence, or maybe some remnant of English reserve. Now, after riding with so many silent country folk, I'm beginning to suspect that it's the bush that is the true home of the taciturn Australian.

Near Tambo, Paul touches my arm and points at an astonishing tree that has a short and grotesquely stout trunk, rising to a bushy head. It looks like a bowling pin with an Afro haircut.

"Bottle trees," he says. "Fattest trees in the world."

I dig into my rucksack's library for a paperback guide to Australian fauna and flora. Bottle tree. *Brachychiton rupestris*. Also known as Australian baobab, or boab. Native to South Africa, Australia, and nowhere else. Girth of up to 59 feet. Sumo wrestlers of the Southern Hemisphere.

Paul turns between two really obese specimens—some kind of sign-post, apparently—and enters a sheep station the size of a medieval principality. It is 6 miles before we reach the manor, a split-level palace with tennis courts and swimming pools girdled round. M'lord and m'lady are in Europe, Paul explains, while the prince and princess are being finished at a boarding school in Toowoomba. But there is a feudal retainer on hand to escort us by motorcycle to a back paddock of the 48,000-acre property. Forty-eight thousand acres. That's bigger than my birthplace, Washington, D.C.—but with a population of five instead of 700,000.

Not counting the animals, of which there seem to be several million. But for some reason our sheep don't want to join this livestock ghetto. As soon as Paul opens the tailgate, the rams retreat into a rugby scrum at the back of the trailer. First in is the caretaker's sheepdog. He barks and howls and emerges a moment later, butted and bruised. We prod at the animals from the sides of the trailer. Still nothing. Finally, Paul crawls in on hands and knees to drag a ram out by its horns. The others follow, as sheep are wont to do.

"Bloody dumb beasts," Paul mutters before catching himself and falling silent. Receipts are exchanged. One vassal nods to another. And a transaction worth several thousand dollars is done without the absentee owners missing a ray of sun on the Riviera. Some among the Lucky Countrymen have ridden far atop the merino's back.

From the "rolling down" country of the sheepocracy we drive into the dusty towns of the wool proletariat. Here the homes are modest, the men brawny from wrestling and shearing sheep. It is late in the day, though, and most are hoisting nothing weightier than a pot of beer. Paul has to keep moving stock, so I pile out at a town called Blackall and retire to the Bushman's Hotel to wash down all that quiet.

Over a tinnie of Fourex, served outback-style in a Styrofoam holder, I learn that a husky lad named Jackie Howe made shearing history near Blackall in 1892. He clipped 321 sheep in less than eight hours (almost one a minute), a feat that took fifty-eight years and mechanized shearing to surpass. The standard-issue singlet that shearers wear has been known ever since as the "Jackie Howe."

The crush of drinkers and the sweaty Jackie Howes give the Bushman Hotel all the jostle and stink of a woolshed. But then, after four days on the road, I'm no rose either. My shorts and khaki shirt are coated in dust. My hair is matted and much too long for soliciting rides, not to mention standing in the outback sun. What better place than Blackall to get the shearing done?

The local hairdresser takes one look at my sweaty locks and decides she is closing early. So I hitch a ride with two shearers deeper into sheep country, deeper into sheep history. Barcaldine, an hour farther on, was the site of the "Great Shearers' Strike" of 1891. Authorities didn't mess around in those days. When the shearers laid down their blades and manned a picket line, the stationmasters brought in scabs and the Queensland government sent troops. Eventually, the strike was broken and the union leaders arrested under an ancient statute barring "unlawful assemblage, riot and tumult." But the strike spawned nationwide union meetings, and later, the creation of the Australian Labor Party.

Northwest of Barcaldine, the land becomes flat and bare again. The map shows almost nothing for some distance after a place named Winton, so just before sunset I hop out at a turn-off to the plainly named town.

If Blackall is the woolly shoulder of Queensland sheep country, Winton is its neglected dag end. Even at tea time the streets are so scorched and dusty that I feel like Lawrence of Arabia navigating from the highway to the business center. The first sign of impending civilization is the public toilet, labeled "Rams" on the men's door and "Ewes" on the women's. I turn on the cold tap and feel my arms scoured by hot artesian water.

Time to consult my tourist guide. Maybe there's someplace more inviting a little farther along. There isn't.

Anyway, the tourist guide tells me that even wretched Winton has its claims to fame. A "large predator" chased some smaller dinosaurs near town 100 million years ago, leaving tracks that are "a tourist must." More recently, a plane carrying Lyndon Baines Johnson touched down on a Winton airstrip. It was twenty years before he became president, but in a place like this, even brushes with fame-to-be are worthy of recording.

Better still to thrust fame upon oneself. Banjo Paterson was working at the Dagworth sheep station in 1895 when he composed "Waltzing Matilda." The station is actually about 60 miles out of Winton—close enough for the town to claim the poet and splash his name on every local storefront. There's the Matilda Motel, Banjo's Motel and the Matilda Caravan Park. In fact, there isn't a business in town that doesn't somehow get Banjo in on the act.

Except for the barber, Victor Searle. I find his shearing shed tucked at the back of a menswear store. That's the first warning signal. The second is a rack of hats by the barber chair, placed, I can only assume, to provide quick cover for customers made sheepish by Victor's work. The final tip-off is Victor himself, palsied and myopic, wielding the scissors like a pair of garden shears.

It seems Victor is determined to break Jackie Howe's old record. The shearing is finished in three minutes flat. But then, at three dollars a head, Victor has to keep mowing the fleece at a rapid clip.

"Cooler now, aren't you," he says, dusting talc onto my neck and down the back of my shirt. Blond locks of hair lie on the chair and floor like so much spilled spaghetti. Cooler, yes, and ready to be done with sheep country, with anything to do with shearing.

Outside, a hot wind blows across the pale, barren scalp. A decapitated hair tickles between neck and shoulder. The jolly swagman feels for his ears, avoids his reflection in a storefront window, and goes a-waltzing on his way out of Winton.

6
BEYOND THE
BLACK DOT

Dawn. Blinding light. In the back of a ute, trying to figure out where I am. Nothing metaphysical; I just want to know my location on the map, which is blowing around my face as I try to pin it against my knees.

I am an agnostic on most matters of faith, but on the subject of maps I have always been a true believer. It is on the map, therefore it is, and I am.

It is, or should be, a town. There's a black dot a little left of Winton, and a comforting, almost suburban name beside it: Bendemeer. But all I see out the back of the ute is dirt and scrub. There is or should be a major road. It's called the Landsborough Highway, a nice red line running straight from Winton to Cloncurry. We're supposedly traveling down it. But all I see is a rutted, unpaved track no wider than a goat trail. And there is no sign at all of the thin string of blue on the map, next to the red line, marked "Diamantina River." No water anywhere in sight.

I have entered the twilight zone of Australian cartography. From now on the map will be filled with mirages; there will be un-rivers (the waterless Todd in Alice Springs), lakes that are not lakes (the giant saltpans of South Australia), and towns that are no more than water towers. Mapmakers have to fill up the space with something. So if there are no true landmarks about, ad lib a bit. Sketch in a dry river, like the Diamantina. Or identify individual properties, such as Bendemeer. It seems incredible to me that farms should make it onto state maps. But there they are, dotting Queensland like the footprints of tiny insects. That's how much impact man has had on the outback.

Outback. For the first time the word fits. There is no agriculture out here. No towns, only black dots. And nothing more than unpaved tracks connecting them, bordered by endless tracts of arid scrub. "Out to buggery," the driver answered, when I asked him where he was headed from Winton. He meant what he said.

Ludwig Leichhardt was one of the first white men to come this way, on an expedition to Perth in 1848. The German explorer posted a letter from a station near Roma, declaring that he was "full of hope that our Almighty Protector will allow me to bring my darling scheme to a successful termination." The only thing that terminated was Leichhardt and his party of six men. No trace of them was ever found. But there's still a dot beside the station where he posted that final letter before vanishing into empty space.

There's another dot beside the coolabah tree where the Burke and Wills expedition unraveled. As any Australian schoolchild knows, the two explorers, and two other men named King and Gray, became the first whites to cross the continent from south to north in 1861. But they took so long that when they returned to their base camp at Cooper's Creek (minus Gray, who died en route), the rest of their party had already retreated south. All that remained was a blaze on the coolabah tree saying "Dig 3 ft NW" for a small store of supplies.

Wills, sun-dazed and half-starved, didn't think to carve a fresh blaze on the tree. So when a rescue party returned and found the old blaze, they assumed no one had been there. Meanwhile, Burke and Wills and King were just a short way up the Cooper, with nothing to eat but the crushed spore cases of a fern called nardoo. Burke and Wills eventually starved, though King was saved by Aborigines. The Dig Tree still stands in southwest Queensland.

Outback Australia is filled with memorials like that: to the confused, the thirsty, the lost. If their maps were anything like mine, it's no wonder so many explorers perished.

· · ·

One thing can be said with certainty, though: when a black dot becomes a town, it begets a pub. Poor diet is still a hazard of outback travel but sobriety is not.

The first town after Winton, after several hours of dirt and gravel, is an old stagecoach stop called Kynuna. Its centerpiece—and raison d'être, now that the coaches are gone—is a weatherboard pub called the Blue Heeler Hotel. Kynuna only has twenty-two inhabitants, but the traffic at the pub often swells the town to more than twice that size. Southbound travelers drink to brace themselves for the rough road to Winton. The northbound drink to forget the drive—or in some cases, the hike.

"Dave and Derry walked to this pub in the mud and rain," says one penciled message on the turquoise-colored walls. "Here two weeks. Jan. 84." And a little to the northwest on the wall: "Curly Tru Blu Longfulla had a slack attack. 23-1-85."

The Blue Heeler is a kind of shrine to the bored, the bogged, or the blitzed bush traveler. Their scribbled testimony has turned the weatherboard into an outback Wailing Wall. In some spots the writing is so prolific that it has spread in lesions from the walls to the ceiling. "Rockhounds never die," says one prominent scrawl. "They only petrify at the Kynuna Pub."

The panels behind the bar are reserved for regulars. There's a pair of underpants with the pub's name scribbled across the crotch, and a faded listing of the tariff for the pub's "answering service for irate housewives." If a wife calls to ask if her husband's there, a drinker may pay hush money to the publican for the following answers:

> *'Just Left'*: 25 cents.
> *'On His Way'*: 50 cents.
> *'Not Here'*: $1.
> *'Who?'*: $2.

Nor are the messages confined to the walls. Outback Queensland is statement T-shirt territory. "You Toucha My Truck I Breaka Your Face" declares the chest of one drinker. It is all bluff, though. He drains his glass, spies my rucksack, and asks if I need a ride.

A few beers do wonders for the scenery. Look at the jump-ups! Red rock! And emus everywhere! The road is a runway for the flightless birds and they sprint down the bitumen like jumbo jets that never lift off the ground. Great rolls of uprooted scrub, or roly-poly, blow onto the road. Then high-rise anthills loom on both sides, each one marking a tree brought to earth by insects.

I am way out there now, beyond the black dot, beyond sheep country, and into the land of precious rocks. They are sprouting up all around in long ridges of iron ore, dotted with spinifex. The landscape is striking, even majestic; it reminds me of some of the weird, colorful formations in the Utah and Nevada deserts.

Is it possible that this journey is about to turn over a new leaf?

I consult my tourist brochure. A black dot, bigger than the others, labeled Cloncurry, lies just an hour ahead.

"We invite visitors to this rugged land of striking contrasts to take in its stark beauty under the midday sun," the brochure announces. "If it is said 'See Naples and Die,' we say 'See Cloncurry and Live.' " As a general rule of thumb, the more purple the prose in a tourist brochure, the more wretched the place described. Cloncurry promises to be a town of unparalleled blight.

I am not disappointed. In Cloncurry at mid-afternoon, the temperature is idling at 110 degrees Fahrenheit. Three hours later, still waiting for my next ride at the western edge of town, a dry wind has cooled things down to 105.

Finally, I abandon my pack and run into a nearby pub to guzzle a lemon squash and two beers. "This is nothing," a facetious barmaid assures me. "You should be here when it's really hot."

January of 1889, for example. That's when Cloncurry (nicknamed, appropriately, "the Curry") earned a spot in the record book: 127 degrees Fahrenheit in the shade, hottest in Australia and something like third best in the world after the Gobi and Sahara deserts. Burke and Wills were obviously stunned by the heat when they trudged past the present site of the town in 1861. Why else would they have given this burnt patch of turf a lilting Irish name like Cloncurry?

I start questioning my own judgment as soon as I leave the pub. Or are those really penguins I see squatting at every street corner on main street?

Closer inspection reveals that the penguins are cleverly disguised rubbish bins. A little printed message encourages citizens to "Do the Right Thing" and shove their rubbish in the penguin's mouth instead of just letting go of their fish wrappings before they collapse in the street from sunstroke.

Unfortunately, no one does the right thing by me. I swelter beside the road until dark. Even after sunset the town holds the heat like a well-oiled wok; if I camp here tonight, I might wake up as tempura.

A neon motel sign beckons: "Vacancy! Air-Conditioned Units!" In fact, the rooms are so frozen that I scale a wall to shut the Kelvinator off. The television isn't so efficient. "Only one channel," says a sign beneath the screen. "You are in the bush now." The TV has adapted to its polar climate; all I get on the screen is snow.

A good excuse to catch up on my reading. *The History of the Exciting Northwest* tells me that Cloncurry is the gateway to one of the richest mineral deposits on earth. Of course no one knew that at first. The big break came in 1923, when John Miles went searching the scrub for a runaway horse and found an odd chunk of rock instead. He lugged it back to the Assay Office at Cloncurry where, we are told, "it lay for several weeks on the floor used as a doorstop." Finally someone cracked it open and found it was rich with silver and lead.

Mining towns seem to thrive on this kind of lore. I have read these tales—tall ones, I suspect—about the opal country of South Australia and the goldfields out West. Horses tripping over massive nuggets. Little boys falling into fabulous lodes. Rain sweeping slurries of gold dust into diggers' tents. No one ever bothers to tell you that most of those who actually dig for the riches come home empty-handed.

My own luck is no better in the morning than it was in late afternoon. The reason, I suspect, is that mining towns attract a rather raffish breed of visitor. When the blow-throughs don't find gold in the ground, they sometimes look in people's pockets instead. So sensible drivers think twice before welcoming a scruffy wanderer into the passenger seat.

Predictably, then, it is a senseless driver who finally weaves over to pick me up. I glance through the passenger window at a unshaven youth with a cigar stuck in his mouth and a half-empty champagne bottle between his legs. Elsewhere I would turn this driver down rather than risk an intoxicated voyage. ("Sorry, mate. Just realized I'm standing on the wrong side of the road. All turned around from my country.") But I can't bear another hour in Cloncurry, so I climb inside.

The driver smiles and hands me a fresh cigar. "Been a husband for twelve days and a father for one," he says. Right now he's on his way to the Mount Isa hospital to collect his new wife and child. "I guess it's a big deal, having a kid. But except for the splitting headache from celebrating, the shock hasn't set in."

The shock sets in for me an hour later, as soon as we catch sight of Isa. In most of the settlements I've traveled through, the skyline is so stunted that you don't know the town has started until you're almost through it. But Isa's mining complex is so big that its smokestacks and slurries can be seen from 6 miles out. And that's just the visible part. Isa's mine is an industrial iceberg, with only 3 miles showing above ground and another 235 miles lurking beneath. Needless to say, this Colossus of Lodes is one of the biggest silver, lead, and zinc mines in the world.

Usually, mines are hidden away from the communities that serve them. But in Isa, the mine squats right at the end of the main street, forming a kind of grayish-red shadow following you everywhere in town. The settlement huddled at its feet has the itinerant air of a glorified mining camp: there are barracks, single men's apartments, and even a few tent houses from early in the century. But it is the mine itself that makes Isa seem so precarious: looming, always lit, always gouging, vast and close enough to run amok and devour the town in one mighty crunch.

The other shock in Isa is hearing accented English on the streets. Since leaving Sydney, I have seen nothing more exotic than chow mein at the ubiquitous Chinese restaurant; the towns are filled with blacks and whites and no shades in between. In Isa, the mine has lured Arabs, Greeks, Yugoslavs and others into a rich ethnic mix of about thirty nationalities. The tourist literature even claims a few Eskimos.

But cultural differences melt quickly in the outback sun. A generation after the immigrant influx, Isa appears as monochromatic as the crusted red earth surrounding the town. K-mart, car dealerships, and fast-food joints clutter the wide, hot streets. There isn't a piece of pita bread or plate of moussaka to be found.

I settle for a meat pie at the Phoenix Restaurant, and a chat with the Hungarian-born cook, named Marta Alpin. "If I served goulash, I'd be out of business in a week," she explains, frying fishburgers and chips for a group of miners at the counter beside me. "Australians, they don't like strange food. And once in Isa, everybody they are Australians now."

The women-starved miners are more eclectic in their marriage tastes. In recent years about four hundred of them have vacationed in the Philippines and returned with local brides. Others don't bother to make the trip. They just pick a face from one of the photo albums passed around by Filipinos already in Isa, then begin writing to their intended. If all goes well, the young woman is flown over, betrothed, and clothed at the miner's expense.

A miner named Alan explains this to me between bites of his Phoenix fishburger. His brother sent away for a "mail-order bride" and he's thinking of doing the same. "An Australian woman isn't worth two bob—unless she's your mum," he says. "And you can't find one out here anyway."

What you will find in Isa are pubs that cover entire city blocks. It's almost as if they were built as an annex to the mine; workers can poke their noses out from underground and head straight for pubs that are as cool and cavernous as a Pharaoh's tomb. At the Irish Club, the multilevel Grace Brothers of Isa watering holes, I count five hundred chairs and stools on one floor. Every seat is filled by eight o'clock. At another pub, the bar is so long that counter meals are announced like numbers at a bingo game—via a crackly public address system. "Eighty-seven, number eighty-seven. Your dinner is now at the counter."

The Wintons and Cloncurrys of Queensland have left me restless for a little nightlife. But at the entrance to an underground dance joint called The Cave, I'm told that my singlet and thongs are not appropriate attire. I need a shirt with a collar and "enclosed shoes" to get in.

Cold down there, I guess; better to stay on the 90-degree street instead. That's where I meet John Wright, a young man seated on a wall at the end of the main street, backlit by the candelabrum of lights from the mine.

"The dress code's to keep the blacks out," he explains. "Anyway, if you go inside you miss all the street brawls." He gestures at the movie theater which offers *Rocky IV* on its marquee. "Who needs that when you can get it out here for free?"

On this night, though, the Wild West is tame. We watch the broad-faced, broad-shouldered miners pull in at the bottle shop ("thirst-aid stops," as they're called in Isa). We watch their weedy offspring, squeezed into tight jeans and tighter skirts, going underground to dance beneath strobe lights at The Cave. And we see nothing more violent than a drunk spewing into the gutter.

"Sorry," Wright says with genuine remorse, as the streets begin to empty at midnight. "Gonna be here next Saturday?"

Not if I can help it. But at this rate, who knows? In a day and a half I have moved 75 miles. Perhaps my darling scheme, like Ludwig Leich-hardt's, will fizzle out somewhere in northwest Queensland.

I rise before dawn, bolt down an indigestible breakfast called the "Mt. Isa Special" (sausage, onion and egg, drowned in grayish-brown gravy), and hike out of town ahead of the morning heat. Past the car dealerships, past the cheap motels, I am swallowed up by the ancient red hills of the Selwyn Range. Ahead lie the Barkly Tablelands and days of travel through territory even more desolate than what I've just passed through. Back east, a lonely smokestack is all that is visible of Isa.

As I hike down the road, away from the rising sun, the shadow of a huge hunched figure is cast before me. But the unshadowed man appears small in the vast outback spaces. Even a sprawling mine—the most aggressive of human industries and the one most contemptuous of nature—seems but a blip on the horizon. And I am something less. Just a blip on a blip of bitumen, waiting for a ride to carry me on.

7
SNORT OF
BLUE

Hitchhiking can sometimes feel like lying on a riverbank with a line in the water.

With yourself as bait, and only the road and sky for company, you wait with the patience of an angler for a passing car to nibble at your fingertip. And like a fisherman, you pass the time with dreams of hooking something really good.

The best catch I know of was made by my friend Rich Ivry in 1978. He was hitching through the hills of central Oregon when a fire fighter named Annie pulled over to pick him up. As I write, Rich and Annie are being married in the mountains at Bend, not far from where she stopped for him eight years ago. It is a union that has always been blessed, I suspect, by the magic of having begun so randomly on the road.

Hitchhiking is strange that way—at once the loneliest and most social of occupations. One moment you're stranded by the highway, as rootless as a piece of driftwood. The next moment you're thrust into someone else's car, someone else's life. Where the driver goes, you will follow. All the way to the altar in Rich's case.

I'm not setting bait for a spouse the morning I hike out of Mount Isa. But after five uncomfortable days, I'm hungry for the Big Strike. An air-conditioned station wagon, say, with room to stretch out and an ice-filled cooler to dunk my head in between snoozes. Anything to escape the heat and glare for half a day.

The fantasy goes through two hours of refinement—from station wagon to sports car to chauffeur-driven recreational vehicle—before the first car appears on the eastern horizon. The sun's in my eyes so I can't see what sort of vehicle it is, but I hold out my finger, steady as a fishing rod, and reel in the hitchhiking equivalent of a muddy old boot. The car is an overheated wreck from the Mesozoic era with no shock absorbers, even less transmission, and the bent remains of a muffler and tailpipe dangling like entrails from the chassis.

The interior looks as if it's been worked over by vandals on the Cross-Bronx Expressway. Abandoned cassettes melt on the dashboard. A plastic skull dangles where the rear vision mirror should be. The seat vinyl is slashed and the windscreen is so cracked that the driver presses his entire forearm against the glass whenever a truck passes in the other direction.

"A pebble could collapse that shield, no worries," he shouts above the engine's cough and grind. If his car had been a fish, I would have thrown it back.

The driver, named Steve, needs a tune-up as badly as his automobile. He is twenty-two, going on forty-five, with teeth and fingers yellow from nicotine. A 10 A.M. shadow of whiskers and grime looks as if it's been painted on his face. His breath smells like Bhopal.

There's also some lethal gear in his car. A bow and quiver in the backseat, a 30.30 rifle in the front, and two dozen rounds of ammunition strapped to Steve's belt, beside a hunting blade the size of a small machete. The only thing missing is a surface-to-air rocket perched on the car's bonnet.

I inquire gingerly about the bow and arrows.

"You never know what you'll see by the road," Steve says. I gaze out at the blank landscape and wonder what hazard could possibly require so much artillery.

Again my host is less than reassuring. "Got in trouble with the law back in Townsville," he tells me. "Thought I'd head for the Northern Territory and get a fresh start."

I calculate the possibilities. Mercenary. Gunrunner. Armed robber.

"What in?" I ask.

"Auto parts. A mate of mine in Katherine says he can set me up in sales." (I can hear him selling accessories well enough: "With a little firepower, this old sedan could be a bloody Sherman Tank, no worries . . .")

Hitchhiking, among its other virtues, forces you to converse with people you'd otherwise cross the street to avoid. And as we roll through the Queensland scrub, I realize that Steve, for all his martial appearance, is as gentle as the tiny bull terrier that scrambles over the seat and nestles in his lap. Steve strokes the pup's chin and serenades it all the way out of Queensland with the country-and-western tunes of Slim Dusty.

"This song describes me exactly," he says, loading the cassette deck with his only functional tape. Slim sings about "the black sheep of the family." Steve waits a few beats then joins the mournful refrain: "the bigg-EST DIsappoint-MENT was me."

Disappointed his parents ("ran away, see"), let down his parole officer ("breaking and entering") and finally just split to try his luck on the open road. He flips the tape and lets Slim do the talking again.

> *It's freedom that I feel sitting here behind the wheel,*
> *Rolling, rolling, rolling down the long highway.*

Steve keeps up this syncopated rap—first Slim, then him, then the two of them together—all the way to the state border. He even has a song ready, disc jockey style, as we approach the last town in Queensland. "Now I know that love was won and lost in that little town of Camooweal."

There isn't much love lost for Camooweal itself. Overpriced beer and fuel are the town's only visible means of support, and drivers have no choice but to pay the ransom and grumble onwards. "No petrol for 270 kilometers," says a sign at the western edge of town, just in case you forgot to tank up.

The border sign that comes soon after is so covered in graffiti that it's impossible to tell whether it says "Northern Territory Border," "Leaving Queensland," "Welcome to the Never Never," or something altogether different. Then comes a cattle grid, then the bleached bones of cows that withered in the heat before making it across. It is a border with all the warmth and welcome of the Berlin Wall.

The only real change is in the road. Queensland's narrow, bumpy bitumen becomes a two-lane highway as flat and smooth as a pool table. Except that someone's ripped the felt off, leaving a rocky and treeless semidesert for 300 miles. Even properties disappear from the map. The only landmarks are dots labeled "microwave repeater station," as if to remind the traveler that he is passing through an elongated inferno.

It is an unrewarding stretch of road under any circumstances. But in Steven's armored wreck, at 45 miles an hour, it is like being lowered slowly through the circles of hell. The midday sun blazes through the cracked sunroof and windscreen, scorching the black vinyl interior. We drape the seats with towels so they won't burn the backs of our legs. The beer we bought in Camooweal has to be swilled within minutes of leaving the cooler; otherwise it turns too hot to swallow. And when I roll down the window to hang out my sweaty head, the desert air scorches my face like the first hot blast that greets a cook on opening an oven door.

Earlier explorers had more sense and turned around. The government began selling properties in the Northern Territory in the 1860s. Soon after, most of the buyers were demanding their money back. Australia later offered the governments of Japan and India free steerage to any immigrants willing to settle in the Territory. Both nations turned the offer down.

The main obstacle to farming—or just surviving, for that matter—is that there's virtually no surface water in much of the Territory. This may explain why its scattered inhabitants irrigate themselves so heavily with beer. Territory drinking was once legendary. It is now a matter of statistical fact. Fifty-two gallons of beer per annum, per man and woman and child—enough to earn Territorians a listing in the *Guinness Book of Records* as the greatest beer drinkers in the world. A Society for the Prevention of Alcoholism in Darwin folded ten years ago for lack of interest.

Darwin residents don't waste their beer tinnies either. Every June they beat the cans into tin boats and float them, like latter-day ironclads, into the Timor Sea. This ersatz America's Cup is known as the Beer Can Regatta.

In the Territory, beer has also supplanted the metric system as a unit of measure. At Barkly Homestead, the first piss and petrol stop after

Camooweal, I ask the barmaid how far we have to travel to the next dot of humanity.

"It's about a carton to the roadhouse at Three Ways," she says, "then another six-pack from there to Tennant Creek."

I check the homestead's map, dividing twenty-four beers into the number of miles between here and Three Ways. We will have to down a beer every eight minutes to reach the roadhouse on schedule. I question the barmaid's arithmetic.

She laughs. "This is a good road, mate. On a dirt track it would be twice as much."

The Territory has also floated the dollar.

"How much to fix up that tailpipe?" Steve asks the roadhouse mechanic.

"About a carton, I reckon. That's if we don't need parts."

Steve doesn't have that kind of money—or beer—so we drag the tailpipe out of Barkly and into another 125 miles of nothing. When Slim Dusty melts on his fiftieth tour of the tape deck, Steve stops singing and delivers a lecture instead. To survive in the Territory, he explains, the traveler must become fluent in drinking as a second language.

"Get the nouns straight and she'll be jake," he says. The principal rule here is that beer is identified by its markings, not its name. Hence Foster's becomes a "blue can," Victoria Bitter a "green can," and so on through the spectrum. The one irregular noun is Castlemaine XXXX, a beer held in particular contempt by Territorians. If you must order it, don't ask for a yellow can. Just say "barbed wire," XXXX. Get it?

This color and picture coding may reflect a highly developed frontier aesthetic. But I suspect it's simply a shred of common sense in an otherwise senseless place. After driving a carton or so along Territory roads, you can still lean over the bar and identify the color of the beer can, even if you can't read the name on its label.

And if the colors blur, you can ask instead for "a tube" or "a snort" or "a charge." They all mean tinnie in Territory-speak. The morning after, there's always a "kicker over" to get you back on the road again.

I need a kicker over or two by the time Steve deposits me at Three Ways. Like Barkly, Three Ways is an artificial settlement, built around a camping ground, a petrol pump, a restaurant and a pub. No one really lives here; it's just a supply point for itinerant miners, oil field workers and Aborigines who wander in from neighboring camps or stations. When I arrive in late afternoon, all of the above are crowded at the bar.

The first thing I notice is that the Aborigines are much darker-skinned than the toffee-colored blacks I met in New South Wales and Queensland. And they don't seem to speak English, at least not as a first language. A group of fifteen huddles by the dart board, chatting rapidly in a swift singsong that doesn't sound like anything I've ever heard.

The miners at the bar speak English, but their faces are so smeared with black dust that it's hard to tell the two races apart. Pale-faced, and obviously a blow-through, I feel uncomfortably conspicuous—and unnerved enough to forget everything Steve has just taught me.

"Stubbie of Foster's," I say to the barmaid, realizing instantly that I should have said "snort of blue." But she cuts in before I have a chance to correct myself.

"Darwin Stubbie?"

I nod. Apparently, my error has gone unnoticed and I've stumbled onto a local brew. Judging from the raised eyebrows of the miner beside me, this Darwin beer is serious stuff.

A moment later, the barmaid returns with a Foster's bottle the size and shape of a NASA rocket. In the Byzantine lingo of Territory drinking, Darwin refers to the quantity of the beer, not the make. And it seems five quarts is the going rate for a snort at Australia's Top End.

There is no room—in me, or in my pack—for this oversized bottle of beer. So I sheepishly ask for a snort of blue instead. The miner gives me a sympathetic nod.

"It's only a six-pack to the next pub, mate," he says. "One ride and you're there."

8
GETTING MAN

There is a pause between beers and in that pause a glimpse of something altogether different.

The break comes in Tennant Creek, one of the few black dots between Darwin and Alice Springs that deserve the appellation of "town." A gold rush in the 1930s turned the quiet telegraph station into a sprawling miners' camp; it was the last place in Australia where a man could just peg out a claim and start digging with a hammer and tap. Then most of the mineral wealth played out, leaving Tennant Creek with the raw, ugly face of a boom town gone sour. The low-slung façades of empty stores and takeaway restaurants line the main street. Abandoned shafts and Aboriginal humpies dot the fringes. And the stench of blood from a horse-killing abattoir is the first landmark that greets motorists descending from Darwin.

When I arrive at sunset, Tennant appears dark and forbidding, except for a bonfire glowing at the northern edge of town. Predictably, I'm dropped off at a pub. This time it's a rough-and-ready, stand-up saloon called the Miners Bar. Waiting for a beer, I find myself standing beside a black man who has a hook where his hand should be. Not knowing what else to say, I ask him about the flames I saw licking into the evening sky.

"Ceremonial business at the Waramungu camp," he says, in clipped and accented English. In the nonmaterialistic world of black Australia, it is traditional ceremony, not commerce, that is the community's "business." The blacks of this region have held on to their rituals more tightly than Aborigines "back East."

The hook man introduces me to a drinker who has kin among the Waramungu people. He is happy to take me to the camp and introduce me to an elder, or, as he says, "one of the senior men."

The Waramungu camp is a collection of dilapidated concrete buildings scattered through the scrub. Children ride bicycles along the dusty paths between buildings, and women chat quietly, seated in circles on the ground. There are no men in sight, but a chorus of male voices is singing in the distance, by the bonfire.

My companion speaks with an old woman then heads off toward the fire. It is pitch black now, and I walk closely behind him so as not to tear my leg on the prickly scrub. My guide seems to know his way along the narrow path without the aid of light.

A hundred or so men are gathered in a wide circle around the bonfire, stamping their feet and singing. One of the senior men greets us at the edge of the circle. I explain that I'm traveling through and ask if it's okay to watch the ceremony.

"That's fine, mate," he says, smiling. "Can you hold a tune?"

I can't, but he takes my arm anyway and leads me to the circle's inner ring. Between songs, he explains what is going on.

The business at hand is an annual initiation of Waramungu men. Or rather, men is what they shall become after a long night of song and dance, ending at dawn with circumcision. The delicate operation will be performed by one of the senior men, using a well-sharpened pocket knife.

As a Jew, I have a passing acquaintance with that sort of tribal business. It isn't something I think of as a jolly event, at least not for the young male at center stage. But the scene I stumble on in Tennant Creek is as raucous and joyful as a wedding party. Except that there's no alcohol, and no women. Just a dozen dancers and an audience of other men, their faces lit by the bonfire, shouting in pidgin English or their own Aboriginal tongues.

"He can move it, eh?"

"Dance! Dance!"

"Shake it some more, man. Shake!"

The ceremony is a curious mix of the primitive and the twentieth century. Traditionally, the dancers decorated themselves with turkey feathers and elaborate handmade headdresses. Now the feathers are fashioned from cotton diapers, the headdresses from cardboard beer cartons. Only the boughs of bloodwood trees, wrapped around the dancers' ankles, remain of the original costume.

The boughs swish the ground like skirt hems as each dancer stamps quickly at a designated spot before the flames. Their movements—a sort of rapid running in place, all legs and no arms—are set to the music of six senior men, arrayed behind the fire like background singers in a Motown band. They bang boomerangs together, stamp their feet, and urge the dancers on to faster contortions. "Move it, man, move!" "Shake!" Or a playful "That's no good, man. Go back to the end of the line."

The dance is designed to ease the pain of four adolescents who will be circumcised at dawn. The boys are painted in ochre and feathered like the rest, sitting quietly behind the fire with blankets slung in their laps. It is this night, and alone in the bush afterward, that they will "get man."

Boomerangs. Bloodwood boughs. Two hundred feet stamping. The sounds are hypnotic, and for several hours I am drawn into the music, watching one man after another repeat his dance before the flames. During the brief pauses between dancers, men approach me and ask if I have cigarettes. But otherwise, no one seems to pay me any special attention.

In the early-morning hours, there is an unexplained intermission and I decide to leave. I am still a stranger to this culture and unfamiliar with its etiquette. Something in me senses that it is more appropriate for the final drama to be played out in privacy from white eyes.

But no one tells me to go. Here, as in Cunnamulla, Aboriginal society is open wide. For the Waramungu, an expression of interest and respect is all that is necessary for me to share the intimacies of their ritual, their man business.

When I return the following day, the men are flaked out across the camp like battle-weary soldiers, sound asleep in the burning heat. I think of myself groping toward a motel air-conditioner in the night and envy them their ease.

In the afternoon I speak with some of the dancers about the initiation. Their answers are polite but oblique. "I cannot say." "I do not own that knowledge." "Ask one of the senior men. They can explain."

Grant, a bearded, middle-aged man, is one who can explain. He tells me that a young man can be speared or clubbed for speaking indiscreetly about the ceremony; womenfolk in particular are to know nothing of what goes on. I missed my cue and regret having been so inquisitive with the other men.

Grant tells me that the boys are now healing in the scrub, alone. Only designated members of their clan, or "skin," can visit and bring them food. In a few weeks the teenager will return a "free man"; free to take the wife that has been promised to him, and at liberty to wander away from his parents' home. No one can swear at him because he is a Waramungu man, to be treated with respect.

"That is all that I know," Grant says, ending the conversation abruptly. "You will have to ask one of the older men if you want to know more. We are not like white fellas who write it all down in books."

Grant has other business to attend to. There is a service at a local Christian church and many black men will attend. Again, white society has colonized Aboriginal culture but failed to subjugate it. The men regard Christianity not as a system of belief, but as a badge of their opposition to alcohol. "I go to church to keep away from the grog," one of the men explains. "In this town you are either a Christian or a drunk." Western curses, it seems, require Western cures.

I leave the camp at sunset and go for a swim in the shallow waters of the Tennant Creek. It is the first running water I've seen since southern Queensland and it feels as clean and soothing as a quiet bath at the end of a long day's work. No lurching on and off the highway, no heat and dust. Just a gentle current carrying my naked body into the slipstream. Two Aboriginal boys skip rocks across the black water. Giant red anthills loom like mini-Ulurus on the riverbank. Cicadas wail as loudly as fire sirens.

I let my ears dip below the water and gaze up at the desert sky through the silver boughs of a ghost gum tree. The world becomes still and strange and silent. And I feel far away, farther away that I've ever felt before.

I think about the Aboriginal business, about my own business, and how as an adolescent in America, hitchhiking was a way for me to go bush and "get man." This time it is something different. A way to "get boy," perhaps—to rediscover some part of me that is still adventurous and open to whatever comes my way.

I spend a lot of time at home composing lists and filling date books. I like to follow stone cairns when hiking through the bush, even if it's a route I've traveled many times before. My life normally has all the order and direction of a five-year plan.

But it is always the detours that move me, like meeting another culture by firelight, or swimming at first dark in a desert stream.

The American writer Annie Dillard has a theory about these moments. Insight can come to those who wait for it, she says, but it is always "a gift and a total surprise."

"I cannot cause light," she writes. "The most I can do is try to put myself in the path of its beam."

The calm that comes over me in the black water doesn't have the force of a vision. It's simply a gentle feeling that I have put myself in the path of that elusive beam. As the desert sky falls dark over Tennant Creek, I make a silent wish that I can keep my foot on the path when the journey turns homeward again.

9
THE ALICE IS ONLY
BEERS AWAY

"I never miss a pub," Bill Gillholey says by way of introduction. "No chance."

I am back in the white fellas' Territory, on a motorized pub crawl from Tennant Creek to Wauchope to Tea Tree to Alice. Each settlement a pub, each pub a snort or two of blue. Then back on the road, like two men in a canoe, weaving down a river of beer.

"Europe, it has the culture," Bill says, holding the steering wheel in one hand and spilling a beer with the other. "Australia, Australia it has the pubs."

Bill left his native Hungary after the Communist takeover in the 1950s. He opposed the new regime and couldn't find work as a mining engineer. Bill hasn't found engineering work in the Territory either, but he's stayed, laboring as handyman on outback stations and moonlighting as a pub crawler of Olympian dimension. He even adopted the surname of an Irishman he met over a green can somewhere in Darwin. At the Top End, it seems, beer helps cement the ethnic mosaic together.

Beer is also the lifeblood of the Territory's road traffic. There is one central artery, the Stuart Highway, running from Darwin to the South Australian border. Smaller vessels feed into it all along the way, carrying goods and traffic from the body corporal into the greater flow. It is at the junctions that the roadhouses appear to pump and prime the system with gas and beer.

There is nowhere else to stop along the hot dusty drive down "The Track," as Territorians call the Stuart Highway. So the same faces appear at every pub. Travelers drink and nod at one another, then move in a convoy to the next hotel. By Alice Springs, I will know everybody at the bar.

If I don't lose consciousness. Pub crawling with Bill makes me realize how much I still have to learn about Australian-style drinking. Americans don't necessarily drink less but they do drink differently. A beer or two after work. Cocktails before dinner. Maybe a blow-out at the weekend. Like everything else in the United States, drinking is done at prescribed times, for a prescribed purpose. And there are still "dry counties" in the Bible Belt where drinking isn't done in public, at least not legally. Elsewhere, there is a growing rebellion against anything caloric or intoxicating: "lite beer" and diet cola are the products of a lingering Puritanical strain.

In Australia, I soon discovered, this toehold of discipline doesn't exist. Drinking is done at all times, for no specific purpose. Down a drink at an 11 A.M. press conference, no worries. Knock back a bottle of wine at lunch and head straight back to work. Drain the hotel mini-bar, just because it's there. Don't let a little grog get in the way of whatever else it is you're doing.

So for a year I drank and learned and drank some more. I learned that it's bad form to make a social visit without a bottle in hand; still more gauche to leave the pub before it's your turn to shout a round. I even accustomed myself to the pub around the corner from my Sydney home, an "early opener" where the dockworkers gather for a quick beer before their shift begins. At 6:30 in the morning.

The Territory is my graduate education. Bars can be crowded at any hour, any day of the week. The distinction between public bar, saloon and lounge dissolves altogether. And as the roadhouses become more isolated, the atmosphere becomes more bizarre. Aviaries and zoos are a common feature. Usually the wildlife is just a camel or emu milling about outside, but sometimes the animals wander inside as well. Other roadhouses host special events. The tiny settlement at Wauchope, for instance, holds an annual cricket match against the world. The home team has an advantage, of course; Wauchope's so remote that it's difficult for challengers to field a team.

But it is the heroic drinking that is the distinguishing feature of outback roadhouses. Again, etymology is the key to Territory thinking. A ten-ounce glass of beer isn't a schooner, or a pot; it's "a handle." Apparently, ten ounces is what's needed to get a handle on yourself before returning to the road. Just don't forget to take away a six-pack of blue tubes to hold you until the next hotel.

"The esky, it is just for back-up," Bill explains, emptying a carton of Foster's into his cooler outside the Wauchope roadhouse. "Even if I'm loaded up, I never miss a pub. No chance."

One pub in particular. South of Wauchope, in the middle of a sand-blasted, sun-bleached desert, there is a road sign painted on the trailer of a capsized road train: "Barrow Creek Hotel—21-1/8 km." It is the first time since entering the Territory that I've seen the distance between two points calculated, well, as distance. Never have I seen it measured so precisely.

The pub that appears two tinnies farther on doesn't look like much, but outback pubs rarely do; a plain collection of iron and timber, piled onto concrete blocks. The rest of Barrow Creek consists of a few houses, a windmill and an old building that once housed a repeater station for the Overland Telegraph. When the telegraph was built between Adelaide and Darwin in the 1870s, Morse code couldn't leap more than 200 miles at a time. So outposts such as Barrow Creek were set up to keep the dots and dashes moving along.

Now it's the road traffic that must be resupplied. Not that anyone will emerge from the pub to pump fuel.

"I have a rule—never go out to serve petrol," says the publican, Lance Pietsch. "If you've got some competition, then you have to do something. But Barrow Creek? If they don't fill up here they're stuffed. And if I don't come out, they come in. Then I've got them drinking beer, buying pies and T-shirts. That's where I make my quid."

It is the first clue to Pietsch's proprietary thinking. The second is a photograph of himself hung crooked behind the bar. Pietsch is a big-shouldered bloke with the broad chest and thick arms of a butcher. But no harm in making himself even more picturesque by turning the portrait askew.

"I hang everything crooked," he says. "Gives the place character."

The entire establishment is an essay in calculated kitsch. There's a pet kangaroo hopping around behind the bar, an emu somewhere out the back. And the walls at Barrow Creek make the artwork I've seen in

Queensland pubs look like cave paintings. Nude photos and rude bumper stickers are the main adornment. Then there's a row of tattered stationmasters' hats hung like headstones in a medieval cathedral: Telecom Tom, Shim Ree, Tossa Reidy. Each man remembered by his hat, and by a short epitaph.

"Been there—done that," says the writing beneath Tossa Reidy's crumpled hat. "Has a very short fuse and prolific swearer."

And beside Telecom Tom's: "Just passing through, 1952. Been here ever since."

And he still is, a crinkled, khaki-clad figure perched atop a bar stool marked by a plaque that says: "Reserved for Barrow Creek superannuated citizens." In a community of fourteen people, he is the only one.

Tom once took part in a dingo cull. He was paid by the number of ears he turned in as proof of having killed the wild dogs. Tom put a few ears on top and filled the rest of the bag with dried apricots. "No one ever bothered to look too close," he says with an impish grin. "The smell's too revolting."

Nearby on the wall is something really revolting: an icon labeled "Genuine Northern Territory Bullshit." It's a large and convincing blob attached to a framed piece of cardboard.

Pietsch swears it's the real thing. "Genuine cow turd, fair dinkum," he says. "I nailed it up myself and held it together with hair spray." I'm dubious but not dubious enough to poke a finger into the thing and find out if he's telling the truth.

The hotel's pièce de résistance is a tapestry of dollar notes hanging on a wall behind the bar. It's called the "bush bank," and there are smaller branches at several other Territory pubs. Drinkers can plan their financial future by signing a note—$2, $10, even $100—and pinning it to the wall. Then, when passing through at a later date, drinkers can simply make a withdrawal by reclaiming their note, and keep on drinking. Foreign currencies are also accepted.

The bush bank is obviously a liquid investment, but not a foolproof way of saving money. Most of the depositors are station hands or oil workers who return to Barrow Creek infrequently, if at all. When there is a run on the bank, the money usually lasts about as long as chips at the roulette table. "I've never seen a bloke claim his money without spending it before going out the door," Pietsch says. "The house always wins."

Sometimes the drinkers don't make it out the door either; they collapse on the wooden floor instead. One binge during an annual horse race went on for five days. "Blokes just fell off their stools, woke up and started drinking again." Most days, though, the hotel stays closed between about midnight and 7 A.M. Eight of Barrow Creek's fourteen inhabitants work at the pub, filling beer glasses or making beds. The dead of night is their only break between shifts.

"But if a bloke needs a beer real bad at four A.M., he'd probably get served," Pietsch says. "Bush rules."

After all, it's about 60 miles to the next pub. Only a heartless publican would exile a man into that much desert empty-handed.

Pietsch claims to have been a candidate for the priesthood before becoming a publican. He was deep in the classics, Latin, and Greek when he landed a summer job as a station hand. That's when he discovered drinking, smoking, and sex. "I asked myself, 'How long has this been going on?' and gave the seminary a miss."

It's been downhill ever since; first as bookmaker, then as a barkeeper in South Australia. "My only claim to fame was thirteen convictions for being present at a two-up game," he says. "Occupational hazard." Genuine Northern Territory bullshit, perhaps. But out here, who's to know? Who's to care?

Barrow Creek's isolation helps Pietsch escape another hazard of his trade: the regular drinkers. Pietsch hates them. "In South Australia they'd come in every day for six years and say 'How's it going, Lance?' They couldn't even remember being carried out the door the night before."

At Barrow Creek, the only face he sees on a regular basis is Telecom Tom's. Almost everyone else is passing through. Myself included. I deposit a two-dollar note at the bush bank, just in case, and head out into the desert with Bill again.

"Europe, only Europe, you find a Prado, a Uffizi, a Jeu de Paume," Bill says, becoming more grandiose with every swallow of beer. "But tell me. Where in Europe you find a Barrow Creek Hotel?" He puts his tinnie between his legs, presses the tips of his thumb and forefinger together and kisses them. "Nowhere." For Bill, Barrow Creek is the Louvre of outback pubs.

It is in a beer daze somewhere south of Barrow Creek that the scattered images start coming together. Tattersall's Hotel at the border of New

South Wales and Queensland. The Blue Heeler Hotel in Kynuna. And now the picturesque watering holes of the Northern Territory. They are kin to one another, but kin to nothing else I've ever seen.

At first I regarded these pubs as eccentric outposts on the way to the Main Event. Somewhere "out there," I subconsciously supposed, a scene or character would bound off the horizon screaming "This is it, mate! Fair dinkum Australia!" I would stumble across the gem (like the mythical prospector at Cloncurry) and carry its wealth with me back to the city.

Travel rarely pays out in that fashion, least of all in Australia. The civilization is too far-flung to allow for many generalizations. And in the outback, home and work life is usually sealed away from view, way off in the scrub.

The lonely roadhouse offers a window into this remote society. And peering blearily through it, I see an irreverence and whimsy that intrigue me: if not the real Australia, at least something more exotic than the international gloss of Sydney.

A Michelin Guide to the outback would, like Bill Gillholey, never miss a pub. No chance.

10
CENTERED

Two cartons later I land in the town called Alice.

My arrival is as indirect as the pub crawl that's carried me there. Bill bypasses town and drives to a rocky slope facing west into the Mac-Donnell Ranges. No verdant Blue Mountains here, just eroded ridges of red rock, winding into the desert. But it isn't the scenery Bill's after. Unable to be a mining engineer by profession, he has taken up mining as a hobby. And this arid hillside is one of the best places in the Territory to scrape for amethyst.

"In my country, every inch of earth has been turned," he says, sinking his pickaxe into the stony red earth. "Here, who knows what is still buried beneath the ground?"

His passion for precious stones is contagious, particularly after a dozen beers. So for several hours we take turns with the pickaxe, then sift through the upturned dirt for the purple-black shimmer of amethyst. All we find are tiny shards, nice enough to keep but not of any value.

"Some day," Bill says, cracking our final tube of blue, "some day I hit it big. I not come halfway across the globe to live like a peasant."

Bill leaves me at a bottle shop in Alice. He will do some electrical work for a friend, then head back to the Top End around midnight; best to have some beer on board, just in case.

I wander into Alice, drunk, covered in dirt, and loaded with gemstones, like an outback digger ready to blow his hard-won claim. But

I've walked onto the wrong set. Alice has none of the frontier character of the outposts I've passed through en route. The town's old center has been torn down for a pedestrian mall. The once dusty streets are paved now with tourist gold; a casino, gift shops, and Kentucky Fried Chicken have been grafted on top like so much alien skin.

At a coffee shop I hear a middle-aged man with an American accent and go over to greet him. We exchange the obligatory "Where ya from?" and then he invites me for a hamburger at a nearby restaurant. "Almost like home," he says, sinking his teeth into a thick slab of ground beef, hidden inside an enormous bun. Remarkably, it is.

The man works at Pine Gap, or the "space base," as the satellite station is known in Alice. Not known, really, because everything about Pine Gap is a secret. Everyone assumes it's a CIA base, but the U.S. won't confirm or deny this. Everyone "knows" that the strange white domes in the desert are a listening station, taking in data from spy satellites—but, again, that's unofficial. Christopher Boyce, the California communications technician who sold secrets to the Russians and whose story is told in *The Falcon and the Snowman*, said at his trial that his work for the U.S. involved "day-to-day deceptions in our transmissions to Australia." He didn't go into any detail, though he later named Pine Gap as a conduit for the false information. Again, no one knows.

And this employee, munching his hamburger and chatting amiably about baseball, isn't about to make me any wiser. We talk about the Los Angeles Dodgers ("headed for the World Series next season, no fuckin' doubt about it"), the difference between American and Australian beer ("Aussie stuff makes our beer taste like dishwater"), and the weather in Alice ("fan-fuckin'-tastic"). But neither he, nor another American I meet, utters a clue as to what it is they do at Pine Gap.

"My job's so classified even my wife doesn't know what I do," one of them tells me, "and she used to work at the base herself."

I ask how the two hundred or so Americans at the base cope with the isolation. He says that they join as many clubs as possible to give them some "neutral ground" to share with their Australian neighbors. Baseball clubs. Bridge clubs. Astronomy clubs. Make as many friends as you want, just don't ever mention what it is you do for a living.

It is an apt commentary on Alice Springs. Like the space base employees, Alice has traded its identity for a patch of neutral turf to unfurl for the world. Tourists can come from Anywhere, Western World, roll dice at the casino or pitch and putt at the golf course, and never feel too far from home.

Far from home is how I'm feeling, though, standing at a street corner with a rucksack, a heavy beer buzz, and 2,000 miles of sweaty travel behind me. It is the kind of faraway feeling that has me squeezing into a phone booth with enough twenty-cent pieces in one pocket to counterbalance all the amethyst in the other. I've called Geraldine two or three times for a quick reconnaissance ("I'm in such-and-such . . . all in one piece . . . I miss you. . . ."). But we haven't had a proper conversation.

Nor do we now. I let the phone ring and ring, then call again to make sure I've dialed correctly. Still nothing. I stand there in the booth for a moment, feeling despondent, then phone my coordinates in to the newspaper office. After all, I secured my escape with the promise of writing some stories about the outback. Seems like a good time to "check in."

The phone call goes something like this:

STD LINE:	*bleep bleep bleep.*
OFFICE:	Chief of Staff's desk.
HITCHHIKER:	G'day. It's Horwitz. [*Triumphant pause.*] I'm in Alice.
OFFICE:	Good on you, mate. [*Phones ringing, fingers clattering against keyboards.*] Now how about some real work?
HITCHHIKER:	
OFFICE:	Right. I'll transfer you to Saturday Review. They want something on the Rock.

For once the office switchboard functions and another editor comes on. He wants to know if I can go to Uluru. Yes, I guess. Feature on tensions after the handover of the Rock to Aborigines? Sure, why not. Two thousand words? By Saturday? Well, okay. Click.

The telephone wire has reeled me into shore like so much played-out tuna.

.   .   .

Part of me is relieved to make contact again. Alice was my destination, as much as I had one. I'm not sure whether to go deeper into the scrub or begin making my way back to Sydney. Now, at least, I'll have a few days to decompress before figuring out my next maneuver.

And a few days to travel on the company budget, slamming down a desert track in a souped-up Detroit roadhog with the radio and air-conditioner blasting at full tilt. ("Top unit, mate," the Hertz man said, slapping his palm on the bonnet. "A real ripper.") The road is a thin line of bitumen and my rented Ford is sucking it up, 5 miles at a time . . . 60 . . . 65 . . . 70. . . . I am moving too fast and I know it. But after days of trudging by the road, waiting for someone else to carry me on, I am intoxicated by horsepower, by my own control.

A massive, flat-topped mountain tears my eye off the road and almost sends me flying into the scrub. There are skid marks all over the highway; obviously, I'm not the first to be fooled by this warm-up to the Rock, called Mount Conner. After days in the flatlands, the eye rediscovers altitude with all the enthusiasm of an adolescent recognizing, for the very first time, the sublime beauty of the female breast. Then the mountain fades into flatness again.

There is no mistaking the great red beast that struts onto the desert stage a short while later. William Gosse, the first white man to reach the Rock in 1873, called it "the biggest pebble in the world." Rising 1,115 feet into the air, the Rock is remarkable because it is absolutely freestanding. The Olgas are only 12 miles away but too far to make the Rock part of any range. So there it sits, all alone on the desert plain, looking from a distance like an oversized loaf of bread: a huge, mis-shapen damper, baked in the midday sun and left to petrify for a few million years.

Up close, the loaf becomes animate, even sensual. From one angle it is a Rubens nude, all thighs and buttocks turning pink in the desert heat. A bit further on it is a stone fortress, or a castle of sand. Then curves and breaks appear and Uluru becomes many rocks, locked in an awkward polygamous embrace.

It is this chameleon quality that has made Uluru one of the world's most photographed lumps of stone. Like its weird, rounded neighbor, Mount Olga, the Rock is as ambiguous as eddies in a stream. Shift the light a bit, or move back a step, and the landscape takes on a whole new dimension.

Ernest Giles understood that, although it was Mount Olga that obsessed him. William Gosse was the first to reach the Rock, but Giles was the first to see it, on an expedition to the center in 1872. He was so tantalized by the center that he staggered through the desert twice more to rediscover the spot.

Giles's notes on the three expeditions read like the musings of an adolescent rummaging through a drawer for different personae. At one moment he tries on the scientific mien of Charles Darwin; at the next, the muse of Percy Bysshe Shelley. And then he is just a heat-dazed Englishman again, wandering through the arid heart of the Antipodean desert.

Giles's first entry describing Mount Olga in 1872 is prosaic enough: "It is formed of several vast and solid, huge, and rounded blocks of bare red conglomerate stone," he wrote, "being composed of untold masses of rounded stones of all kinds and sizes, mixed like plums in a pudding."

His second go at Mount Olga is more architectural: "It displayed to our astonished eyes rounded minarets, giant cupolas, and monstrous domes." On a return visit in 1874, he becomes painterly, almost psychedelic. The Olgas suggest "five or six enormous pink haystacks leaning for support against one another." Loosening up now, he sees "the back of several monstrous kneeling pink elephants . . . or [a] Chinese gong viewed edgeways."

Animal, vegetable, gong—whatever. Now for the Rock. "Mount Olga is the more wonderful and grotesque; Mount Ayers the more ancient and sublime." Reminiscent, perhaps, of Shelley's ode to Ozymandias. He writes without shame: "Round the decay of that colossal rock, boundless and bare, the lone and level sands stretch far away."

Sadly, a Romantic imagination didn't count for much in those days. To the land-hungry colonists, Giles's expeditions did little more than demarcate vast tracts of arid territory to be avoided. He found neither an inland sea nor land of any pastoral value. And the landmark for which his journeys are best remembered is a desert—the Gibson Desert, named for the member of his party who died while trying to cross it. Giles published his journals and saw out his days as an unsung clerk at an office in the Western Australian goldfields.

But it is to Giles that we owe the name of every second bump, claypan, and riverbed between Adelaide and the center. One mountain suggested Shakespeare to him and he named it Oberon. A salt plain evoked Spain and so became Lake Amadeus, after King Amadeo. And when he felt less inspired, or depressed by the hardships of desert travel, Giles reached for blunter labels: Mount Desolation, Thirsty Glen, Stinking Pit.

Yet this prolific name dropper was struck dumb by his first view of the Rock. He came within 18 miles of it in 1872, made notes in his journal about an unnamed range south-east of the Olgas, and turned back to Adelaide.

So the Rock's christening was left to William Gosse, a surveyor who journeyed to the center a year later with four white men, three Afghan camel drivers and a "black boy" named Moses. If Giles carried all of English literature in his head, Gosse stuffed his brain with the name of every dignitary and benefactor in the young colony of South Australia. And compared to Giles, his journals read like notes from the least memorable of geography lessons:

Saturday, July 19.

Camp in Spinifex Sandhills, Barometer 28–12 in, wind south-east. Continued same course, in direction of hills, over the same wretched country. The hill, as I approached, presented a most peculiar appearance, the upper portion being covered with holes or caves. . . . I have named this Ayers Rock, after Sir Henry Ayers.

That's as lyrical as the story gets. Having named the Rock for the South Australian premier, he was of course obliged to climb it. After "scrambling two miles barefooted, over sharp rocks," he "succeeded in reaching the summit, and had a view that repaid me for my trouble." He busily set about naming the surrounding ranges—after the governor and the surveyor-general of South Australia—then scrambled down. One wonders what Ernest Giles would have splashed on the same canvas.

As it is, we are left with a Rock named Ayers, and with the curious Western compulsion to scale every mountain, no matter how arduous the ascent. "The climbing of Ayers Rock was one of his lifelong ambitions," declares a metal plaque at the mountain's base, in memory of a Newcastle man who died of a heart attack on the way up. There are a dozen memorials beside it to fallen or coronary-stricken climbers, which makes for a grim caveat emptor to all who begin the ascent.

To most whites the Rock remains what it was for Gosse: a kind of geological freak, an oversized pebble to be gawked at and conquered. But to Aborigines, it is Uluru, the place where totemic beasts met in a Dreamtime Battle of Hastings. Uluru is still etched with the lines of battle. Kuniya, the Carpet Snake, was victorious over another serpent named Liru, and the Kuniya still lives inside the Rock. The Devil Dingo won control of the summit, while the Hare Wallaby retreated from the field, leaving creases down the mountain's face. The Aborigines who dwell beneath the Rock—Uluru's traditional "owners"—still honor these ancient deeds and derive their kinships from them. Uluru is "a kind of continental navel," writes Thomas Keneally, "the point at which the Aboriginal demigods, the ancestor heroes, half human and half animal, cut the umbilical cord connecting earth to heaven."

My tutor at Uluru is a Pitjantjatjara man named Tony Tjamiwa. As Grant explained to me at Tennant Creek, there is no textbook of Aboriginal belief. But because Aborigines lack well-defined hierarchies as well, it is hard to find anyone who will speak for the community as a whole. Tjamiwa is one of those rare spokesmen, pressed into service by the crush of curious whites at the Rock.

Even so, it is very slow going. We meet at Mutitjulu, a community of several hundred blacks near the base of the Rock. He understands little of my language and I not a word of his; Pitjantjatjara seems impossibly cluttered with the letters j, g, and k, and delivered in a high-pitched singsong that mushes the words together.

"Ananguku ngura nyangatja Tjukurpa." He points at the Rock and sketches a serpentlike creature in the dust. "Tjuta tjuku-tjuku." More scraping in the dust. Our "talks" have almost broken down when a white ranger arrives to provide a rough translation from Pitjantjatjara to English to Pitjantjatjara again.

The concepts Tjamiwa is trying to explain are as foreign as his dialect, which is one reason Aboriginal belief is so poorly understood by whites. Take the central concept of Tjukurpa. Our clumsy translation of it—Dreamtime—suggests a kind of Old Testament fable with Freudian overtones. But to Tjamiwa, the Dreamtime is past and present and future rolled into one. It is not only his history, but also his law; a seamless fabric of knowledge and belief.

Aboriginal art is also opaque to Western eyes. Even the fanciful Giles found little to say about the cave paintings he discovered at the Rock; they were "ornamented in the usual aboriginal fashion," he wrote, with "parallel lines with spots between them." Tjamiwa shows me a bush tucker bowl, used to collect berries and nuts. It has an abstract design burned into the quandong wood—at least it looks abstract to me: swirling lines and circles, much like the lines and circles on other bowls he shows me. But to Tjamiwa it tells a particular and whimsical Dreamtime tale about two women who chase a goanna deep inside a cave. At the bottom of the pit the women meet two snake men, whom they eventually marry.

Uluru dominates Tjamiwa's visual and spiritual landscape. He built a hut recently, making sure that the doorway opened directly on to a view of his "Dreaming Trail"—the creased north face of the Rock to which his people are connected. "I do not own this thing," he says of Uluru. "It owns me."

I envy Tjamiwa the security of having his history, his law, his roots all preserved in a massive piece of stone. But this strength of Aboriginal belief is also its greatest vulnerability. Lose the land, or become alienated from it, and Aboriginal culture loses its very soul.

Even as Tjamiwa speaks, Uluru's face is covered by tourists: "minga juta," he calls them, which translates as "lots of ants." Greater armies still—advertisers, developers, promoters of every stripe—are clamoring like Visigoths at the gate. A New Wave band wants to set up a stage, using Uluru as a backdrop for a televised concert. A film crew asks permission to crash an airplane into the Olgas. Another wants to roll boulders down the Rock. And a self-promoting hang glider doesn't even ask: he just jumps from the summit and floats to earth again.

Somehow, though, Tjamiwa and his kinsmen remain calm in the face of this onslaught. Perhaps it is because the magic of the place seems to rub off on all but the thickest skinned of visitors. Australians may litter beaches and bush trails but here the land is unspoiled. Tourists, particularly Americans, often display an odd impulse to shrink even the grandest of natural wonders to human size. "Majestic doesn't appeal to us," writes Garrison Keillor in his gentle satire of Midwestern America, *Lake Wobegon Days*. "We like the Grand Canyon better with Clarence and Arlene parked in front of it, smiling."

But Uluru seems to humble and inspire respect, even from the Clarences and Arlenes. I meet a few of them—"Idaho potatoes!" they exclaim—armed with Instamatics and Budweiser caps, clustered at the base of the Rock. When I tell them about the stories Tjamiwa has shared with me, they ask if it's blasphemous to climb onto Uluru's face. I sense that it is, and as we follow the dashes of white paint marking the beginning of the climb, something feels awkward. With a few of the others I retreat to the base and circumnavigate the mountain instead.

At sunset, the tourists gather to watch the Rock begin its dance through the spectrum, from red to orange to pink to purple to red again, then brown and black. An expectant hush falls over the audience, like the quiet at first dark in a theater. Only the sound of camera shutters breaks the silence. And when the show is done, the audience drifts away, leaving the great desert beast to bed down in peace for the night.

Even in midsummer the warmth drains from the desert air as soon as the light is gone. I dig my toes into the still-warm sand, as if to grip the elusive spirit that dwells here. I feel centered now, peaceful, ready to move on. . . .

It is morning and the rented Ford speeds toward Alice like a steed that smells the barn. I touch my foot to the accelerator and seven hundred horses of power pound off through the scrub . . . 60 . . . 65 . . . 70. . . . . Nothing but empty road and empty space to measure myself against . . . 75 . . . 80 . . . 85. . . .

I reach for the radio dial, catch a wheel in the road's soft shoulder, swerve once, and spin off the bitumen backward.

The Ford swan dives off an embankment. Then it begins to roll. There is an instant when I realize that the car is going over and in that instant I wait for the vertebrae to crack, the skull to cave in. I do not wonder if I will die, just when. The last thing I see is a blur of sand and stone, upside down, rushing up to meet me. Fade to black.

I wake, suspended by the seat belt, hanging upside down, with my head pressed against the car's crushed rooftop. Blood drips slowly past my face and onto the ceiling. Outside, the wheels still spin, the engine still spits and groans. And inside, the radio drones along: "After nine overs of play, Australia is none for 30. . . ."

I was trying to find something other than the cricket when I reached for the radio and skidded off the road.

Slowly, I start taking stock of the damage. There is broken glass in my nose and under my tongue. I lick my front teeth; having chipped them twice before, I assume they will be the first thing to go. But the enamel is intact. I try to wiggle my toes. They wiggle. I feel gingerly for the leak that is still draining blood down my chest and onto the ceiling. A deep gash in my thigh, a bloody nose, a sliced arm. I am bumped and bruised, badly shaken, but otherwise fine. Lucky boy.

I undo the seat belt and scramble through the space where the windscreen used to be. My leg hurts, so I crawl on hands and knees to the road. Here I am again, lying in the hot sun by an empty highway, waiting for a ride to carry me on.

My fortune knows no bounds. On this lonely stretch of road, a car happens to be just a few minutes behind me, and not just that: the driver is an off-duty cop from Alice. Immediately he takes control. Two strong hands plant themselves under my armpits and pull me onto the backseat. Two strong legs disappear over the embankment to collect my possessions, which have been thrown from the boot of the Ford like so much confetti. Then the man stands by the highway staring at the car and nodding in disbelief.

"Don't know how you walked away from that one, mate," he says.

Only then do I take my first look back. The rented Ford has become what is known in insurance circles as a "write-off." It looks like a tinnie that someone has stomped on with steel-toed boots. The only bit of uncrushed metal is a small cocoon around the steering wheel. The rest is a steel and chrome coffin.

There have been close calls before this: at gunpoint in America and once at the mercy of a piece of chicken lodged inside my throat. But on those occasions, I faced my possible demise with disbelief and a childlike sense of invulnerability. Somehow, some way, everything would turn out all right.

Careening off the road at high speed is different. Like everyone else, I am too well acquainted with the statistics of roadside death to feel indestructible in that situation. And in a way, I had it coming. "Mr. Leadfoot," my father used to call me, as I sped through suburban streets as a teenager. In ten years' time, I hadn't changed.

They say the last words of airplane pilots, picked up from black boxes in downed planes, are usually "oh shit" or "dammit"—more an expression of annoyance than of terror. A black box in the Ford would have picked up a kind of mournful sigh: an unreformed speed demon wishing he could hit the rewind button to tape that part over again.

Now, slumped in the backseat of the policeman's car, I feel like I'm lying in a bathtub with the water draining out. Someone's pulled the plug and I'm going down, way down. This is what shock is, I guess. Not fear or hurt, just a huge, gaping emptiness, like one of those bottomless pits in television cartoons. There is nothing to do but try and fill the hole, which I do by chattering at the policeman for the hour-long drive to Alice. If he gets in a word, I don't hear it, so busily am I shoveling noise into the void.

In Alice my mind goes on automatic pilot. There are police forms to fill out, car-rental papers to sign. At the police station I sheepishly confess to driving over 75 miles an hour. "No worries," the officer says, "most people burn down the Track at ninety." It is all as straightforward and painless as paying a parking fine.

The officer asks if I want to go to the hospital. Suddenly, all I want to do is be home. The image of nursing my wounds in Alice, with nothing but my own thoughts for company, fills me with a strange sort of terror. The officer seems relieved. He calls a tow truck to collect the Ford for transportation to a metal grave. Then he rings a taxi for me and goes back to watching cricket. "Matthews has faced eighty-eight balls on this wicket. . . ."

It is on the way to the airport that the numbness finally wears off. My leg feels as if someone's planted a kitchen knife just above the knee. And my head spins every time I think how much worse it could have been. I feel light-headed, short of breath, panicky.

Then absurdity intervenes. I rush onto the plane forgetting that my nose, shirt, and trousers are still caked with blood. I look at the faces lining both sides of the aisle and feel about as welcome as a Palestinian arriving late at a Jewish wedding.

I go to claim my assigned seat, which is in between two other passengers. The man to my left throws on his headphones and presses his entire torso against the plane window. The woman to my right tries to squeeze into the ashtray on her armrest.

As soon as we're aloft, a stewardess with huge false eyelashes rushes up to ask if I "require assistance." A moment later I am in the galley sipping Scotch while she examines the gash in my thigh.

"Well, that's one sure way to get a girl to take off your pants," she says, bandaging the wound.

I bolt into full consciousness again. Back in the world of the living. Life is as real and banal as a bad joke told by a stewardess with eyelashes as long as her nose. I can't stop laughing. The stewardess thinks I'm crazy, which temporarily I am.

11
HALLEY'S
COMET

The leg heals quickly but there's a hole in my head where the road keeps winding in.

Usually it's the highway south of Alice and I'm speeding down it in the big rented Ford. I reach for the radio dial, the car flips up on two wheels and begins to roll. And there's the scrub again, upside down, rushing up to meet me. I reach for the radio dial, the car flips up on two wheels and begins to roll. . . .

My mind keeps replaying the moment like a needle reaching for a scratch in a record over and over again.

But there's another image as well, less haunting, more familiar. It's a clear blue outback morning with a hitchhiker leaning against his pack, a map spread on his knees, imagining what the next stretch of highway will bring. He folds the map as a car approaches and sticks out his finger. *Cummon, baby. Don't say maybe.*

The car slows and the hitchhiker climbs inside. Then the phone rings and I am back in the tall gray building where I work downtown. No windows in this office, just the fluorescent glow of letters moving across a computer screen. A reporter at the next desk flicks his cigarette into a half-empty cup of coffee. It sizzles for a second and a small stream of smoke lifts off the gray-brown liquid.

Deadline, mates. Where's that copy? Horwitz, where's that copy? Horwitz? HorWITZ!

It is a month before the crash begins to fade, and another month before there is a chance to return to the road once again.

I have changed my habits with the hemispheres, but there is still some internal rhythm that comes alive in April. Eliot's month, "breeding/ Lilacs out of the dead land, mixing/Memory and desire, stirring/Dull roots with spring rain." The great thaw begins and life seems ready to blossom all over again.

That's what "spring fever" in the Northern Hemisphere is all about. Here, of course, April carries the melancholy of summer ending and winter closing in. But why let Australian weather patterns get in the way of good poetry? Can't my dull roots be stirred in autumn as well?

Dull is how I'm feeling in the slipstream of the morning, when the first rush of caffeine has rippled through my nervous system, leaving me an hour short of lunchtime, tired, irritable, restless. I wade listlessly through the mail on my desk. Is this how Ernest Giles felt, his journeys ended, pushing paper at some clerk's desk in Western Australia?

I plod through the hate mail ("Dear Sir, it has recently come to my attention that in your misleading article of . . ."), the press releases ("Did you know that Matchbox Toys Pty Ltd, one of the most respected names in the Toy World . . ."), the announcements of boring events ("The Brickmakers Association of New South Wales will hold its annual . . .").

All the usual stuff. Then, a wrist flick away from the rubbish, one envelope marked "Northern Territory Government" wins a last-second reprieve.

"Alice Springs has been named by leading astronomers as the best point for viewing Halley's Comet," it says. "Has your newspaper given thought to sending a correspondent to Central Australia for this once-in-a-76-year-special-guest-star appearance?"

If it hasn't, it will now. I fold the press release in my shirt pocket, straighten the knot on my tie, and stride off to the glass boxes where the editors reside. The script is ready by the time the secretary waves me in. A few stories on the "guest-star appearance," a feature or two on the outback, then a story of my own to finish, on my own time. Half a continent, still unexplored.

. . .

The three-hour flight from Sydney to Alice makes my earlier journey seem as tortured and slow as a drunken weave home from the pub. But just as flying shrinks all sense of distance, so too does it sharpen contrast. Before, the center of Australia seemed no more remarkable—or un-remarkable—than the bleached and barren scrub I had hitchhiked through to get there. This time, climbing out of Sydney smog and easing down through the cloudless blue of an outback afternoon, the center seems as light and crisp as the celery in my Bloody Mary. I stare out the window at the squiggly ridges of sand, swimming like minnows across the surface of the desert, and feel as I did so many months ago, when I flew over Australia for the first time and imagined that I was descending onto an alien planet.

"The land is here, sky high and blue and new as if you'd never taken a breath out of it," D. H. Lawrence wrote to an English friend in 1922, soon after arriving in Australia. "And the air is new, new, strong, fresh as silver. . . . The country has a fourth dimension and the white people float like shadows on the surface."

Close to Alice there's something else floating on the surface: the huge white domes of the Pine Gap satellite station, lying on the desert floor like giant golf balls caught in the world's biggest sand-trap. If the goings-on inside are supersecret, the location of the CIA base is obviously not. And with skies this clear, you could photograph Pine Gap from the other end of the solar system.

For genuine mystery, the Soviets would do better to train their cam-eras on Alice Springs, at least on the day I arrive. At the center of town, several hundred people are sprawled on a grassy bank, guzzling beer and staring into a dust storm. Then the dust clears for an instant, two canvas sails tack past each other, and the crowd begins to whoop and cheer.

"With winds like this it's anybody's race!" shouts a muffled, micro-phoned voice somewhere inside the maelstrom.

I have arrived during the early heats of the Henley-on-Todd, a bush parody of the annual regatta on the Thames in England. Parody begins with the Todd River, a dried-up channel of sand snaking through the heart of Alice. Then there are the "sailors": teenagers mostly, in sneakers, with their legs poking out from underneath bottomless boats. Standing inside the hollow crafts, holding the sides at waist height, they wait for an "admiral" to fire the starting gun, then sprint down the riverbed, around two oil drums, and back to the finish line, canvas sails flapping in the windless desert air. A thin stream of spilled beer is the only moisture in sight.

"Some fine sailing there!" the admiral shouts as two boats butt each other and capsize, like toddlers wrestling in a sandbox. "But I'm afraid both ships have been disqualified. The judges are waiting to see which one brings in the biggest bribe."

It has the look of Page-One stuff to this reporter's eyes. Better get some background information. At the beer tent I meet the regatta's founder, a laconic, gray-bearded man in a sailor's cap named Reg Smith. He dreamed up the regatta twenty-five years ago, while working in the weather tower at the Alice airport. The job was undemanding: Alice skies are almost always clear, and in those days there was only one airplane arrival each day. So Smith sat there, staring into space, until he was struck by one of those thunderbolts of outback inspiration— the same kind of vision, say, that spawned the first bush bank or Darwin's Beer Can Regatta.

"Racing boats down a dry river just seemed like the logical, sensible thing to do out here," Smith explains. Behind him, the sailors rest while two rowboat crews paddle through the Todd with sand shovels. "Of course when we started, the race was a little more primitive than now."

So primitive that yachts snagged their sails on overhanging gum trees, or foundered on sandbars in the Todd. Then one year the riverbed had the temerity to fill up after a rare burst of rain; water had to be channeled off so the boats could "sail" undisturbed. The trees and sand have since been tamed, and the race sponsors now have an insurance policy against the Todd ever flowing again at race time.

But a certain primitive spirit has remained unevolved. The day's final contest pits two boats, mounted atop four-wheel drives, in a gladiatorial duel to the death. In one corner a three-masted pirate ship called the HMAS *Nauteus*, and in the other a boat called *Bite Ya Bum*, which claims as its insignia a huge middle finger raised defiantly on the stern.

The crew members look like riot police on R and R. Wearing gas masks and crash helmets, they are heavily armed with water cannons, gravel, paint, flour bombs, water bombs, smoke bombs, and anything else that makes a mess and is easy to throw.

The battle is no more of a spectator sport than the America's Cup. A huge cloud of dust and smoke envelops the duel, and the crowd waits expectantly, trying to judge from the groans which ship has the upper hand. Then a broadside of water and paint clears the dust for a moment. There is a glimpse of the *Nauteus* crew clambering over the gunnels of *Bite Ya Bum* for hand-to-hand combat, and the battle is quickly done.

The victorious crew heads straight to the beer tent to sink a few more schooners. "We stole most of their ammo before the race," the *Nauteus* skipper says, pulling back his gas mask to swallow a beer.

And down in the Todd, a group of Aborigines reclaim the polluted riverbed, bemused by this strange white fellas' Water Dreaming.

Alice, meanwhile, has been transformed into a ten-ring comet circus. Even the Pine Gap spooks come out of the closet for this one, turning a small park called the "Space Base Picnic Ground" into the venue for a "Stargazers Bush Ball." Hoping to learn a little more about the base, I travel down the well-paved but unmarked road to the satellite station, 12 miles out of Alice. The road dead-ends at a guard tower, flanked by high fences and surveillance cameras. An amiable, heavily armed guard points me to a grassy picnic area. And sure enough, there they are: CIA wives, disguised in aluminum foil space suits, barbecuing hot dogs and hamburgers just a few yards from Pine Gap's barbed wire fences. That's as close as anyone in Alice ever gets to the spy station.

Back in town, I sample celestial food—moon rock buns, flying saucer doughnuts, galactic gumbo, aspic aurora—and the celestial junk jettisoned into every bit of vacant space: Halley's sweatshirts, comet beer coolers, computer-enhanced postcards of Halley's streaking like a fireball over Alice in 1910.

"It's like a super convention into all things cosmic!" exclaims a local tourist honcho, whom I interview for the "official viewpoint." Outside, on the streets, it looks more like a United Nations meeting that has got freakishly out of control. There are stargazers from every corner of the globe, falling over themselves to confirm national stereotypes . . . Japanese with enough camera gear to cover a coronation . . . English astronomers, flesh untouched by ultraviolet light, shielding themselves from the desert sun with umbrellas and masks of sunblock . . . and, of course, the Americans, thousands of them . . . "oll" men from Dallas wearing ten-gallon hats and huge buttons declaring "Proud to be Texan!" . . . good ol' boys from Florida in Bermuda shorts, football jerseys, and duckbill caps with cotton koalas climbing up the back . . . New Yoikers staggering through the wide streets, stunned by the open spaces . . . "Harry, willya look at that park? Empty, absolutely empty."

And then, the gaudiest visitor of all, live, from the far side of Neptune, the one, the only, Comet Halley!

At least that's what the hype has been promising. As night falls over Alice, and everyone gathers around telescopes at a racecourse outside town, I find my cynicism slipping away. After all, I'll be 103 the next time this comet whooshes by. My great-grandfather lived that long, but he had to read the newspaper with thick spectacles and a magnifying glass. Whatever shape I'm in, I certainly won't be here, in Alice Springs, Australia, on a clear night at the planet's best spot to take in the show. Better to see it now. Then I can lean on my stick fifty years hence and tell, in a hoarse grandpa croak, how I was once a young feller bumming around the bush in '86. . . .

I stare hard into the night sky. Nothing but stars. I edge over to eavesdrop on a group of Australians who are pointing into space and talking in stage whispers: "Go down from the Milky Way . . . See that tree? . . . Then go a little to the left."

I follow their directions. Still nothing.

"Little further to the left, mate."

And yes, a smudge of light flickers just above the horizon. A man offers me his binoculars. The smudge gets bigger, smudgier. I move to a telescope the size of a howitzer; a smudge within a smudge, smudgier still. I look at my fellow stargazers. They look at me.

"That's it?"

"That's it."

We grope for the proper metaphor (after all, grandchildren will demand details). A smudge. A blob. A blur. A headlight coming through the fog. A headlight with a weak bulb seeing through the fog. A faint star. A flop. A fraud. A bloody fraud. A bloody flop of a fraud.

Nearby, some proud-to-be-Texans are splayed out on banana chairs, staring through telescopes at their first view of southern skies.

"Herb, where's the comet's tail?"

"You're looking at it, hon."

"Not *that*? That's just a bunch of fuzz."

"That's right, hon."

We came all the way from Dallas to look at *that*?"

"Uh hunh."

Silence. Quiet calculation of plane fares, hotel bills, banana chair rental. Herb has the dismayed expression of a man who has just sunk a dry well somewhere in west Texas.

A stockbroker named Arnie is more upbeat.

"Herb, it's the concept that's important," he says in a bullish voice. "This guy named Halley makes these calculations and they turn out right. That's what makes it so exciting. It's not going to be a huge flash of fire in the sky, if that's what you're looking for."

Silence again. Evidently, that's what Herb and Hon were looking for. If they wanted to see a goddamn cotton ball they could have done that ten minutes from Dallas.

"I knew it wasn't going to be as good as they said," moans Hon. "But it's a *whole lot* not as good."

"Cummon," says Herb. "Let's go watch the astronomy movie they're showing. Maybe we can find it in the film."

So the pride of Texas march off, leaving Arnie and friends to discover an unsuspected interest in the Trifid Nebula, the Magellanic Clouds, globular clusters, and other deep-space phenomena.

"That's the twenty-fifth dimmest object in Centaurus."

"No kidding?"

I wander off after Herb and Hon and find them watching slides of the barren red surface of Mars. The pictures bear a distressing resemblance to central Australia. The central Australia I am about to hitchhike into.

12
ON THE ROAD, AGAIN

The First Commandment of Hitchhiking is also the easiest to disobey: "Thou Shalt Not Make a Plan." It is a sin that brings swift and cruel retribution. Plans unmade, routes rerouted, shortcuts un-shortened into tedious detours. If you want to get to a certain place in a certain time, don't hitchhike; take a bus.

But I've been off the road long enough to forget all that, and to be tempted by the security of a plan. So after three nights of watching a smudge in the sky, and writing stories about people watching a smudge in the sky, I spread my map on a motel floor in Alice, take a few swigs of mini-bar bourbon, and play Abel Tasman.

Three deserts block my circumnavigation of the rest of the continent: the Gibson, the Great Sandy, and the Great Victoria. I choose the Gibson—Ernest Giles's desert—and plot the following course:

1. Fly to Ayers Rock, thus bypassing the ill-fated patch of scrub where the rented Ford found its resting place a few months ago.
2. Hitch west along the unsealed Gunbarrel Highway, a desert track into 600 miles of townless, empty desert. The most direct route to Western Australia and the most desolate. I want to get Way Out There.
3. Proceed via the goldfields all the way to Perth, where I will arrive in a week's time, before moving up the coast to Broome and Darwin.

It's all as clear and effortless as running my finger along the map. If I stick to this itinerary and don't linger too long in any one place, I can cover the rest of the continent in the time I have before returning to work.

The only hitch, so to speak, is that I need permission to cross the Aboriginal lands west of Ayers Rock. One call and I'm there.

BUREAUCRAT: Mr. Horwitz, are you sure you want to do this? We're talking about a desert track, not the Autobahn.

MR. HORWITZ: What's the problem? Isn't there any traffic?

BUREAUCRAT: Heaps, Mr. Horwitz. Three cars a day on average.

MR. HORWITZ: I reckon I'll risk it.

BUREAUCRAT: Suit yourself. I'll give you a permit for ten days.

"Ten days!" the macho Mr. Horwitz says to himself, on the flight to Ayers Rock. "A camel could hump it to Western Australia faster than that."

Then, to himself again, un-machoed after three hours of burning roadside heat: "A man's not a camel." The only thing that's moved west all day is the angle of the sun. Now, instead of roasting my face and arms, it's blowtorching the back of my neck. Another few hours and I'll have a body coat as red as Ayers Rock.

The first sign of traffic is a cloud of dust on the western horizon, coming from the direction of Docker River, which is where I'm headed. It's a four-wheel drive that looks like one of those mythical beasts I read about in outback motoring guides, equipped with two extra tires on the roof, a spare everything in the boot, and enough food and water to survive a nuclear holocaust. Or a three-day dust storm, which is what the driver appears to have just traveled through.

"The only cars I saw going your way were broken down." The driver's voice is muffled, as if someone's shoveled sand into his lungs." Anyway, the cars are so filled with jerry cans of petrol that they wouldn't have room for an extra body."

I once saw a hitchhiker in California who stuffed all his clothes in a gas can. The idea was to make drivers think he'd just run out of fuel and become tired while hiking to the next station. The ploy worked; a car passed a queue of other hitchhikers to pick him up. That's the kind of Yankee ingenuity I need right now.

An hour later, the bright idea strikes. Start walking. If I don't, I'll melt right here on the road within view of the Rock. I doubt they'd give me a plaque at the Rock's base for that.

The problem is, which way? It's 6 miles back to the Ayers Rock resort, and a bit further to the Olgas, on the way to Docker River. Which way?

Having sinned once by making a plan, I will repent by letting the rides decide the way from here. I'll start walking back to the resort and stick out my finger at any car that passes, going east or west. If the rides so decree, I will retreat to the Stuart Highway and go south toward Adelaide, entering Western Australia by crossing the Nullarbor Plain. The long way around, but so be it. Let the rides decide.

An hour later, a van winds down from the Olgas, heading east. I run across the road and point my finger back toward Alice. The van slows, a side door swings open, and a hand pulls me into the tenth reunion of an astronomy class from Tokyo.

"How you do?" says a grinning young woman named Atsuko. She is the only member of the group who speaks any English. "We, how do you say, go bush? And you?"

"Bush. Great. Yeah, I go bush too." And off we drive, east, back the way I came.

Inside the minibus are four young Japanese, five telescopes, and the entire contents of a Nikon warehouse: flashes, autowinds, tripods, monopods, telescopic lenses. Most of the equipment hasn't shed its cellophane wrapping. Atsuko says the lights from the Ayers Rock resort made it difficult for them to see the comet, much less photograph it. So they're hoping to find a remote spot between here and Alice to set up camp again.

"Many people out there?" she asks me, pointing at a blank spot on the map. It is as thickly settled as a Siberian missile range. When I shake my head, she smiles and communicates the news to the rest of the van.

It is the first hopeful moment of their Australian expedition. They had expected to see kangaroos everywhere and have spotted only one, flat on the bitumen. They'd hoped to feast on inexpensive lamb and beef, but couldn't afford the Rock's pricey restaurants and had to settle for meat pies instead. As for the comet, well, the comet has been no more spectacular in the Australian desert than it was in suburban Tokyo.

"The comet my grandmother see in 1910, she say it was a fire in the sky," Atsuko tells me. So bright and close in fact, that the Japanese worried that the comet's vapors might poison them. Atsuko's family filled up bicycle tubes with spare oxygen, just in case.

"But this time, the comet, it is all head and no tail." Atsuko says. "We think if we go bush, maybe the comet grow some tail."

And maybe pigs will fly. Another few days of cometless skies and there could be thousands of Japanese and proud-to-be-Texans running amok through Alice, stringing up travel agents.

Atsuko puts a hand on my arm as the van skids to a halt. There, a hundred yards into the scrub, a big red kangaroo is sniffing at the ochre-colored earth. Within seconds the van's arsenal of photographic gear is wheeled into action. High-powered lenses poke out the windows like guns along a firing squad. Click. Wind. Click. Wind. Reload, Click. Click. The van fires off a few dozen rounds of film before the kangaroo hops out of range. Everyone is smiling now and chatting with excitement. Proof of their Australian journey is well in hand.

At a roadhouse by the Stuart Highway, two hours east of Ayers Rock, their path leads north to Alice; mine south toward Adelaide. But not before we've climbed out of the van and lined up so a camera on a tripod can snap a time-release photograph: four Japanese and one American, standing against a backdrop of empty scrub. We shake hands and they drive away, leaving me to imagine myself a few weeks hence, projected onto a living room wall in Tokyo between three dozen slides of the big red kangaroo and one slide of a dim, blurry fuzzball called Halley's Comet. "This hitchhiker, he go bush . . ."

The chronicle of my own journey is in a holding pattern over the center. I had planned to be chugging into the sunset west of Docker River by now, or firing up a billy of tea with Afghan camel drivers (who, I fantasized, still roam the desert out there). Instead, I've retreated 125 miles east, in time to watch the sunset turn the Desert Oasis Roadhouse from gray to brown to black. Ayers Rock it ain't.

Even more distressing is a message flashing by the roadside like so many dots and dashes on the Overland Telegraph. Scratched, painstakingly, onto fifteen separate rocks, it reads: C-O-O-B-E-R P-E-D-Y P-L-E-A-S. Decoded into hitch-speak, that means "God help me, I've been sitting here for days and I think I'll spend a few hours scratching my destination onto stones so I don't go crazy or worse."

It seems the poor bastard couldn't spell, unless he got a ride before completing the "pleas." Either that or the heat finished him off and a pack of dingoes picked his corpse clean before I got here.

I have just begun scratching an "e" onto a nearby stone when another messenger of doom appears, this time in person. Emerging from the Desert Oasis is a scruffy-looking man about my own age, with a rucksack over his shoulder and a cardboard sign under his arm. He is the first hitchhiker I've seen in the three months since Phil "Boots" Harris hustled me at cards in rural New South Wales.

Fortunately, he's headed the other way, toward Alice. Unfortunately, he's just come from South Australia and he can't wait to tell me all about it.

"Mate," he says, crossing the highway to greet me, "mate, if you have any sense, you'll turn around. I spent sux days getting from Adelaide to here. Worst sux days of my life."

The hitchhiker's accent tells me he's from New Zilind. The hitchhiker's stench—and the battalion of flies buzzing around his head—tells me he knows of what he speaks.

"Mate," he says, sitting down on his pack now, "it was horrible, let me tell you." And he does. Two days in Port Augusta, in burning sun, with no one stopping to pick him up. A ride finally to Coober Pedy—"hell on earth, mate, hell on earth." Stuck there for another two days. Then a ride with two Aborigines who broke an axle in the middle of nowhere, and just abandoned the car—and him—to wander off into the scrub. He finally flagged down a car for the last stretch, which was the worst of all. "Mate, imagine a bedspread that's all crumpled, except that it's made of rock, and you're driving over it. That's what the road is like. I needed back surgery by the time we reached the Northern Territory."

There's more ("plenty of it, mate"), but a car is coming the other way. So he crosses the highway and sticks his finger out. When the car stops, he chats with the driver a minute, then comes over and asks if I want to go to Alice. No thanks, I tell him. He shakes his head as if seeing me off to the front line of some distant battlefield.

"Take this," he says solemnly, handing me a road map and tourist guide to outback South Australia. "And take care, mate. I hope you make it."

With that he vanishes toward Alice, leaving me with his flies, which busily begin crawling into my eyes and up my nose.

As twilight descends, C-O-O-B-E-R P-E-D-Y P-L-E-A-S takes on the eerie aspect of a headstone. I retreat to the roadhouse, but no one's there to ask for a ride. So I settle in over a beer and begin a crash course on South Australia, which I hadn't planned to travel through at all. The fine print of the Kiwi's road guide makes for a grim introduction: "Coober Pedy to Kulgera: 465 kms—100 kms bitumen and 344 kms gravel and earth road in fair condition only, with bad corrugations, thick bulldust, loose sand and stony surface a hazard."

Dislocated vertebrae. Bruised coccyx. Emphysema from the dust. No wonder there's no traffic on this road.

I'm interrupted by two girls, aged about seventeen, coming in for a cup of coffee. They flash me friendly smiles so I wander over and inquire which way they're headed.

"Darwin," they answer in unison. "How about you?"

"Darwin, but I'm going the long way around."

They look at each other and shrug. Crazy Yank.

When I ask about their plans, I get a bubbly report about how they just left Tasmania and are on their way to work on a cattle station near Darwin. Jo likes to cook. Maryanne does laundry, but she wants to be a "jillaroo," which seems to be the female equivalent of a cowboy, or "jackeroo." Except that on this particular station, there are a whole lot of jacks and no other jills.

"Three hundred and sixty blokes, and just the two of us." Jo giggles. "Can you imagine?"

I can. Hooting. Pinching. Rape. Gang rape.

Maryanne has higher aspirations.

"I'm just hoping to find one guy to go out with," she says, her mouth wrinkling into a serious, meditative knot. "What do you think?"

I think I would vote this comely Tasmanian most likely to succeed of any woman in Australia, and I tell her so.

Jo, the flirt of the pair, breaks into a toothy smile. "Sure you don't want to go to Darwin the direct way? We've got plenty of room."

Bloke number three hundred and sixty-one. No thank you. I just wish my own prospects were that good: car upon car, headed south, and I the only hitchhiker to choose from a zillion empty seats.

. . .

The seat I finally get, two hours later, consists of a few inches of vinyl, wedged between 500 pounds of baby food and a lifetime's supply of diapers. And Ken and Anna and baby in the front seat, driving home to South Australia from a shopping expedition to Alice.

"The stores aren't much in our town," Ken explains, shouldering aside a mountain of shopping bags to make room for me in the back. "So once or twice a month we go for a big splurge in the city."

The city being Alice, being only an 800-mile round trip from their home in Mintabie, South Australia. Not much worse than popping around to the corner deli, once you get used to it.

Shopping isn't the only thing that's a bit limited in Mintabie. Strapped to the car roof is a pile of timber, fresh from an Alice lumber yard. "That's for our walls," Ken says. "Right now all we've got is corrugated iron." Apparently, the few hundred inhabitants of Mintabie are too busy mining opal to worry much about what their houses are made of. Anyway, they'll strike it rich any day now, which means they can move out of Mintabie. So why bother building a real home?

Ken sold his farm near Adelaide a year ago to buy mining equipment for digging opal. "You don't make a million dollars talking about it at the pub," he says of the career change. You don't make it digging for opal either, or at least Ken and Anna haven't. But everyone they know seems to be hitting it big.

"They don't actually say so, but you can kinda smell it on their trousers when they've found something," Anna says. A new truck, maybe. An aerial sticking up from the corrugated iron. Then the final tip-off: they leave Mintabie altogether. That's what keeps the rest of the miners scratching in the desert soil. Maybe one day they'll get lucky and then they can leave Mintabie too. In the meantime, well, there's always the fifteen-hour drive to Alice and back for entertainment.

"We've got all our money sunk into the mining now anyway," Ken says. "We couldn't leave if we wanted to." The wonder of free enterprise is that people can be so enterprising in finding ways to un-free themselves.

Around midnight, Ken pulls in at a roadhouse near the South Australian border to secure the rooftop cargo before plunging into 125 miles of gravel and bull dust. He tells me that the turn-off to Mintabie "is about as lonely a place as a man would ever want to see" and recommends I bed down here instead. "At least you can get some water at the roadhouse if you're stuck." Then, unable to resist adding one more blighted thought for me to sleep on, he says: "Anna and I will be back up this way in a week or so. If you're still here, we'll pick you up."

The roadhouse is shut; there's not even a light in the back to hint at any humans about. Just me, a gas pump, and a night sky as unpolluted by smog and city lights as any I've ever gazed at. As soon as Ken's headlights disappear, a brilliant tapestry of stars opens up overhead. Even the comet is a bit more of a smudge tonight—a piece of lint, say, instead of a speck of dust.

Most travelers dream of rolling out their swag in unspoiled bush like this. Not me. Sleeping out has never been one of my talents; nor, for that matter, has sleeping in. Outdoors, my natural insomnia is compounded by a stunning ineptitude for the basics of camping. I'm hopeless at pitching a tent, unless there are floodlights and a civil engineer on hand. Nor do I have much hope of starting a fire without a quart or two of lighter fluid.

I also have an unfailing nose for the Bad Bivouac. That first summer hitchhiking across America, I met up with a young artist in San Francisco named Trish. She was curious about the road, but afraid to travel it alone and asked if she could tag along with me as far as the Canadian border. At seventeen, with a one-track mind and a twenty-four-hour erection, I couldn't believe my good fortune. Not only could she travel with me, she could—and of course would—share my sleeping bag. How could she possibly resist after I'd displayed my savoir faire of the road?

Day one went according to script. We hitched easily through the hills of northern California, picnicked on roadside blackberries, and found ourselves at first dark wandering the banks of an Oregon river in search of a camping spot. I trotted ahead in the dark until the trail opened onto a small clearing, so close to the river that you could hear the water lapping gently against the shore. The only thing missing was a minstrel strumming a dulcimer in the woods behind us. I spread out our groundsheet—managed a smoldering fire even—and prepared for what I knew would be the start of a memorable romance.

Trish wasn't impressed. "Something smells funny," she kept saying. Nerves, I reckoned, no reason to rush things. There's always tomorrow night. So I curled up alone in my bag and popped off to sleep, which I was able to do at seventeen.

A few hours later Trish nudged me awake. "This place is weird," she said, wide awake. "Something's rotten here. I swear it is." I smiled the smile of the road-weary traveler. "It's always spooky your first night out. Relax." And I rolled over for another few hours of untroubled sleep.

At dawn I awoke to find Trish dressed and packed, studying my map. "I'm getting out of here whether you're coming or not," she said, hollow-eyed after what was obviously a sleepless night. I jumped out of my bag, threw on some clothes, and pulled up the groundsheet to stuff inside my pack.

Trish gasped. Beneath a corner of the cloth lay a grave-sized pit filled to the brim with nets full of fish heads, fish tails, fish guts. I had chosen for our bedroom the favored fish-cleaning spot of every angler on the Columbia River. Trish and I parted company that night at the Canadian border. I haven't heard from her since.

There are no such hazards at the South Australian border. In fact, I doubt that there's a stream or puddle for 500 miles in any direction that's big enough for a tadpole to swim in, much less a full-sized trout. Just flat, hard scrub with the occasional cow pad about.

I toss down my rubber mat and blanket, then lie on my back, gazing up at the brilliant night sky. Let's see now . . . Halley's . . . the Southern Cross . . . the Trifid Nebula. For the first time all day I am comfortable and contented. Back in the bush, a free bird, with only the constellations for company. The shooting stars become sheep, and counting them I begin to drift slowly off to sleep. Who knows, I wonder dreamily, an eye movement away from unconsciousness, maybe I'll turn over a new leaf. . . .

A new leaf . . . a leaf . . . a leaf blowing in the wind . . . a wind blowing me like a leaf to South Australia. . . .

I jolt awake to discover huge clumps of roly-poly gusting past. My blanket is wrapped around my ankles, and a collection of clothes and books are scattered across the scrub downwind of me, like fuselage from an airplane crash. Only my rucksack, half-emptied, is lying on its side where I left it a few hours before.

I sit up and the blanket takes off after the rest of my gear. The foam pad rolls itself and blows up against my pack. I stand up and am blown back to the ground again. Half-naked and shivering, I start crawling around the scrub collecting my scattered possessions. A shirt is lying at anchor in a pile of cow dung. My blue jeans have thrown themselves against a barbed wire fence. T. S. Eliot is doing slow, awkward somersaults across the wasteland. "What are the roots that clutch, what branches grow out of this stony rubbish?"

On the other side of the barbed wire I find a shallow trench and throw myself in. The wind still gusts across my scalp but at least my torso is protected. I prop my pack against the fence as a windbreak. Huddled behind it, I pull on two pairs of pants, three shirts, four pairs of socks—my entire wardrobe in fact, except for the dung-covered shirt and five pairs of elastic-waisted underwear. No room for dignity here, at the center of a cyclone. I put the jockey shorts over my head, one pair at a time, fitting the fly over my nose to let a little oxygen in.

A soothing calm envelops me with each added layer of cotton. I lie down, stop shivering, and listen to my own heavy breathing and the muffled gusts of the wind above. Much better than the hard ground, this trench. This underwear trick's not bad either; I'll have to give it a try on an insomniac night in Sydney.

It is the surreal logic that precedes sleep. I laugh out loud. Lying in a ditch with jockey shorts over my head—an appropriate end to a day that has seen nothing but headlong retreat. At least I've kept my camping record intact.

13
NOODLING

There's only one thing I dread more than setting up camp at night in the Great Outdoors, and that's breaking camp at morning in the Great Outdoors. At least in the dark you can just curl up in your bag and be done with it—if there are no cyclones lurking about. But mornings are pure hell. I like to wake slowly, over a cup of coffee and the sports page, not scramble around in the dawn chill for socks and shoes, then hike off for a "dingo's breakfast"—a pee and a good look around. That's my idea of a lousy way to start the day.

Weathering a hurricane has one advantage. Since I've got my entire wardrobe on already, all I have to do is shed a few layers into my pack and hike out to the road. The night breeze has died down, from cyclone to mere gale-force winds, so I'm reasonably cozy, propped against my pack with a blanket around my shoulders.

If I only had some food. It is part of my poor camping technique to never have victuals on hand when I'm a million miles from nowhere. And there's still no sign of a proprietor at the roadhouse. Maybe he's asleep, as any sensible person would be at this hour. Maybe I should wake him up. Maybe he's awake already, cooking me two dozen flap-jacks with six fried eggs smiling on top, and coffee strong enough to kick-start a cadaver. Then again, maybe he's off shopping in Alice.

I try to distract myself by reciting "The Love Song of J. Alfred Pru-frock." I memorized the first few stanzas between Sydney and Alice, but now, in the middle of the poem, I keep getting stuck on the same two lines: "I have measured out my life in coffee spoons" and "Would it have been worth it, after all, after the cups, the marmalade, the tea." The whole poem's about breakfast if you read it right.

My imaginary marmalade and tea is interrupted by a very unpoetic roar down the road. bbbbbbrrrrrr. BBBBBrrrrrrrrr! I squint at the horizon. It looks as if the night wind has blown away all the trees, hills and scrub. The landscape is so flat and bare that I feel as if I might be able to see all the way to Alice. But all I can pick out is a tiny speck, coming toward me, going bbbbrrrrr, BBBBBrrrrrr! It is moving at a pained, slow crawl, like me before my morning coffee. A few minutes later, the ute limps to a halt beside me. There are four Aboriginal men staring sullenly out from the cab and a dozen jerry cans of petrol vibrating in the back. Judging from the noise, there's some kind of prehistoric beast with pins stuck in its nose stuffed under the bonnet.

"Where ya headed?" I shout at the driver, a very black man with a massive bush of hair. He looks at me blankly. I point at the southern horizon and bob my head up and down.

"Pedy," he mumbles. I point at the back of the truck, then at myself and bob my head again.

"Hey, mate. Okay," he mumbles. I scramble into the back and squeeze myself between two petrol drums, like a stowaway on an oil tanker. We rumble off at 12 miles an hour and the hideous noise starts again. BBBRRRRRRRRRRRR! I have gone from the eye of a hurricane to the belly of a sick, screaming whale. BBBBBBBBRRRRRRRRRRRRRR! I toss the blanket over my head again and the noise goes down a decibel or two. BBBbbbbbrrrrrrrr. It's beginning to look like another underwear job.

It's also beginning to look like a very slow drive to Coober Pedy. Ten minutes down the road, the driver stops and feeds the monster a drum of petrol. Then he rolls the empty barrel into the scrub and hops in beside me, letting someone else take the wheel. I offer the three words of Pitjantjatjara I picked up at Ayers Rock—*Uluru*, *paya* (thank you), and *rama-rama* (crazy). He offers his sum total of English—okay, hey, mate, yes. We shout our three words in every possible combination, then smile and nod at each other for 125 miles.

Actually, it's hard not to nod when you're swerving and bumping over a road that's like gravel laid over choppy surf. Only the oil drums keep me from going overboard. And there's nothing to look at except a cloud of dust shooting out behind the truck, with glimpses to either side of baked and empty desert. By mid-morning, the heat becomes staggering; even in the windblown rear of the ute, I can feel the sun burning every inch of exposed flesh. Nothing to do but huddle beneath my blanket, wedge some of it under my bum as a shock absorber, and tough it out.

A few hours later my companion squeezes up front again with his mates. Then something strange happens. The ute veers off the main road (such as it is) and onto what looks like a dingo trail. I clutch the side of the truck as we bounce between bushes and churn through deep sand. I have a hitchhiker's distrust of detours, particularly when the main road is itself a detour from any habitable territory.

I bang on the back window and get no response; apparently, there's some kind of domestic squabble going on up front. The ute lurches to a halt behind a clump of mulga and the four men pile out, talking loudly in Pitjantjatjara and gesturing at me. All I know is that something ugly is about to happen, and whatever it is, I'm along for the ride.

One thing's for sure; I'm not going to talk my way out of this one, whatever it is. All I can do is listen to their chatter and let my paranoia run riot in translation. ("How much money do you think he has?" "Do we kill him or just leave him here to bake?") Nor can I sort of mosey off into the scrub—"Some other time, fellas"—and run for it. Not here, at the center of the bottomless dustbowl that is outback South Australia. I'd make it three hours at the most before collapsing of heat exhaustion, dehydration, or worse.

"Hey, mate!" It is the driver speaking. He is walking toward me, sweating nervously, with one hand clutching something in his pocket.

"Hey, mate!" He pulls his hand out and thrusts it toward me. I freeze. Then his fist uncurls to reveal a pile of crumpled two-dollar notes.

"Okay, yes!" he shouts.

I look at him blankly. Yes, what? He's exhausted his English and his body language isn't helping. Nor does my extensive Pitjantjatjara vocabulary seem appropriate. Rama-rama? Uluru?

"Grog, mate," says one of his companions. "Black fellas can't buy us grog."

We move to dust language now and he draws a map headed back the way we came. South of the spot where we turned off, he sketches a square, and what looks like a bottle. "Black fellas can't buy us grog," he repeats, handing me the money and the key to the ute. "Two, mate."

Slowly I get the picture. They want me to take their money, and their truck, and drive to the roadhouse to buy two cases of beer. For some reason—a racist publican, I assume—they can't buy it themselves. They'll wait here until I return.

The request says a lot about their trust and my lack of it. All I have done to win their confidence is utter three words of pidgin Pitjantjatjara. All they have done to lose my trust is talk loudly in a language I don't understand. Paranoia took care of the rest.

My first reaction is relief that nothing sinister is afoot and that I can atone for my suspicions by helping them out. For the first time on my journey, I feel as if I've violated the unwritten contract of trust between hitchhiker and hitchhikee. But they don't know that, and anyway, I can make up for it by buying a few beers.

But as I dodge sand traps on my way back to the main road, another dilemma surfaces. I am not by nature an interventionist on the matter of personal habit. Live and let live; drink and let them get drunk. That's the reckless half of my hitchhiker's valor. The discreet hitchhiker in me is screaming caution. We are still 200 miles of rough empty road from Coober Pedy. With a case or two of beer on board, it could be a long, even futile journey.

Or is this prejudice again, welling up in the background as it threatened to do a moment ago, when I began hearing the racist chorus of Territory voices I've managed to ignore until now? . . . "Don't turn your back on a black fella . . ." "An Abo will cut your throat faster than you can say boomerang. . . ." "Whatever you do, mate, don't take a ride with boongs."

My contact with Aborigines has consistently contradicted these dire warnings. From Cunnamulla to Tennant Creek to Ayers Rock, I've been treated by blacks with an openness and generosity not always evident among whites. This last incident is further proof of Aboriginal goodwill. How many white drivers would entrust a scruffy hitchhiker with their piggy bank and sole means of transportation?

That's what makes me nervous; there is a whiff of desperation about the request. But the real problem is, I have no way of knowing if this will lead to a blow-out, and no way of coping if it does. North of Alice, there was the occasional roadhouse at which to abandon ship. Here, nothing; we haven't even seen another car in four hours. The barrier between us isn't racial, it's linguistic. If things get sloppy, which they easily can after two cases of beer, we'll need more than dust drawings to sort the situation out.

As the roadhouse comes into view, I am leaning toward a compromise. My instinct is confirmed by a huge sign above the bar, which announces that it's illegal to buy alcohol before heading into Aboriginal territory. Two cases of beer might make me conspicuous. Two six-packs won't, and it also won't be enough to leave me on a walkabout in the South Australian desert.

The publican is the only person in the pub and he doesn't ask any questions. So I load up the beer, and fill my tucker box with stale bread and overpriced cheese. Then, just for security, I order a meat pie as well. After hours with no food, the microwaved chunks of meat go down like coq au vin. Picky eaters don't survive a day of roadhouse cuisine.

My companions appear unsurprised when I return with most of their money unspent and only a dozen beers. And the speed with which the tinnies are drained, crushed, and tossed into the scrub quiets any qualms I had about disobeying orders.

I am about to pass around my bread and cheese when two of the men begin helping themselves. Their offhand manner makes me realize that the gesture is neither rude nor ravenous. Rather, it seems that food and drink are assumed to be public domain. Every twenty minutes or so through the morning, a waterbag and a lit cigarette were passed to me in the back of the truck. This was my ration, my right as an occupant of the ute. It would be inappropriate—even insulting—to suggest that my food was anything but part of the collective. We eat a few slices each, share the waterbag and cigarette pack, and climb aboard for the long drive to Coober Pedy.

This time my companion in the back is Joe, he of the "black fellas can't buy us grog." His English is good enough for a halting dialogue interspersed with sign language and sketches on the dusty side of an oil drum. As far as I can make out, the men are traveling from their home on a reserve in the Northern Territory to spend a few weeks "noodling" for opal around Coober Pedy. Noodling, as Joe describes it, is a leisurely sort of look-see through the piles of rubble left by white miners and white machines.

"White fellas always go, go go," Joe says, pantomiming men driving drills and pickaxes into the ground. "They miss so much riches that way." Noodling, it seems, is not a bad metaphor for the difference between our cultures.

Indeed, Joe doesn't miss a beat along the 60 miles of unsealed road we travel after stopping for beer. Every ten minutes or so he touches me on the arm and points off toward an empty horizon. Each time there is an emu or kangaroo, almost invisible to me, but obvious as a skyscraper to Joe. The foreground is clear enough, though; long lines of abandoned automobiles stretching beside both sides of the road, like parallel queues to a scrapyard just over the horizon. Burnt cars, stripped cars, overturned cars. The place looks like a training camp for terrorist car bombers.

"Black fellas bad with cars," Joe explains. "No buy fixing out here." At least there are plenty of dead cows to keep the car bodies company. But otherwise, nothing. It is as bare and bleak a landscape as I've ever clapped eyes on.

For several thousand miles, I've been struggling for un-superlatives to communicate the un-ness of outback scenery. The towns and people are easy enough; they have faces, buildings, features. But what can you say about a landscape that is utterly featureless? A landscape whose most distinguishing quality is that it has no distinguishing qualities whatsoever? Flat, bare, dry. Bleak, empty, arid. Barren, wretched, bleached. You can reshuffle the adjectives but the total is still the sum of its parts. And the total is still zero. Zot. Nought. Ayers Rock has a lot of blank space to answer for.

To the early explorers, this arid region north of Adelaide was simply Australia's "Ghastly Blank." Charles Sturt set off into the desert east of here in 1844 to find the inland sea, and so sure was he of success that his party included two sailors and a boat (as well as eleven horses, two hundred sheep, thirty bullocks and four drays). "I shall envy that man who shall first place the flag of our native country in the center of our adopted land," he declared. But after staggering for some months through the desert, Sturt reached neither sea nor center—just the dry expanse of Lake Torrens. "The desolate barrenness, the dreary monotony, the denuded aspect of this spot is beyond description," he wrote in his journal, having described it rather well. Daniel Brock, a member of Sturt's party added, "This scene is the Climax of Desolation. . . .

Miserable! Horrible!" Not long after, Sturt launched his boat on the Darling River and then retreated to Adelaide.

Looking out the back of the ute I am amazed that Sturt made it as far as he did. Desert to the right of me, desert to the left of me, a plume of car dust shooting down the middle, I claim this spot as the landing pad for the alien probe I imagined my first day in Australia. The alien probe that drops down, declares "No life," and heads back to outer space. The probe people could sniff around her for a few hundred miles in every direction and come to the same conclusion. No life. No bloody way.

Just the sort of place you'd never want to break down in; just the thought that comes to me as the engine coughs and goes silent, leaving the ute half on and half off the highway. It seems the moaning beast under the bonnet has finally been put out of its misery.

The four men pile out and take turns staring through the steam rising out from under the bonnet. They study the ute's Japanese repair manual, upside down. Then they begin staring vacantly off into space. It is the noodling school of car repair. We are about to join the long queue of automobile corpses. Looking out at the empty desert, I don't like our chances either.

I am an automotive moron, a clod when it comes to all things mechanical. But desperation makes for marvelous self-improvement. Studying the manual, and then the tangle of metal under the bonnet, it becomes obvious to me that we no longer possess a fanbelt, if indeed we ever did. Also, whatever water the radiator once held is now evaporating on the ground at the rate of about 50 quarts per second.

Joe fashions a fanbelt by knotting the spare rubber flapping around under the bonnet. But feeding our meager supply of water to the radiator seems a little risky. If we do, and the ute still doesn't move, we'll be fashioning straws to drink from the radiator within a few hours.

So once again I am called into service for the purpose of liquids procurement. While the four men huddle out of sight—or as out of sight as you can get in a desert, which means behind the ute—I wait for a passing car to beg some water from. It seems that for black fellas in this stretch of outback, water is as difficult to come by as beer.

The first car to pass is driven by a Romanian refugee named Milos. He's headed north from Adelaide to "see some bush" and is happy to give me his entire water supply, all 2 quarts of it. I explain to him that there's no Danube running through South Australia and hand him his water back, along with the tourist guide the New Zealander gave me yesterday.

A short while later, two Aborigines pull up in a battered truck. When my companions hear the familiar, accented English of fellow blacks, they pop out from behind the ute like guests at a surprise party. The six men chat away for half an hour, then conversation is followed by a pirate raid on the newcomers' water, tucker, and cigarettes. Then everyone begins chatting again. I assume that I'm witnessing a chance reunion of long-lost friends or relations. In actual fact, one of the newcomers tells me, they've met only once, on an earlier noodling expedition to Coober Pedy. The color of one's skin can be as powerful a bond in the outback as it can be a barrier.

An hour later, the party gets around to fixing the radiator. Water doesn't revive the ute. But with the truck pushing us from behind, the engine kicks into life again, or a tubercular version of it. We cough and wheeze down the highway for a hundred yards or so—before everyone decides this is cause for further celebration. So we pile out, chat, and smoke for another half hour, then get kick-started again down the road toward Coober Pedy.

Relieved, I let out an Indian war cry—*Yihaaaa! Yi-HAAAAAAAAAAAAA!*—and Joe imitates me for the hour-long drive. "Do it one more," he says, as if prompting a singer to repeat a favorite refrain. "One more time, Tony." The two of us are roughly the same color from the waves of reddish-brown dust we've been swimming through all day. So there we sit, two red-skinned Apaches, belting out war cries all the way to the opal fields of South Australia.

Late in the day we reach Coober Pedy with the fanbelt still intact, the radiator cool. I climb out of the ute, shake each man's hand . . . "Hey mate, okay" . . . "Yes" . . . "Okay, yes" . . . and hoist my pack over one shoulder. It feels like a bag full of wet fish is crawling down my back. I yank the pack off and discover that one of the cans of diesel fuel has been leaking onto it for the past ten hours or so. The frame-and-canvas pack looks and feels like a soggy spring roll, abandoned in the grease for a few days. I think of all the lit cigarettes passed between Joe and the cab during the day, directly over the diesel-soaked pack.

One stray ash and my clothes would have launched into outer space.

If they had, they might well have touched down in Coober Pedy. Lunar landscape is too generous a metaphor for this ugly, eerie place. Imagine, first of all, an endless plain of sand-colored cones, spreading like an abandoned tent camp all the way to the horizon. That's the outskirts of town: a man-made—or man-ruined—expanse of dirt kicked up by the picks and bulldozers and explosives used to uncover opal.

The town itself is in perfect harmony with its surroundings, which is to say, as raw and ruined and forbidding a settlement as you'll find anywhere in the outback. It looks like an inhabited vacant lot. Abandoned and burnt-out cars litter the streets and yards like so much rusty lawn furniture. Discarded timber and sheets of corrugated iron are strewn about as well. And the dust is so thick when I arrive, several hours before sunset, that cars motor through slowly with their headlights on, as if piloting through fog.

Getting your bearings in Coober Pedy requires a kind of twisted sixth sense. There are few street signs and few real streets to speak of; just a dusty tangle of unpaved trails cutting every which way between the burnt-out cars and litter of timber and iron. Finding the inhabitants is almost as difficult. According to the tourist guide, there are 5,000 Coober Pedians, "give or take a thousand." Many of them are underground, if not in the mines, then in subterranean homes called "dugouts." All you can see from outside is a doorway set into the ridge, like the entrance to a mine shaft. That's home.

This molelike life-style began after World War I when miners rushed here to scratch for opal. Veterans mostly, fresh from the trenches of France, they got the bright idea of escaping the dust and blast-furnace temperatures by gouging underground. The habit survives today because it is cheaper to light a dugout than to air-condition an aboveground home through months of desert heat.

"This wing was started with pickaxes, then blown out with dynamite," says Edward Radeka as nonchalantly as if he were showing off an addition to his split-level suburban home. In fact, he is leading me down a black tunnel to a room in Radeka's Underground Motel. "Nice and quiet, don't you think?" The room is a cave, literally, with a bed and a chair beneath a canopy of shot-out stone. No windows, no natural light, just a few drawings hung from the stone and a small airshaft winding up to the earth's surface to let in a little oxygen. It looks like the kind of place where you could go to sleep and wake up in the next century.

Washing up isn't so easy. The name Coober Pedy is derived from an Aboriginal phrase meaning white man's burrow, or boy's waterhole, depending on which tourist brochure you look at. But whatever waterhole there once was has long since dried up. Now fluid comes in by truck or pipe and it costs about twenty dollars just to water the lawn. This explains why the only lawn in town belongs to the pub, which gets a helping hand from spilt beer. At the motel, Edward Radeka says I can have a bucketful of soapy water to wash with so long as I toss it on two of his stunted trees when I'm done.

The diesel fuel washes out well enough. But after an hour of drying on a Hills Hoist above the motel—that is, at ground level—my clothes are coated with a dense layer of reddish-brown dust. At least now they're color-coordinated, with one another and with the color of my skin.

At sunset I wander through town past underground homes, underground restaurants, underground bookshops. You can even pray underground in Coober Pedy at the Catacomb Church. About the only thing you can't do underground is find much opal, at least not anymore. Apparently, the easy pickings are gone and most of the serious miners have moved off to Mintabie or other settlements. The only new work in the last few years came during the filming of *The Road Warrior*, when about 120 locals were hired to loll around as extras. They didn't really have to act, nor did the town require any modification; it is already a natural setting for a postnuclear fantasy.

After an hour of sightseeing—abandoned cars, humpies, broken glass—I stop to ask a man for directions to the nearest pub.

"You want to buy opal?" he answers in a strong Eastern European accent. I repeat my question and he repeats his. "You want to buy opal?" I shake my head and he points me to a pub up the street. I have just had my first sip of beer at the bar when a man at the next stool edges over and whispers hoarsely in my ear: "You want to buy opal?" Is this some kind of password or is every Coober Pedian a portable gem shop?

"Not many miners have a luck anymore," the man explains. "But you can't sell small bits of opal so easy. So we make our tucker money by selling this way."

Stief ("No last names, please. I not pay tax in nineteen years") is a

Yugoslav by birth, as are many of the miners in Coober Pedy. The town is so isolated that ethnic differences have been preserved in a kind of Southern European aspic. Croatians gather at one end of the bar; Serbians at the other. And Italians and Greeks go to a different club altogether. "Every nation in this place, except fair dinkum Aussies," Stief says, wandering off to hustle another tourist at the bar. The phrase "Want to buy opal?" is the Esperanto that joins all the different cultures together.

I leave in search of a souvlaki to fortify myself against the procession of pies and pasties on the road ahead. At nine o'clock the streets are almost silent. It seems that all the life has been coaxed out of Coober Pedy, along with the opal. Except for the gem sellers, of course. I am propositioned three times between the takeaway and the motel, twice by the "Want to buy opal?" set and once by a tall, painted lady, whispering from the doorway of an opal shop.

"You have money I give you a sex."

No, thank you, I have a sex. I have a souvlaki. All I want to do is get to my cave and go to sleep.

But there is one more voice in the night.

"Hey mate, okay!" It is Joe and company, greeting me from the ute, which is parked on the main street. Their eyes are glazed over with beer.

"Rama-rama," I say, casting my arms around the town. Crazy.

Joe smiles. "Say it one more time, Tony. One more time." I shake my head, exhausted. So he does it for me, letting loose with a blood-curdling war cry into the desert air over Coober Pedy.

"*Yiiii*HAAAAAAAAAAAAAAAAAAAAAA!"

14
THE UNBEATEN
TRACK

In the morning I enjoy the leisurely wake-up of the Motel Man. Or in this case, Cro-Magnon Man, crawling from his cave, squinting once at the sun, then sloping off into the cool gloom of Radeka's Underground Restaurant for a cup of coffee and a look at the morning newspaper.

The opal fields seem even stranger in the matter-of-fact newsprint of the *Coober Pedy Times*. "SEALING CELEBRATION FOR STUART HIGHWAY," screams one headline. "WATER AT INDULKANA," shrieks another. And then, "WEATHER: NO RAIN FOR APRIL." Elsewhere, sealed roads and running water, from ground or sky, would be taken for granted; here, they're lead stories. And the crime reports are written in a curious sort of Newspeak. One story tells of "a drastic increase in the number of cars taken and used without the consent of the owner"—car theft, I guess—and another of "night shifts in the opal fields," which apparently refers to miners making midnight raids on other people's claims.

The home improvement section is most primitive of all. "EXTEND YOUR DUGOUT!" says one advertisement, beneath a dimly lit photo of a man in a bulldozer, clawing at the rock wall of someone's living room. "NO JOB TOO BIG OR TOO SMALL!"

All this underground action is making me claustrophobic. So I linger over the recipe page (Camel Stew, straight from the Goanna Grill in Mintabie), then go out to face the day. By dusk, Coober Pedy had been homely enough. In the morning glare it is a wrecked and hideous hag. Staggering past burnt-out cars and dilapidated humpies, a piece of cardboard as shield against the blinding heat and light, I feel as if I'm touring Ground Zero after the bombs have hit. I have never wanted to get out of a town as much as I want to leave Coober Pedy.

Unfortunately, the desire to escape a place is usually in inverse proportion to one's luck in catching a ride. It's as if drivers can read the scorn beneath your insincere smile and return the favor by letting you stand there and suffer.

So I wait outside Coober Pedy all morning, with nothing for company but blinding sun and swarms of blowflies. Since I gave up on insect repellent back in New South Wales, drivers have offered me about a hundred home remedies for the Great Australian Fly Plague. Gum leaves rubbed all over my body. Garlic. Mint. Prayer. Not one has worked. Mute tolerance is the only defense. Close-mouthed silence, that is; otherwise, the flies might crawl down my throat.

It is midday before I'm finally picked up—by a ute that looks as if it was rescued from the same junkyard as the one I rode in yesterday. The muffler and shock absorbers have been surgically removed. And of course there's not a spot of room in the cab, which is occupied this time by three young whites. No choice but to spread my fly-bitten limbs like strips of bacon across the hot metal surface of the ute's open rear.

At least there's no oil to fry in this time. Instead, I am accompanied in the back by a huge wood-and-Styrofoam coffin with three eskies of beer entombed inside on a bed of ice. Every twenty minutes or so, the driver pulls off the road, unlatches the coffin and pulls out four bottles of beer (one for me, of course). In between beer stops, the driver pulls off the road, and the three men pile out to urinate on the hard, baked ground.

"Watch where ya piss, goddammit," a drunk named Barry yells at a drunk named Darryl, who is urinating somewhat recklessly against one of the ute's tires.

"Aw, get stuffed," slurs Darryl, wetting his own leg, then laughing. "This little piggie is gonna go wee wee wee all the way home."

Home is the wheat-farming country near Kimba, on the Great Australian Bight. The three cockies are in their late twenties but look older, with the rugged, sunburnt faces of men who make their living from the land. Barry, a brawny, solid-looking sort of bloke, and Reg, the half-sober and sarcastic driver, wear visored caps that announce what kind of tractor they use. Darryl is boyish, too big for his singlet, with eyes so blue that they pop out of his sunburnt face. He is also the butt of the jokes, most of them scatological.

"Goddammit, Darryl, one more fart out of you and you're walking the rest of the way."

"Whaddya want me to do?"

"Put a lid on it. Keep your mouth shut."

I pick up bits and snatches of this dialogue as we irrigate the dry road running south from Coober Pedy. At piss stop number eleven, I learn that the three men have spent the past few weeks scratching for opal in Mintabie, which they do during every slack season to earn a little extra cash. The opal fields seem to be South Australia's answer to Las Vegas: a casino off in the desert where ordinary people can come toss their money on the ground and hope their number will come up. Like every other opal digger I've met, Reg and Barry and Darryl have crapped out. But they got their money's worth of fun, just hanging out with one another, drinking and farting and swearing, a day's drive away from the humdrum of life on the farm.

"You put your crops in, you take them off, you fix a fence or two, then you put your crops in again," says Reg. "Sometimes it's good to get on the piss and piss off to the opal fields for a while."

The drive home, it seems, is the final grand piss-up before returning to the family, the farm, the fertilizer. When the coffin of stubbies empties out, we pull into a roadhouse for a few glasses of beer to add a bit of variety. Then we load up again and head off the main highway onto a dirt track that runs all the way to Kimba.

"Hard to find good navigators these days," Reg complains as Barry and Darryl fall out of the truck, giggling. "Just piss wrecks." He hands me a topographical map. "Keep an eye on it and let me know if it looks like we're getting off course."

It is my first real venture down Australia's unbeaten track. Instead of plotting a course from town to town, or even station to station, we hop from "Haggard Hill" to "Numerous Small Claypans" to "No. 19 Bore" to "Skull Camp Tanks." Picturesque as these landmarks sound, they aren't exactly jumping off the horizon. For one thing, the dust is so thick that I could be in sub-Saharan Africa for all I know. When it clears, and a sandhill comes into view, it's hard to tell whether I'm looking at "Hunger Hill" or "Dingo Hill" or some other hill altogether.

I can't even use the location of the sun as a reliable guide. One moment it's straight in my face, the next moment it's burning the left side of my face, the next moment it's throwing the shadow of my hat onto the truck.

Then we make a 90-degree turn at the top of a sandhill, and a shimmering plain of salt spreads like a white quilt across the landscape. I look at the map, and nowhere between Kingoonya and Kimba do I see anything that looks or sounds salty. I begin banging on the back of the cab and Reg skids to a halt.

"We're lost, I think."

"How's that?"

"Look at that," I say, pointing at the salt plain. "Tell me they'd leave that off the map."

Reg squints at one sandhill, then another, and then at the map.

"That's Lake Everard, ya mug," he says with a laugh, climbing back in the cab. "We're way out to buggery now."

Sure enough. A ghostlike patch on the map marked Lake Everard. The beer has obviously got to me. Why else would I be so stupid as to expect a body of water to actually have water in it? After all, the biggest lake in South Australia, Lake Eyre, is so hard and dry that a racing car driver set a land-speed record tearing across it. Land-speed record. On a lake. If you're looking for permanent running water—or even standing water—in outback South Australia, forget it. There isn't any.

After that I stop worrying about the map and take in the scenery instead. Except for a few windmills and an abandoned sandstone out-station, I see no sign of human life for 200 miles. What I do see is the wildlife that humans normally chase away. Not just a lone kangaroo or two, but herds of them hopping across the scrub. Emus too, and wild goats, wild horses, and even a pair of wild, humpless camels— descended, Reg says, from the camels that Afghan drivers once prodded across the scrub.

The setting is so wild and unspoiled that even our lonely ute seems an intrusion of massive dimension, blaring fiddle music by the Bush- wackers and trailing a plume of dust that obliterates the landscape for some minutes after we travel through it.

At other times the intrusion is more violent than that. In late after- noon, Reg almost skids off the track for what I assume is an emergency piss stop. But turning around, I see that he's swerved to avoid two men wrenching at the grillework of a truck, which is stalled in the middle of the narrow track.

"Any damage?" Reg asks out the window.

"Naw, just the grille," one of the men says. Then, gesturing at a heap of flesh by the roadside, he adds: "Want some dog tucker?"

The kangaroo, of course, is dead.

By sunset, my three companions are almost incoherent. Round upon round of beer seems to have washed away the years in a kind of drunken regression. The conversation has winnowed to wanking.

"For Chrissake's, Darryl, stop playing with yourself."

"I'm not playing with myself, dickhead."

"Yeah? You'd do it with your grandmother if she gave you half a chance."

"You'd do it with an empty bottle. Bang it like a dummy door."

My own grip on sobriety is slipping away, as is my grip on reality, or at least my place in it. Here I am, drunk in the back of a ute with three drunk cockies racing from nowhere to nowhere in the South Australian scrub. If I bounced out the back at the next hairpin bend, what would they make of my body? A dusty, ragged hitchhiker with the smell of diesel fuel about him: no name, no known address, no occupation apparently. Does the fact that I have a name, an address and a job make my other life real? Can I be both people at the same time? Do I want to be?

I am not the only one in the throes of an identity crisis. At sunset, after a pub stop at a place called Bungleboo, I squeeze up front to keep warm for the last hour to Kimba. And as home approaches, the gaiety of the day-long drive begins to sour like week-old milk. Reg and Darryl start arguing over the best way to control weeds: spraying or driving them out by tractor. Barry worries out loud that his wife will yell at him for coming home three days later than scheduled: broke, drunk, and filthy. And Reg wonders where he's going to get the money for the next tractor payment.

"It's a good life, farming," Reg says. Then he reconsiders. "Not really. Particularly not now. You can't make a bloody quid out of it."

"Yeah, but what's a bloke to do?" Barry says, taking up the yoke.

"Get out now, or wait to see if it picks up again, pay your bills, and get out altogether?"

It is Darryl, strangely sober now, who has the final word. "Problem is, mates, what the bloody hell else are we going to do?"

The journey home is silent for the final half hour.

At the Kimba pub we settle in for another round before calling it quits. There are a few wistful jokes about the opal fields, then a meditative quiet as we finish off our beers.

"One for the road, mate," Darryl says, hoisting his glass at me in the smoky saloon. "Wish I were you." The four of us clink our glasses together, toss them back, and head off into the night.

My way leads in a slow weave from the pub to a nearby camping ground, a five-star joint with trees and water and indoor toilets. The rumble of trains, wheat trains, serenades me as I roll out my swag. It is a romantic lullaby, full of yearning for distant places; the sound of freedom, a kind of locomotive counterpoint to the welcoming skid of a car hitting the gravel as it stops to pick me up.

But I imagine the wheat trains have a different resonance for the piss-wrecked cockies. Tonight they are beyond hearing. But tomorrow, when they return to the fields, hungover, their vacation over for another year, how will the wagons of wheat sound to them?

I will be well down the road by then, headed west with the trains.

15
WESTWARD HO

I wake up on Sunday beneath a three-towered silo that rises like a cathedral over Kimba. No chiming of bells from this monolith—just the deep, digestive rumble of wheat traveling into the silo's large intestine. Another doleful reveille for the cockies.

The desert ended during the final hour of last night's drive. In Kimba there's even a whiff of the sea blowing up from the south. I feel like lingering, but it's Sunday and all the world's asleep. Might as well hit the road and get an early start.

I have barely raised a finger toward the rising sun when a bloated sedan drags a trailer out of the caravan park. Experience tells me I needn't bother to eyeball the driver; vacationing families are either overloaded or loath to let strangers into their domestic sanctum.

The squeal of brake pads tells me I'm wrong. I wedge in the backseat between a pimply teenager and a two-year-old in a baby chair with a toy seal clutched to his breast. Unprecedented. I haven't even showered or shaved to deserve this.

I've landed in the lap of miners again. Not opals; gold. Used to be tin, explains the mother of the family, whom I will call Edna. That was back in Tasmania. Then Norm, that's my husband, the one that's driving, he got retrenched, so he got a job with a gold-mining company in Kalgoorlie. That's where we're headed now after a week's vacation in Tassie.

Such is the trickle-down lottery of international metal markets. The price of gold's strong, the price of tin's not, so another Tasmanian family loads up the car and migrates to Western Australia.

Not that this family seems to care, at least not Edna, who does all the talking. Only too happy to put a few thousand miles between themselves and the "bloody greenies" who are "hung up" on Tasmania's wilderness.

"What's the harm of a few little mines?" Edna bellows. Viewed from the backseat, she has the neck of a heavyweight boxer and the voice of a circus barker. "Do you want to drive up the whole coast of Tasmania and look at nothing but rain forest?"

I offer the gentle suggestion that rain forest might be nicer to look at than the moonscape of overmined hills across much of western Tasmania. She throws me a quick expert glance that tells her I'm "one of them"—them being some evil stew of greenies, pinkos, homos, and freaks. Then she returns to studying the map, as if she's searching for a particularly desolate bit of the Nullarbor Plain at which to let me out of the car. I decide to keep my mouth shut after that.

Not Edna. From greenies she moves on to bloody dole bludgers, bloody unions, and Bob bloody Hawke (the prime minister). She'd like to shoot the whole bloody lot of 'em. She even hates kangaroos: "The only good one is the one that jumps in front of your car."

No one else in the car dares to try and get in a word; they just tune her out. I try to adopt the same glazed manner and after an hour or so, Edna's voice is no more irksome than a revivalist preaching on a radio in the next room. It becomes monotonous, almost soothing, like the fur-lined backseat, which feels as therapeutic as a Swedish massage after two days in the back of utes.

The scenery is pleasant but dull, rolling past like the vast midsection of America—plains of wheat and grass to be crossed en route to more exciting places. Even our frequent stops do not make so much as a ripple in this tide of blandness. At each town, Edna directs Norm past the pubs, past the coffee shops, past any spot that might offer some local color, and into the identikit tourist traps that sprout beside interstate highways. The family piles out to buy postcards at Penong, spoons at Ceduna, stubbie openers with opalized wombats at Nullarbor. Washed down with a steady stream of pies and pasties and chocolate-covered Cherry Ripes. Then back in the sedan, windows rolled up and air-conditioner booming until the next roadhouse, the next round of Cherry Ripes. Two hours west of Kimba, I assume the cool repose of a package of processed meat in the back of the refrigerator.

I come out of the deep freeze at a sign announcing the start of the Nullarbor Plain. The most striking thing about the Nullarbor is how unstriking it is. Australia's symbol of bleak despair is not even all that bleak—at least not compared with the forbidding desert I passed through to get here. In fact, it's only something like 12 miles between trees at the Nullarbor's most barren stretch.

Not that a little greenery gets in the way of what is a numbingly monotonous journey. Just north of here, the rail line runs dead straight for almost 300 miles—the longest such stretch in the world. And as Agatha Christie found when she pondered the mystery of the Australian bush in 1922, open spaces don't have to be dry to be dull. "I had never imagined a green grassy desert—I had always thought of deserts as a sandy waste," she wrote, "but there seem to be far more landmarks and protuberances by which you can find your way in the desert country than there are in the flat grasslands of Australia."

One landmark that is unmistakable—to my American eyes, at least— is a sign warning of camels, wombats, and kangaroos for the next 60 miles. It is one of those small but startling reminders of how far from home I am; like pinching myself and saying, yes, you are in Australia, 12,000 miles from your natural habitat. America has only the occasional deer or cattle crossing, or maybe a "Beware of Falling Rock" sign to break up the monotony of interstate driving. Wombats never.

My reverie is broken by Edna again. Wombats, it seems, are almost as verminous as kangaroos. "But the worst of all are Tassie devils," she says, as if reading my mind to find my favorite of all Australian creatures. "They'll eat anything. Bones, bolts, nails. If we had any sense we'd shoot the bloody lot of 'em into extinction." I look at her closely to see if she's joking. She isn't. Her face is red with rage at the thought of the marsupial hordes crowding her out of all that empty space.

By midday I've exhausted my patience for the scenery as well as my repertoire of goofy faces to make at the baby. Comfort is giving way to claustrophobia. The stink of cigarette smoke and sickly sweet Cherry Ripes is thick and heavy. All I can do is close my eyes and console myself with memories of the truly awful road trips of my childhood. As the youngest of three children—hence, the baby—I was born with a lifetime sentence to the middle of the family car's backseat. No matter that I was, by the age of thirteen, an awkward, fidgety adolescent as big as my sister and more of a window person than my brother, who has been known to sleep through the Great Smoky Mountains, the Rockies, and the Painted Desert. My spot in the pecking order doomed me to be forever squeezed in the center, with no place to put my feet and nowhere to turn my head.

On one trip when I was six or so, I got the bright idea of actually renting out my lap for twenty-five cents an hour. My brother, a virtual narcoleptic, had no choice but to pay and I did rather handsomely on the ten-hour drive from Washington to Cape Cod. My parents took it as a sure sign of my budding entrepreneurship. It was the last sign they would ever see.

But one skill has endured from those childhood road trips. I am a Grand Master of the well-placed elbow, the sudden shift of the hip, the sharp kick of the feet into the well of space behind the driver. Attila the Hun couldn't occupy vacant car space and hold its boundaries more ruthlessly.

Anyway, I have just established a comfortable *Lebensraum* in the backseat of the Tasmanians' car, crowding the adolescent up against one window and the baby and seal against another, when the family decides to make its first extended stop of the day. We pull off at a lookout somewhere along the cliff-lined coast of the Great Australian Bight and Edna announces that we have twenty minutes, and twenty minutes only, to take in the view and a breath of sea air.

Father and son lean against the car and smoke cigarettes rather than stroll 55 yards to peek over the cliff edge. But baby bounds out of the car like an animal freed from its cage, laughing and screaming and rolling on the grass. Before he can so much as manage a somersault, Edna lassos him with a huge, knotted leash and ropes him in around the waist. "He's too game," she declares. Any less game and this family might go the way of the Tasmanian tiger (now extinct).

On Edna's orders, Norm has a listless go at the video camera, taping his wife and baby in a pose that looks like a drill sergeant walking a pet chihuahua. Silent teenager stirs himself to urinate over the cliff edge, then spits overboard as well, watching the saliva drift down to sea. And chaperone stakes out a window seat until we reach Western Australia.

After we cross the border, the towns dwindle into marginal communities that appear to subsist solely on rabbits and roadhouses. The element of choice is eliminated, so when it comes time to refuel with Cherry Ripes, Norm is forced to pull in at a combination grocery and hotel. I slip off to the pub, only to find everyone at the bar staring at me as soon as I order a beer.

"Beg yours?" the bartender says.

"A Foster's, please."

"One more time, mate."

"A Foster's. Victorian Bitter. Whatever you've got."

The man smiles and winks at the half-dozen regulars gathered at the bar. " 'E's a fair dinkum Yank, 'e is." Then, with great ceremony, he presents me with a rolled piece of paper from beneath the bar, like a dean awarding a university diploma. I unfurl the parchment to find a drawing of a yacht with a secret keel—in the shape of a hugely erect penis. Below, a captain reads: "How We Fucked the Americans."

The whole bar breaks out laughing. They have obviously been waiting some time to snare an American for this particular prank. It seems only fair that I take their bait.

"We'll see who gets fucked this time."

" 'E's game, 'e is," the bartender says to his audience, then to me again. "Tell me, chappie, where's the spunk going to come from? Not Mr. Dennis Conner, surely?"

"A winged cock, maybe," I mumble. "Yankee know-how. Now how about my middie of beer?"

"My shout, chappie," the bartender says, smiling broadly. "But it's just called a glass of beer in this state. And it'll have to be Bondie's brand." Sure enough, the tap shows only Emu and Swan Lager, both owned by the Perth brewmaster. A horn starts honking outside, so I toss back the beer and rush off to reclaim my seat in Cherry Ripe Land.

"See you in Fremantle, chappie," the bartender shouts after me. "In 1990."

There is something open and up-front about the pub that is refreshing after the taciturn machismo of so many outback hotels. It has a whiff of Texan brashness about it that seems approachable, pleasantly familiar.

There is something familiar as well about the traffic on the highway.

Soon after crossing the border into Western Australia we are joined by a legion of home movers, travelers, drifters. One car has two mattresses strapped precariously on the roof, another is towing a trailer with chairs and a refrigerator poking out the top. A third, with "Just Married!" scrawled above a Victorian license plate, has a vacuum cleaner sticking out a rear window. I feel as if I'm in a traffic jam of Okies, fleeing the dust bowl for the glittering dream of California.

Fleeing too fast, perhaps. In late afternoon we came upon two trucks that have just sideswiped each other before careening off the road. One has capsized with its cab crushed against a tree. The driver is lying on the ground nearby with a blanket thrown over his head. A blood-spattered torso sticks out from beneath the makeshift shroud.

"Sort of sobers you, doesn't it," Norm says, slowing for a moment then accelerating back to 75 miles per hour.

The tape in my head starts playing again. . . . I reach for the radio dial, the car flips up on two wheels and begins to roll. And there's the scrub, upside down, rushing in to meet me. . . .

I feel sweaty in the palms, short of breath. I want to tell Norm to slow down, stop for a minute maybe. Instead, I close my eyes. In a suburb somewhere, the phone is ringing as the truckie's family sits down to tea. A phone call and a dot on the map is all the family will have to make the death seem real. Truckies' wives must live in dread of an unfamiliar voice trailing the bleep-bleep-bleep of the STD phone line.

After dark there are kangaroos all over the road, so Norm decides to call it quits at a roadhouse named Cocklebiddy. I thank the family, tell them that I'll try to hustle a ride from someone at the pub, and sprint off through drizzling rain.

"Tell him to get a 'roo or two for Tassie," Edna yells after me.

I manage a ride as far as Caiguna, 60 miles farther on, but it's still raining so I ask the roadhouse keeper about indoor accommodation. "I can give you a room for forty-nine dollars, a bus for ten dollars, and a car for five dollars," he says. I opt for the coach, a gutted old school bus with beds set in where the seats used to be.

As sleeping quarters go, it is comfortable enough. But the rain, and the long dozes through the Nullarbor, have left me wakeful, vaguely uneasy. I turn on my torch and study my reflection in the bus's rearview mirror. It is the first good look I've had at myself in three or four days and already the sunburned, unshaven face in the mirror looks unfamiliar—as if it's been placed in front of a fire and then had its red cheeks planted with scraggly, bleached-out grass.

It is the same creeping sense of unreality I felt in the cockies' truck yesterday; part of me here, in this beat-up bus in the Nullarbor, and part of me in Sydney with Geraldine. And then a third self, in another place still farther away—a childhood bedroom in the attic of an old shingle house at the other end of the globe. "Which I is I?" the poet Theodore Roethke wonders. I am less and less sure.

The farther I travel from home, the more I feel as if I could just drift off altogether, like a boat breaking loose from its moorings and easing out with the tide. Identity seems a brittle thing sometimes, particularly when you consider how easy it is to end up by the side of the road with a blanket over your head.

Remembering the truckie fills me with the same strange giddiness I felt for a month after my own car accident. If the rented Ford had rolled another way, I would have ended up like the truckie. But it didn't, and I'm still here, living on borrowed time—more like a handout, really.

And thinking about it now, the crash seems both inevitable and good. I used to nibble at each day's goodies like a child who pushes the best bits of every meal to the side of his plate, saving them until after the spinach and lima beans. Going for the moment—"going for the gusto"—was something people did in beer ads, not in real life.

Running off the road changed that, at least for a while. All I wanted to do was live fully; to work, but also to blow it off and go to the beach for an afternoon if I could get away with it. Better to go for the moment than to wait until it's not there to go for anymore.

Then, gradually, the old compulsiveness came back. If I miss this ferry, what will I do with the thirty minutes until the next one pulls in? If I have another glass of wine now, will I feel like working in the morning? And if I don't finish writing this news story by the end of the day, how will I get the feature done by the end of the week? Somehow, when I was done cramming together all the minutes and seconds, there'd be no time left, no room to move.

It was the same time sickness that helped send me off the road, rushing toward Alice when there was really no reason to rush at all.

The scar on my thigh is tanned now, but there's still the ugly pink-and-white crosshatching where the stitches went in. I need to keep the scar tissue in my head just as close and easy to get at; I need to roll back some trouser leg in my mind from time to time and be reminded. Otherwise I'll just pick up speed and run off the road again.

16
A CERTAIN SIRE AND
A CERTAIN DAME

On any other morning I would have ducked into the bushes as soon as I saw the car approach. And had the driver seen me scrambling out of sight, he would have happily sped on past. But not here, on the edge of the Nullarbor, with the rain spitting down. So when the Tasmanians see me, and I see them, there is really no choice but to climb aboard again.

Edna picks up where she left off the night before. As we pass a flock of crows, breakfasting on dead kangaroo by the highway, she rolls down the window to cheerlead: "Good on ya, mates! Good on ya!" Then it's back to bloody unions, bloody greenies, bloody dole bludgers, and Bob bloody Hawke.

Two bags of Cherry Ripes later, we reach Norseman, the first real town in Western Australia. I decide to duck out and have a poke around before choosing whether to go north through the goldfields or to take the coastal road to Perth.

"I'll stop in when I pass through Kalgoorlie," I lie.

"Love to have you," Edna lies back. She doesn't bother to offer an address.

It is 11 A.M. Monday when I disembark in Norseman. The gold miners are halfway through the day shift, their wives are shopping in town, the children are all at school. And I am shuffling down the main street with a rucksack: no appointments, no deadlines, no errands. Beats the hell out of Monday morning at the newspaper office.

But my waifdom is not so complete that I can walk by the first news agency I've spotted since leaving Alice. In fact, the very idea of a newspaper makes me weak at the knees, like a junkie giving in to the needle again.

What I get is a kind of newsprint Methadone.

"The *Norseman Today* is a paper without character," declares the editorial in a three-day-old copy of the local rag. "It never has any controversial articles printed in its pages. . . . All it does is report school news, Lions news, and various other sports club news."

I open to the inside pages and sure enough: school news, Lions news, various other sports club news. I return to the curious editorial. "Have you noticed that *Norseman Today* never writes about accidents, deaths, or anything remotely unpleasant? Well, that probably will not change." And that seems to be the point of the editorial—to assure readers that they'll continue to be fed a steady diet of school news, Lions news, and various other sports club news.

After all, there's enough unpleasantness in Norseman without the local paper rubbing it in. The town seems to have been in a slow state of decay since 1894, when a horse named Norseman stumbled over a gold nugget and the mining fever began (yep, the old horse-trips-over-nugget-story). Jerry-built houses huddle beneath a huge slag heap left by the mines. All commerce seems to have fled with the gold, leaving a row of Victorian shopfronts with "for sale" or "for lease" signs in the windows, and iron rooftops sagging almost onto the footpath.

One of the few businesses actually open at noon on Monday is Amelia Jones's rock and empty-bottle shop. She spies me peeking through the window at her granite and glass, and comes out for a chat.

"Business is kind of slow," she confesses, stopping to rearrange a few chunks of amethyst in the front window. "And I guess this isn't the best kind of business for a town where people are always moving in and moving out. They don't want to load themselves down."

I decide to go with the flow and move out as quickly as I can. But the same rule applies here as in Cloncurry and Coober Pedy; the more blighted the locale, the harder it is to escape. Norseman has the added disadvantage of being a gateway to Western Australia, and hence a point of entry for fugitives, criminals, and drifters from the eastern states. If the *Norseman Today* hadn't been so busy reporting Lions news and various other sports club news, it might have told me what Amelia Jones reports: namely, that three days prior to my arrival, a pair of hitchhikers bashed and robbed a driver who had been so unlucky as to offer them a ride out of town. No wonder, then, that the only person to pull up beside me all afternoon is a policeman who wants to check my identification.

Until Elsa. There's a bit of fable that passes among male hitchhikers the world over. It's called "The Woman in the Sports Car" and like any good story it gathers a bit of lint in the telling: A Holden might become a Porsche; an average-looking woman may start to resemble Sophia Loren. But whatever the version, it is a story that brings together two essential threads in Hitchhike Dreaming: the unattached, attractive woman and the comfortable car. Jackson Browne popularized the fantasy with his song about standing on a corner in Winslow, Arizona: "It's a girl, my lord, in a flatbed Ford, slowing down to have a look at me."

The song ends with Jackson wailing, "Open up, I'm climbing in." But that only happens to rock stars. My friend Rich—the one who married a fire fighter he hitched a ride with in Oregon—is a one-in-a-million case. In fact, Annie was the first woman to ever offer him a lift. Beginner's luck.

Unaccompanied women are understandably afraid of letting strange men into their car. Some will even stop to tell you that as they un-pick you up. "Sorry, if I weren't alone I'd give you a ride," or a similarly apologetic phrase.

The fact that drivers of luxury cars stop as rarely as lone women is more complex. Perhaps they're simply worried that a scruffy wanderer with a rucksack will scratch a polished leather seat. But having hitch-hiked now on three different continents, I suspect there's more to it than that; some universal law stating that the higher one climbs on the economic ladder, the lower becomes one's quota of generosity toward strangers. The converse is also true. If anyone ever put together a group profile of hitchhikers' most frequent patrons, it would come out looking like the lobby of a welfare office: Mexican fruit pickers in America, Turkish laborers in secondhand Volkswagens on the Autobahn, Aborigines and hard-luck cockies in the bush. It is the disadvantaged who are also most likely to offer you a seat at their dinner table or a bed for the night. Meanwhile, those who can afford to share their petrol and tucker very rarely do.

Enough for social theory; all I'm thinking of in Norseman is a ride, any ride. I don't care if it's an old man in a horse-drawn buggy, I just want out. For my humility I'm rewarded with a young doctor popping past in a zippy roadster, then turning around to offer me a lift.

"Hop in," she says with a wide, welcoming flash of perfect orthodontia. "I'm just headed down to have a look around the coast. Plenty of extra room." I click a mental snapshot to pull from my wallet at the next hitchhikers' convention.

Elsa is a GP from Perth, putting in a few months at a clinic in Kalgoorlie. She's also the first kindred soul I've encountered in several thousand miles. Kindred in that she's an outsider who has left the city in a self-conscious effort to see some bush. Kindred too in that she's a little burned out and anxious to chat about city things for a while. After a steady conversational diet of fertilizer, farting, drinking, and killing kangaroos, I'm only too happy to oblige.

So we speed south of Norseman, through Salmon Gums, through Grass Patch, through Gibson, noshing at plays and movies. We sip at English literature. We hoe into politics. We dessert on the differences between city and country life. And it is all as smooth and satisfying as a long lunch over chardonnay by Sydney Harbor.

But my movable feast with Elsa causes a strange sort of indigestion. While I was traveling through the scrub with opal miners and cockies, or across the Nullarbor with a family of Tasmanian geeks, there was little to remind me of home—and hence little to make me homesick. But chatting with this amiable and attractive young doctor, I begin to miss Geraldine with a palpable sense of longing. I can see her right now in Sydney, in the bathtub, newsprint smudged on her thighs from the paper she's reading. I can see her now, smiling as I climb into the tub beside her. . . .

Elsa's company is to Geraldine what reading *Norseman Today* was to my news junkiedom. Methadone treatment again.

There's a related discomfort, less acute but more perplexing. Elsa breaks the spell of my adventure, in the same way that the Tasmanians' air-conditioned car removed me from the rawness of desert travel. After a few days of drifting, my identity is suddenly secure. And as soon as I've become the Young Educated Urbanite again—albeit, transplanted to the bush—I want to shed the familiar luggage and be back in the slums of outback hitchhiking.

The scenery conspires with the chat to shrink all sense of away-ness. I am suddenly out of the scrub, rushing toward the sea through rolling, verdant heath. Grass. Trees. Orchards. I haven't seen so much green since my first day hitching out of Sydney. Approaching the coast from the sunparched interior, it is easy to see why Australians crowd the shoreline despite all the open, untamed spaces farther in.

The seasons have also changed. In the outback the only seasonal gradations are hot, very hot, and unbearably hot. But when I leave the warmth of Elsa's car in Esperance, I step into the chill and wet of a late autumn evening. Still clad in a singlet and shorts, I feel like an Australian bumpkin climbing off a plane in wintry London. I decide to hibernate at the nearest pub and console myself with a hot meal and a warm, early bed.

I would have done better to camp in the rain. The pub meal is Rabelaisian in quantity and grotesque in quality, even by comparison to the chicken rolls and pasties I've been living on for the past several days. For entrees I devour a basket of stale white bread and a thin gruel with grease bubbles floating on the top, called "soupe du jour." The main course appears to be an entire haunch of lamb, swimming through a swamp of brown gravy, with a massive collection of vegetables dipping their toes in the ooze: three greens, two baked potatoes, a pile of canned carrots and canned peas. There's also a side salad of egg, more potato, beetroot, and sweet canned fruit sailing through the muck on a wilted leaf of lettuce.

I eat it all but the meal is so poor that I feel unsatisfied. So I order dessert and get a lemon meringue that a mining engineer couldn't drill his way into. Washed down with coffee that looks suspiciously like the soupe du jour.

Of course, it could have been worse. Ernest Giles's first meal after surviving the Gibson Desert was a small sick wallaby, which he ate "living, raw, dying—fur, skin, bones, skull and all. The delicious taste of that creature I shall never forget." Nothing like a few words from the wretched explorers to put your own misery in perspective.

I stagger upstairs to a lounge room where a dozen hotel boarders stare blankly at a sitcom on the television. The volume is so loud that even lying in bed, I can hear the TV's canned laughter wafting in. Dampness hangs on the hotel's walls and blankets. My chapped lips and dried skin soak up the moisture like a happy sponge, but so do my joints and neck, which begin creaking as loudly as the bed in the room above me. The creak upstairs gets louder, more furious, almost shaking the walls. I think again of the bathtub in Sydney and feel as lonely and low as at any time during my Australian journey.

In the morning I restore my spirits—and my resemblance to the rest of the species—with a long shower and a trip to the Laundromat. Between the wash and the rinse cycle I meet three Englishmen named Paul, Nick, and Nick, touring Western Australia in search of the elusive Halley's Comet. They offer me a lift to their next viewing spot, a few hours inland from Esperance.

The company makes me feel as well-seasoned and Australian as a nineteenth-century bushman. In England, Paul, Nick, and Nick work as pharmacist, physicist, and computer programmer. In Australia they merge into a three-headed parody of the Pommie nerd. Paul the pharmacist drives like a half-blind pensioner, with Nick the computer whiz in the navigator's seat, yelling in panic whenever a scenic lookout or roadhouse doesn't appear with the precision of a software program. At one point he even orders Paul to turn around and retreat 12 miles to Esperance. The gas tank is half empty; better to go back and refuel rather than to venture into 30 miles of wilderness.

Meanwhile, Nick the physicist shifts uncomfortably in his proper leather shoes and stretch slacks, complaining of the "heat bumps" covering his pale white body. While the deep space he's gazed at through the telescope has been underwhelming, the Australian space outside the car has him reeling.

"I get agoraphobic out here," he confesses, gazing at a landscape of sheep and farmhouses that is downright cluttered by Australian standards. "In England there'd be three villages out there. Here, nothing."

I think of the hardbitten men I traveled with in the center, and of explorers like John Eyre, who walked much of the way from Adelaide to Esperance in 1841, and muse at how quickly *Homo Australis* has evolved from the English weed that first took root in the Antipodes.

Hitchhiking with tourists has a singular advantage: namely, that they are doing the same thing as you—sightseeing. Riding with a truckie, or with a local driver through the flow of their daily work, you can't very well blurt, "Pull off here so I can snap a picture," or "The travel guide says the best view of the coast is just ten kilometers south." Tourists do it for you.

So three Poms and a Yank amble through the countryside, stopping to gawk at Pink Lake (an algae-ridden pond that is as pink and artificial-looking as cotton candy) and to photograph each other standing atop a dune overlooking the Great Australian Bight. We even go in search of the famed Western Australian "rabbit fence," erected by graziers and farmers some years ago to keep bunnies from migrating west. It didn't work. There's no sign of the fence anymore; just rabbits hopping all over the highway.

Hitchhiking with tourists has the singular disadvantage that they, like you, are strangers to the territory. Only the surface of the landscape is touched and understood. Not since Kimba have I crossed the line from tourist to fellow-traveler. So at a town called Ravensthorpe, where the Englishmen stop to set up camp for the night, I decide to pick my own ride instead of letting it pick me.

Nine head of cattle stare out from between the wooden slats of a truck parked at the gas station. I wait for the driver to fill his tank and flash my most plaintive "I-need-a-ride" smile. He smiles back and waves me into the passenger seat.

It is a fortunate selection. Andrew Cabassi is as rare and fine a breed as the bulls he is carrying to a "Beef Week" auction in Albany: a successful man of the land, as contented with his lot as the Kimba cockies were discontented with theirs.

"If you want to grizzle, you can grizzle, and most cockies do," he tells me. "But at the moment I can't think of anything to grizzle about." When I ask him what he specializes in, he hands me a finely printed business card with "Advanced Cattle Production Consultant" written beneath his name. "Just for show," he says, fingering the card with a curious mix of pride and embarrassment. "Anyway, it only tells half the story."

The card should read: "Andrew Cabassi, cattle consultant, stud breeder, sperm exporter, vegetable farmer, and lucky son of indigent Italian immigrants." A generation ago, his bloodline was still scratching two acres of stony hillside in Tuscany, as it had for the previous few centuries. Then his father fled to Western Australia and started scratching a few unstony acres of soil near Perth. Andrew left school at eleven ("Still can't do anything but sign the checks"), married with 200 pounds sterling to his name, borrowed, increased, and eventually bought his own farm. He has been growing fat off the land ever since.

"Fat as a sow," he says with the hearty squeal of a pig rolling in the mud. The good fortune includes a few thousand head of cattle grazing across 3,000 acres of land. Also, the highest price ever paid in Western Australia—$22,000—for the last bull he sold at the Albany market. It broke his own record set a few months before that. "And I've had some bloody fun, all the way to the bank," he says.

Success has gone to Andrew's pocket but remarkably little of it has gone to his head. He could easily afford to hire someone else to drive his bulls to market. But he prefers to do it himself. And when he gets to Albany, well before dawn so his bulls will be first off the auction block, he'll sleep in the back of his truck rather than check into a hotel.

"My blood is *contadino*—peasant blood—and as soon as I forget where I came from, I will be a peasant again," he says. "Just because I have money doesn't make me better than the next bloke. Just happier." He laughs again. "As happy as a bull in a paddock full of dames."

Andrew talks about cattle with the passion of a vintner discussing his finest burgundy. "See that one in the corner?" he says, pointing through the slats of his truck. We've pulled off the road so he can illustrate a point about breeding. "Good muscle, nice and wide across the top. But not real masculine. Sort of sloppy. You want more muscle through the rest of the body for red meat."

He lectures me about sperm rights, about "teaser" cows that lure the bulls into the pen, and about the rubber bags—soft and water-filled to duplicate a vagina—used to collect the specimen. "Doesn't take 'em long, let me tell you," he says with a chortle.

But all this expertise has affected Andrew even less than the money. In the middle of his dissertation—"Am I boring you?" "No, not at all." And he isn't—he pauses to ponder the magic that unfolds every time chromosome X meets chromosome Y.

"Use a certain sire with a certain dame and it comes up trumps," he says, concluding the lecture. "Works almost every time. Isn't that something?" Still as wondrous to him as his own success at engineering it.

Part of the appeal of newspaper reporting is that it gives you daily glimpses into the lives of people you'd otherwise never encounter. Hitch-hiking magnifies the same experience. Instead of calling ahead and arranging an appointment, you are thrust into the full stream of their working day. No time for them to fix the makeup or alter the normal pattern of events. Just raw and unedited life; as raw as a truck full of bulls, rumbling toward a "Beef Week" auction in Albany.

We drive slowly through the twilight, with Andrew pointing out the farm of one customer, then another; the road is as familiar as a milk run to him. And as dusk gives way to dark, we share the sandwiches his wife prepared—"home-grown veggies, not a chemical on the lot of them"—and talk about the future.

Driving at night seems to unlimber the soul. Eye contact ends and the cab becomes a confession box, with nothing but murmuring voices in the dark. The small distractions of the workday are shoved aside.

Andrew tells me about his marriage of thirty years and I ask him how to keep it strong for all that time ("Stay patient and keep your fingers crossed," he says. "Let her window shop if she's restless, so long as she doesn't buy"). He tells me about his sons at university—"one in med sci, one in ag sci"—and asks for advice about keeping them away from drugs (I tell him that I experimented and came through all right—I think). I ask him about success and he tells me, "Trust your instincts and don't listen to the next guy."

And finally we talk about death, or our fears of it. Pushing fifty, Andrew looks as strong and well fed as his cattle. But still he worries. "I'm just hoping one of the boys will take over the farm, then I can die happy." I tell him about the tape that keeps playing in my head whenever I'm in a car that picks up speed, and about the truckie I saw by the road in the Nullarbor. He tells me that all I've done is grow up fast.

"When you're young, you feel like Superman, like nothing can touch you," he says. "Then some bloke you know, strong as an ox, keels over in the paddock one morning. So you slow down a bit, spend more time with the missus, try to enjoy things a little more."

And then we both go quiet for the last half hour to Albany, feeling a bit astonished at having opened up so easily to a stranger of three hours' acquaintance.

But Andrew has one parting piece of advice. As I climb down from the truck to wander into town, he gives me a stock tip—not of the Hereford kind either. He tells me the names of several small companies that he's "got a hunch will be worth a bloody fortune some day." I want to ask how I can invest in him instead. As it is, he will be remembered in a private collection of all the memorable faces I've met on the road. Andrew Cabassi, the Happy Farmer in the Lucky Country. We shake hands and go our separate ways in the night.

17
RIDING THE
RAILS

Something strange and wonderful is about to happen. A freight train is chuga-chug-chugging up the track and in a moment I'm going to climb on and ride it somewhere, where, I don't really know.

At least that's what I've been telling myself all afternoon, lying in this ditch at a railroad crossing west of Albany.

"Two o'clock, sure as night follows day," said the cockie who dropped me here, at Elleker, a few hours ago. "They don't stop anymore, at least not to drop anything off. But they fiddle with something on the track."

I didn't think anything of it and started hiking a few miles out of Elleker to catch a ride on the main road running west. Then, halfway there, I found myself turning around and hiking back. As traveling goes, hitchhiking is about as random as you can get. But hopping a freight train, on a line headed who-knows-where, that's a different kind of random altogether.

I also have a private score to settle with freight trains. The score to date is Trains 2, Tony 0. In America there were once thousands of drifters riding the rails, from job to job, or hobo jungle to hobo jungle. Most of them are gone now, with the freight trains. But the myth of the rail-riding rambler still has resonance, at least for romantic fools.

Foolish is what I proved to be at seventeen when I tried to hop a freight train in California. A corroboree of winos was drinking around a bonfire by the tracks, so I figured it made sense to seek out some professional advice. What I got was a long line of drunken bull from one hobo, while another crept around and rifled through my pack. I didn't find out until later that he'd pinched my wallet. That was after I discovered the advice was worthless; the freight trains didn't even stop there anymore.

I tried again a few weeks later on the testimony of a hitchhiker I'd met outside Boise, Idaho. "Just hand one of the guards ten dollars and ask him where there's an open car," he told me. I did. The guard handed the ten dollars back and told me that if I didn't get lost in five seconds, I'd be under arrest. I gave up on freight trains after that.

But Elleker looks easy. No tangle of rails to tiptoe across, no hobos to mislead me, not even a neighbor within clear view to dob me in. Just a few railroad workers a mile farther on, banging listlessly at the track. Cachunk. Cachunk. Cachunk. All I have to do is lie in this ditch, out of sight, and wait for the two o'clock train to come rattling along. Piece of cake.

I close my eyes. CaCHUNKunk. CaCHUNKunk. CaCHUNKunk. That's a heartbeat now, not a hammer. I bolt upright. What if there's a guard on the back? What if there are no open wagons? What if there are?

And who are we kidding? This is me we're talking about, not some stunt man. Me, lily-livered me, who gets sweaty palms on airplane take-offs, who faints at the sight of blood, who hasn't ridden on a roller coaster since he was eleven, and then only because his brother forced him. Who the hell are we kidding?

The truth is, when it comes to matters of physical courage, I'm all talk. That is to say, I'm fine in situations that I can talk my way out of. Even muggers are okay so long as they don't flash any artillery in my face. Words will never hurt me.

It's the sticks and stones breaking my bones that I worry about. I'm the sort of person who watches war movies and wonders why all the soldiers don't lie down in the mud and play dead.

That's the real me; the fantasy me is some kind of cross between Geronimo and Ned Kelly. And the fantasy keeps getting in the way of the real thing, as fantasies have a way of doing. So I end up in situations like this, lying in a ditch in a wretched, sweaty panic, waiting for a freight train to come so I can climb inside it.

CaCHUNK—CaCHUNK—CaCHUNK—CaCHOOOOOOOOO-OO! CaCHOOOOOOOO! CaCHOOOOOOO! CaCHOOOOOOOO-OO! I poke my head out of the ditch and sure enough, there she is, rumbling up the track to meet me. I duck back in the ditch and wait for the long line of cars to pass and then hiss to a halt. CAchoooooooooo. I poke my head out again. The men working on the track are on the other side of the train, out of view. No guard on the back car. No one in sight. No excuses.

I leap out of the ditch and run alongside the train looking for an open wagon. All sealed shut. I run to the back car to see if there's a platform to sit on. There isn't. I sprint back down to find a space between two of the wagons. It's a tight squeeze, uncomfortable, maybe dangerous. There's a ladder going up the side, but riding piggyback looks dodgy. Maybe I should toss myself back in the ditch and play dead.

Too late.

"Hey, mate, what the hell are you doing?" It is an engineer standing a little way down the track. "If you're thinking of riding between those wagons, I wouldn't. Unless you want to be the meat in a very messy sandwich."

The real me is relieved; whatever happens now, it can't be as scary as riding between two wagons. But Geronimo is disappointed; after all, this is about as far as he's pushed himself in the last ten years.

"Got any room for me up front?" I blurt out.

The question seems to catch the man off guard. "I'm just the assistant," he says. "Ask the driver."

I run down the track and look up, way up, at the digits 1592 and the name Shire of Toodjay, and above that the driver's window with a balding man in a plaid shirt looking out. I repeat my question. He looks at me through dark sunglasses, looks down the track, and gestures me aboard with a toss of his head.

"Just remember, you didn't hear me say that," he says as I climb a ladder into the driver's compartment. The assistant climbs in with us and we rumble down the track out of Elleker.

"Where ya headed?" the driver asks.

"Wherever you are."

"In it for the thrills, are ya?" He laughs. "Well, it's no bloody adventure up here. But at least it's safe." Then he tells me why the assistant warned against squeezing between the wagons. Just a few weeks before, a train derailed in the Nullarbor and when they finally pulled the cars apart they found a man in his twenties "well and truly mashed." He was a Yank, too. Probably had the same dumb fantasies about freight trains as me.

My own fantasy is about to carry me north, where the twenty empty cars will load up with wheat. It's not exactly the most direct route to Perth but at least it's not back the way I came. So I settle on the floor by the driver's seat and listen. Yesterday's lesson was artificial insemination; today's will be riding the rails.

"Back in the forties, when I got started at this, there was plenty of blokes like you," Gordon Link tells me. Swagmen usually. But also apple pickers and packers, trying to bum a ride to the next orchard. Officially, freight drivers weren't allowed to carry human cargo. "But most of the time, if I saw someone climbing on in the back, I just looked the other way, unless they were drunk." Or unless they were female. Then he might invite them to ride up front. Even so, they'd have to work for the privilege. "I'd make her swing a coal shovel, same as anyone else."

Then the fruit picking dwindled, and so did the freight traffic. The trains used to carry small goods to drop off at every little junction. But trucks and automobiles cut into that. Now most freighters are restricted to long-distance hauls with coal or wheat or iron ore. Only spots like Elleker, where the track changes, merit any pause en route.

The last hitchhiker Gordon saw was a drunk sailor who jumped ship in Fremantle, went to see his girlfriend in Albany, then hopped on the train to get back to port.

"He reckoned this would be the quickest way back to Freeo. But he didn't realize until too late that we were going the wrong way, and going there bloody slow."

So slow in fact that Gordon doesn't have to do much but settle back and keep a lazy eye on the track ahead. There's no coal to stoke on electric trains, and no real driving to be done. All Gordon monitors is the speed. "I'm just a throttle jockey," he says. "Ease her down at the sidings and get her back up to speed in open country. Sometimes we get up to a tonne—that's a hundred k's an hour—but mostly we just cruise along at eighty."

He slouches in his seat, watching the woods and rolling farmland chug past. It looks as easy as steering toy engines around the Christmas tree. The train's whistle isn't even a whistle now that steam power's gone; it's just a glorified air horn. Gordon yanks it once to warn off a car that wants to scoot across the tracks before he rumbles through.

"Must be a lot of Japs around here," he says. "Always someone trying to do harry karry getting across the tracks."

I doubt there are many Japanese, but maybe a tribe or two of dyspeptic Aborigines. Every second town and river name seems to end with a hiccup: Narrikup, Porongurup, Bolganup, all the way from the Bight to the Indian Ocean. Gordon says it's because "up" means water, which may explain all the hiccups.

Gordon's headed toward the dry interior where all the names end with "in": Wagin, Wickepin, Corrigin, Kellerberrin. And he's a little concerned that some superintendent might spot an unauthorized passenger up front. So at a quiet junction a half-tonne north of Elleker he stops to let me out.

"You should feel privileged," he tells me, yanking the air horn a few times just for the hell of it. "This is the first wheat train to stop in Mount Barker for about a thousand years." Barker doesn't look too impressed. Nor am I, if the truth be told. My foray into freight-hopping has been like going to ride the Ferris wheel and ending up on a merry-go-round.

I spread out my map on a splintery bench by the tracks and plot my choice of hiccups. I can go north on the main road to Kojonup, north-west to Boyup or follow a little red squiggle of a road west to Manjimup and stay on the up and up to Perth. I foolishly choose the squiggle. The region seems so tame and settled after the outback that I've forgotten how much empty space there can be between blips of civilization.

I remember when I hitch a ride as far as Rocky Gully. It is so blippy as to not even register on my map. Just a grocery, a petrol pump, a few dozen houses, and thick timber with a chainsaw mowing away in the middle distance. I keep thinking the noise is a car. But every time I look up, there's nothing but a cloud in front of my face or, rather, coming from my face. That's how cold it is.

The proprietor at the grocery offers some advice. The good news is that there's a hotel a little way down the road; the bad news is that it's the closest you'll ever come to a pub with no beer. "The publican's got rooms but he doesn't let them," she explains. "But you can try. Knock back a few beers and sort of warm him up to the idea. And for Chrissake's, whatever you do, don't ask for tea. He hates cooking tea."

She offers this information with a matter-of-factness that suggests all business in Rocky Gully is run along eccentric lines. After all, why should a publican be expected to let rooms and sell food? But it's dark and cold; I have no choice but to observe the local work rules.

The Rural Hotel is plain brick on the outside and even plainer on the inside. Beside the bar there's a pool table and then a big stretch of floorspace that would be occupied in any other pub by tables, chairs, a jukebox—something. Here, nothing. No people, either. Just me and a sour-faced, white-haired publican, studying a racing form at the bar. A few thousand losing ponies appear to have trotted across his face, leaving it raw and rutted and unhappy.

I climb on a stool, drop a two-dollar note on the bar, and order an Emu. The publican doesn't move. I repeat the order. Still nothing. I wander over to study a few public notices pinned by the door. "Goats. Alive. Wanted to Buy." "Quails for Sale." "Sheep Shorn." The usual stuff. When I return there's a can of Emu and eighty cents change on the bar. The publican is just where I left him, face buried in the racing form.

Four sawmill workers come in and order a round of beers. They are even more tentative than me, waiting patiently while the publican makes a phone call—to a bookie, I assume—then checks the paper again before serving them. The sawmill workers chat for half an hour, softly, as if in church, then order a round of pies. I take the chance to order one myself. The publican glares at us over his paper as if we've asked him to whip up a bit of duck à l'orange. Twenty minutes later, the pies are still sitting on a cool rack in the microwave, apparently forgotten. When the publican goes to the phone again, I ask one of the workers if we should remind the chef of our order.

"Don't rush him or you won't get a bite," he whispers. Ten minutes later a batch of half-warmed pies are tossed on the bar. The sawmill workers thank the publican so effusively that you'd think they'd just been served a roast dinner by their mother-in-law.

"Mmmmmmmm."

"Great pie, real beauty."

At first I take this nonsense for sarcasm, then I realize it's just diplomatic. With no other pub for 50 miles, they can't afford to alienate their only source of grog.

Two beers later, after the workers have left, I pop the big question. "Excuse me, sir? I was wondering whether you'd have a room for the night?" I don't expect an answer and don't receive one. I have learned enough protocol to wait five minutes before repeating the question. He doesn't shift his eye from the television screen and waits a few more minutes before answering.

"All booked out, mate," he says.

Of course, how silly of me. After all, I've had three beers and a lukewarm pie in two hours. Let's not get greedy.

I gaze down the empty bar, read the notices on the wall for the fifteenth time, peek out the window at the cold, dark night. Then shuffle back to the bar and stare blankly at the television for another twenty minutes.

"I reckon we might be able to squeeze you in," he says, unprompted, during a commercial break. I nod. Ten minutes later, when the sitcom ends, he shows me into a back corridor. There are fourteen empty rooms, beds made, towels over backs of chairs. The bathroom is equally pristine. "Push Here for Soap" says the old-fashioned fixture above the sink, which looks as if it hasn't been pushed since 1924. He shows me to a room at the end of the hall and holds out his hand—"Twenty dollars, ta"—and disappears. It is the most I've paid for a bed since Sydney.

The room is as inhospitable as my host. No sooner am I undressed and in bed than a cold wind starts seeping through the walls and floorboards. There is only one blanket—a thin wisp of wool, almost transparent. The bed feels as if the springs have been yanked out and a slab of concrete poured where the mattress should be. I pillage the other rooms for extra blankets and manage to make my resting place about as comfortable as a medieval dungeon. I lie there awake for some time, wondering what quirk of fate has condemned this publican to Rocky Gully, in a role for which he is so obviously miscast. And pondering all the quirks of fate—a love affair, an idea for a journey, haphazard collection of rides—that have landed me in Rocky Gully as his prisoner for the night.

18
THE CUP
RUNNETH OVER

Sound and smell are second-class citizens in the realm of my senses. No matter that the world goes blurry as soon as I take off my glasses; what I can't see I tend not to trust.

But the gloomy mist is too thick in Rocky Gully to see anything. So as I stand by the road at dawn, I have no choice but to listen and sniff at the air as the town comes awake, slowly, like a cat. A wind wafts in from the woods with the odor of pine, nudging the night mist aside. Birds chatter and chirp like noisy children at the breakfast table. Then, as the dawn breaks, a rooster crows the town awake. Dogs bark. There is the smell of a fire burning in someone's hearth. And finally, an hour after sunrise, a human sound; the dull, persistent moan of a chainsaw followed by the heavy thud of timber meeting ground.

A ute rumbles off a gravel side road and pauses to pick me up. Inside is a grizzled old man in woollen plaids. There are a chainsaw and an axe in the back of his truck. A nice start: a lumberjack on his way to the day's first stand of timber. What's it like, I ask him as soon as we rumble off, to be wandering through the woods and come across one of the centuries-old karri trees that tower in the forest hereabouts?

"I reckon if she's got two hundred dollars of lumber in her, I'll cut the cunt down," he says. The interview ends there.

Gazing out the window, I feel as if I've found my natural habitat— or at least the habitat I once enjoyed: rolling woodland and streams, like the Virginia countryside near my childhood home. Thus far in Australia, Tasmania is the only other place that's had that whiff of home about it—initially at least. I went there with Geraldine a few months after migrating to Sydney, and the island's hills and woods and colonial villages made me homesick. In the wild north of the state, we went for a hike up a secluded mountain trail that had been advertised by a friend as "a bit of a scramble." We set off early, with only an apple as baggage, expecting to be back down the mountain by lunchtime. Just a bit of a scramble.

A dimly blazed path led us through thick woods, then to a stony, treeless ridge that led to a stony, treeless cliff and then to another ridge. We struggled up to find another cliff, another ridge, beckoning us with the come-hither smile that mountains so often show to the world. When we finally reached the top, the flies were unbearable. So we retreated, picking our way like billygoats down the steep stony mountainside.

The trail was nowhere in sight. We tried one direction and then another; each ended in sheer drops of several hundred yards. I looked out at the panoramic view, stretching for 50 miles or so in every direction, and couldn't spot one sign of humanity; not a road, not a power line, not even a wisp of smoke. It would be days before anyone knew we had come this way, I decided; many weeks before they found our bodies.

At sunset we found the trail again and made it to the bottom, scratched and bleeding. Not like Virginia at all.

Geraldine still laughs about the hike and accuses me—and many Americans—of being anthropocentric: unless a landscape has a person in it, I become anxious. Hardy Australians, of course, feel at home on desolate beaches and in untouched rain forest. After living here for awhile, so do I. Just spare me the bit of a scramble.

The southwest corner of Western Australia is Tasmania without the wild edge. The woods are open, easy to walk through, and never too far from a weatherbeaten cottage or an old stone chimney where a homestead used to be. All the signs of a land gently settled, long ago, that never grew fat enough to attract less gentle development. Only the soft, unmistakable imprint of a rural counterculture: the Old Bakery Restaurant in one town, the Cheese Factory Craft Centre in another, and brightly colored cabins nestled in the valleys. A hard squint and it could be the Shenandoah.

The hitchhiking also resembles my journeys through rural America. In the outback I have accustomed myself to marathon rides; the towns are so few and far between that your first ride of the day is often the only one. But here, on a weekday morning in the well-settled countryside, I bump along from town to town, climbing out before I've learned the most cursory details of the life I've brushed against. It's a bit like hitching through the first fifty pages of a Russian novel, being introduced to a dozen different characters whose names and faces quickly begin blurring together.

In order of appearance, the cast after Rocky Gully goes as follows:

THE FARMER [*Slows down truck, gestures at unkempt fields of a neighboring hobby farm.*]: Now a good cockie, he'd be mowing that paddock. But you know what? You could knock on that door any hour of the day and some bloke would be there to answer it. Not too keen on work, them folks. Now a bloke that's grown up in these parts, he's keen as mustard. But them folks, they'd rather get the bloody dole.

THE WEAVER [*Sixties-style bug-eyed sunglasses covering most of her face.*]: Perth just became a hassle. Hassle hassle hassle. You know what I mean? Like I was in a real suburban rut. Down here, there's no hassle at all. Just the cockies. You know what I mean? But it's funny, like I thought it would be more private down on the farm. But you know what? It's worse than the city. Everyone knows who drives what car, who's home, who's at someone else's home, whose missus is down at the pub. You know what I mean?

THE FOOTIE PLAYER [*Arms as big as my thighs, car littered like the locker room after a big game: shorts, T-shirts, jock straps, crushed tinnies.*]: I've been lucky so far, all I've had is breaks. (Jaw. Nose. Wrist. Jaw again.) But breaks are all right. They're clean. Snap and you're done. It's when you get into knees and elbows that you have to give the game away. [*Pauses, flashes toothless smile, lifts arm to show off the scabs from last game.*]. See that? Bark's peeling off me all the time.

THE APPLE-PICKER: We'll be well into yellows now and then a spot of red. You're Canadian, right? A Yank? I thought so. But it's safer to ask if you're Canadian. Canucks can't stand being called a Yank. Do Yanks mind being called Canucks? No? That's good. Here, try one of these reds, try a yellow, eat the bloody lot of 'em. If I look at any more apples, I think I'll spew.

THE SALES MANAGER [*Car fragrance on dashboard, company sedan, company tape deck.*]: When I was a kid, Perth was a cemetery—it was that dead. You think I'm joking? It was dead, really dead. Now? Now it's a rat race. People will eat your eyes out if you give them half a chance. Bunbury's the way Perth used to be. Dead. But it's a nice sort of dead.

The rides wind north from Manjimup to Nannup to Balingup to Boyanup. Then the ups give out in Bunbury, and so do the paddocks, the apples, the old stone buildings. Perth is more than 60 miles away but already there is the odor of an encroaching city. One-lane roads merge and swell to two, then four. The traffic is impatient and aggressive, pulling me toward the rat race and hassle everyone has come south to get away from.

Major cities are a nightmare for the hitchhiker. If possible, you find a ring road and plot a bypass around the thumping aorta of urban life. But more often you end up circulating through every capillary before being pumped out at the other end. En route you are likely to be hustled, hassled, robbed, or arrested as a vagrant. Or to find yourself in the thick of a lynch mob on a city bus, about to be strung up for clobbering an old lady with a careless swing of your pack.

Perth's sprawl is anorexic compared with most American cities, but it is still big enough to threaten half a day of moving in and moving out. So I decide to berth south of the city at Fremantle, then set off for the bush with a full day in front of me. Anyway, I can hardly show my face in America again without having eyeballed the one part of Australia that my countrymen may know something about. (Perth, that's the capital, right? . . . No, Canberra. . . . Canberra? Is that near Brisbane? . . . No, nowhere near. . . .)

Fremantle quickly cures me of the lingering homesickness I felt in the countryside farther south. America—or the America's Cup, at least—is branded on the former fishing village like a pair of McDonald's

Golden Arches. I head straight for the water only to find that the Indian Ocean has been imprisoned behind a wall of high-security fences. "America's Cup Defence Headquarters," says an imposing sign on one locked gate, beneath a huge banner with the ubiquitous boxing kangaroo. It looks more like an army compound than a yacht berth.

The real waterfront has been stuffed into nooks and crannies between the marinas, leaving the fishing boats to slither in and out like minnows tiptoeing past sleeping whales.

Fremantle has spent 150 years collecting flotsam and jetsam from the Northern Hemisphere. In the 1850s, convicts were so numerous that soldiers walked the streets at night asking "Bond or free?" Then, as the first stop for ships arriving from the West, Fremantle became Australia's "front door to Europe." A lot of the immigrants who poured off here never got past the foyer; there are still something like seventy-five languages spoken in the town.

But in the run-up to the Cup, Fremantle resembles an Italian village bracing for the arrival of Allied Forces. Or, rather, a patient awaiting the plastic surgeon's knife. Snip and staple the Commercial Hotel, pull out the urine-yellow carpet, put in coachlights where the naked bulbs used to be, and turn it into the New Orleans Bourbon and Beefsteak Bar. Reduce and contour Clarrie Minciullo's panel-beating shop and implant the Harbour Mill Garden Restaurant. Enlarge the old Papa Luigi's café and reshape it into the new Papa Luigi's café, as bloated and artificial as a silicon breast. And when the stitches are out, the old, ethnic town will have magically become a tarted-up clone, like the "international" villages they build overnight for the Olympic Games.

Fortunately, the graft has been uneven, at least up to now, six months before the races. You can redo a Victorian façade in a month but it takes a bit longer to change the people who live behind it. So Fremantle still shows an essentially Mediterranean face to the world: old Italian men sipping cappuccino at open-air trattorias, Greek sailors weaving through the narrow streets with duffel bags slung over their shoulders, Portuguese fishermen slapping their catch on the dock. The same westerly wind that remedies the morning heat and powers the 12-meter's spinnaker—Fremantle's famed "Doctor"—picks up the odor of fish from the docks and blows it through the dolled-up streets.

Of course, a bit of ethnic color enhances Fremantle's tourist trade, which is one reason the traditional scene hasn't been erased, just tidied a bit. And Fremantle has made a career of integratng newcomers; its character can survive where a younger, less worldly town, such as Alice Springs, has its personality trampled by the tourist crush. I find myself hoping that the Yanqui invaders will recapture their Cup and take it home, leaving Fremantle to become a sleepy little seaport again.

Perth, 12 miles up the coast, is a different kettle of fish altogether: crisp skyscrapers, clean streets, and suburbs that sprawl so far that it's hard to find the city for all the brick-and-tile houses. While much of Fremantle is working class and bohemian, Perth's dominant theme appears middle class and provincial. My first and strongest impression is of a kind of seaside Denver: a cow town grown fat and smug, disdainful of the oversophisticated hordes "out East."

"New South Wales is bilge," a good-humored young clerk tells me on the twenty-minute rail trip from Fremantle to Perth. "Victoria's even less than that."

I ask him if he's ever been to the eastern states. "Why bother?" he says. "We've got it all here. Anyway, the big nobs don't want to know about us."

This isolationism is firmly rooted in geographical fact. Bali and Singapore are closer and cheaper to reach than the cities back East. (Due west there isn't another landfall until the island of Mauritius, off the African coast, about 4,000 miles away.) No wonder Perth has become a bit inward-looking, even jingoistic. "It's WESTern Australia," a buttondown bureaucrat intones at a downtown pub, correcting my pronunciation. Then he adds with a smile: "And don't you forget it." When I ask him how long his family's been in Perth, he answers without irony: "For yonks—sixty years at least."

Perth flashes me the same brash amiability I encountered at the Nullarbor roadhouse. Like Texas, only bigger; three times as big, as I'm informed on about five separate occasions. WESTern Australia even has its own little version of the Lone Star state. A wealthy grazier, dubbing himself "Prince Leonard," has seceded from the Commonwealth and declared his property north of Geraldton a free territory.

Nicknames, when pinned to a place and its people, are usually just exercises in public relations. There is nothing in the concrete megalopolis of New York that suggests a "Big Apple," and there is even less sense in its grimy neighbor New Jersey being dubbed "The Garden State." Industrial plants strike me as a rather broad definition of horticulture.

But "Sandgropers" is a peculiarly apt nickname for Western Australians. It conveys the image of a society moving in a kind of sun-dazed, self-satisfied crawl across the beach. "We're doing just fine out here without you," the place seems to say to "t'othersiders" from the East. "There's an empty banana bed by the pool if you want to lie around for a while. If you don't, well that's okay too."

And it is a pleasant enough place to grope about for a spell. I meet a dozen or so people—on trains, waiting for trains, drinking beer—and they are as friendly and laid-back a sample as I've taken anywhere in Australia. One amiable fellow even suggests he might have a job for me at what is probably the quintessential Perth occupation—installing custom-made swimming pools.

"Perth's perfect because it's so suburban and cliquish," he says. "You put in one pool and it runs down the block like wildfire—everyone's got to have one."

I ride back to Fremantle wondering about all those exiles I met farther south, who insisted they could no longer stand the pace of life in Perth. They must have a pretty low hassle threshold; the only rat race I encounter is the real thing, between two rodents scampering down the hotel corridor when I go to brush my teeth.

But I have a very short while to take the pulse of the place. A more experienced and appropriate student of sandgroping is Swami Anand Haridas, also known as Harry Aveling, a local university professor. "Perth's a great place," he once declared, "for the neck down."

19
CALLING EARL

The first white people to visit the coast north of Perth weren't all that impressed. One of the earliest was Francois Pelsaert, whose Dutch East India Company ship, *Batavia*, ran aground on an island near Geraldton in 1629. When he sailed to the mainland for water, he discovered a "bare and cursed country devoid of green or grass." The flies, anthills, and "black savages" also came in for a few unkind words.

There were more shipwrecks in the following decades but no true exploration of the coast until the Englishman William Dampier came along. Dampier was a well-born sailor who spent his youth as a buccaneer in the West Indies. After glimpsing Australia in 1688 he returned on a government-sponsored voyage in 1699. He didn't find anything to loot. New-Holland, as it was then known, struck him as the "barrenest spot upon the globe." He added: "the Inhabitants of this Country are the miserablest People in the World.

"Their Eyelids are always half closed, to keep the Flies out of their Eyes," he wrote. "From their Infancy being thus annoyed with these Insects, they do never open Eyes as other People: And therefore cannot see far, unless they hold up their Heads."

Dampier went back to being a pirate. He also wrote a bestseller called *A New Voyage Around the World*, which did a lot to spread the bad word about New-Holland. It wasn't until Captain Cook arrived in 1770 that an Englishman gave the continent another serious look.

To these flyblown, half-closed American eyes, the landscape doesn't look too promising either. Just north of Perth the highway heads into territory that offers nothing but sheep and wheat, wheat and sheep, forever. So 50 miles out of the city I hitch west until the road meets the Indian Ocean again at Geraldton.

It's easy to see why there were so many shipwrecks up here. Wind buffets traffic across the highway, and roadside trees are so bent by the breeze that their boughs reach all the way over, as if trying to touch their toes.

Geraldton, a day's drive north of Perth, is a town that rides on the crayfish claw. The day begins well before dawn, when the lobster boats start collecting their pots from the rich beds that lie an hour or so offshore. By noon, the crays are landing on the pier, and that's when the processors begin their day: "killers" twisting off the heads, "stringers" pulling out the guts, "horners" scraping the shells for paste. By nightfall, about twelve hours after being plucked from the sea, the crays are on ice aboard ships bound for the U.S. and Japan. Then the cycle begins all over again.

"Dirty, rotten, smelly bloody business," declares a nineteen-year-old named Rob, who has just finished ten hours of disemboweling crays. He is sitting now in the Tarcoola Tavern, trying to wash the day away with beer. He keeps looking at his hands between sips, as if checking for any lingering lobster gut. "I have to bloody drown myself with Brut to get the stink off. Bloody awful."

I ask him if the smell ever turns off girls.

"Sometimes. But the guy in the backseat smells just as bad, so you just fuck and don't worry about it."

Rob and his two mates, Adrian and Steve, are on an abbreviated pub crawl through Geraldton. In other small towns, Friday night is usually the big night out—men's night, when mates drink with mates, and behave like boys. At about eight o'clock, they pick up some fish and chips for the missus and stagger on home.

But in Geraldton the working men's pubs are quiet soon after dusk.

The cray season only lasts half the year, and for those six months the town is like a university during exams.

"When you start work at four in the morning, it gets to be a late night by nine o'clock," says Adrian, a part-time deckhand. The three teenagers drain their beers and head home to catch some shut-eye before another shift at sea or at the lobster plant. I decide to do the same. That way I can get out to the wharf before dawn and hitch a ride on a lobster boat. I have crossed the continent by air, by car, by ute, by road train, by freight train, by foot. Why not have a look at it from the water?

Three A.M. is not man's most generous hour. I thought the boatsmen would be so impressed by my early rising that they'd welcome me aboard. But they don't want to know about it.

"Busy day, mate," the first skipper says when I ask if I can come along for the ride. "Can't afford any extra cargo."

"You'll see the crays better at the restaurant," says the next. "They don't squirm so much on the plate."

A third skipper thinks I'm joking. "This isn't a yacht race, mate, this is hard yakka. Go home and go to bed."

The point's made. These are working men with work to do; they've got no time for dilettantes. So when I spot a sandy-haired skipper struggling with his mooring, I come over to offer a hand.

"Need a deckhand?" I ask. He gives me the once-over and doesn't look overwhelmed.

"Been doing this long?"

"Not really, I mean, I've been on boats—"

"But never on a cray boat."

"Well, strictly speaking, no. First day out."

He laughs. "Probably your last."

"I come cheap—free, in fact. If I'm in the way just toss me overboard."

He laughs again. "I'm short a man. Hop on." Then he tosses a bag full of fish heads into my arms and I follow him aboard. Nothing frivolous on this craft, just a broad-beamed 30-foot workhorse. We load the rest of the bait—cowhides and cow hooves—then shove off into the dark water.

The skipper is a second-generation lobsterman named Kim. He has two deckhands: Gary, who is twenty-five, and a fifteen-year-old named Justin, who is spending his first season at sea.

"I puked my first day out," Justin tells me by way of introduction. "Since then it's been okay."

As we ride out of the harbor it is still dark enough to navigate by the stars. But Kim turns instead to a bank of machines that glow like video games in the dark corner of a pub. There's a mass of green and red dots that shows the coastline, and a blip that shows us moving away from it. Alongside the radar is a gray tangle of lines that tells Kim how many fathoms deep the water is. And another screen, with marks like cardiac tracings, which shows whether the bottom of the sea is hard or soft and how much vegetation there is for the crayfish to hide in.

"Catching crays used to be trial and error," Kim says. "Now it's electronic warfare. I couldn't see what's down there better if I was in a submarine."

Fifteen minutes from the harbor, the boat begins to roll like a rubber ducky in a bathtub. Ten minutes farther into the Indian Ocean, she becomes a washing machine on spin cycle, then rinse. Water pours across the open back of the boat, forcing me out of the air and into the claustrophobic cabin.

"I hope you're not the seasick type," Kim says, yawning. "It got so rough yesterday that we had to turn around." With that, he and Justin retire below for a snooze while Gary navigates out to the crayfish beds.

I can no sooner sleep—or even close my eyes—than jump overboard. Sea travel isn't one of my phobias, but then, I've never ridden a small fishing boat into open sea. As one wave after another crashes into us, I begin clinging like a mollusk to the cabin doorway. This leaves me at the mercy of Gary, one of those conversationalists for whom every second word is a sexual organ.

"Do you know the one about the bloke who goes down on a whore in Las Vegas? You don't? Well, he goes down, you know, and there's all this gross stuff that looks like food coming out of her. So he says to this sheila, 'What's up? You sick or something?' And she says: 'No, but the last guy down there was.' "

He lets go with a loud, wheezing laugh, then starts in again. "Do you know the one about the guy who's having his cock sucked by a nun? You don't? . . ."

All I can think about is getting my stomach pumped. Waves are crashing over the side and washing into the cabin. And it's so dark that I can't even anchor my eyes on the horizon. Just the glow of the radar, tossing around in the black like a drunken firefly. My equilibrium is fading fast.

Gary isn't helping. When he notices I've gone silent and crumpled on the cabin floor, clutching a table leg, he switches from genital geography to scatology.

"If you're feeling crook, the best thing to do is stick one finger down your throat and the other one up your bum," he says. "If that doesn't work, switch fingers."

The dawn light is making things worse, not better. Now I can see what's coming—giant walls of ocean that roll the boat over, then drop it into a trough on the other side, just in time for another wall to tilt it up again.

"You know, it's interesting how many words we have for vomiting," Gary continues. "Spew, chuck, toss, toss your cookies, barf, Technicolor yawn. Talking to the floor. Are there that many in America? Or don't you blokes puke so much?"

I consider the matter. "Whenever a guy threw up in grade school, we'd say he was 'calling Earl.' " (Why in God's name am I telling him this?) "You know, ERRRRRL! If Earl wasn't home, you'd call Ralph. RAAAAAAAALF!"

Gary can't get over that one. As soon as Kim and Justin come up from below, yawning and stretching, he starts telling them all about Earl and Ralph. "You know what Yanks call spewing? Calling Earl. Get it? ERRRRRRRRL!" Gary would have been a big hit on my playground.

Kim cuts off the engine and for a moment my head and stomach stop spinning. "Let's see what the world has for us today," he says, steering around to a buoy marking the first lobster pot of the day. Crayfishing is underwater mining. Each morning the seabed may disgorge paydirt, or a pile of loose sand and starfish. And since deckhands are paid a proportion of every 100-pound bag of crayfish they deliver, Gary and Justin are as anxious as Kim to see what comes over the rail.

The wooden crate surfaces, and a lonely pink cray flaps onto the floor of the boat. "Bloody cacker," Gary says, measuring the lobster and tossing it back in the sea. A cacker is a crayfish that's below the legal limit.

We motor slowly from pot to pot and at each one the story is much the same—maybe one or two decent-sized lobsters, but mostly cackers and starfish, or nothing at all. Machines do most of the work, pulling in the crayfish pots and automatically coiling the rope. While Gary empties the crays into a water tank, Justin and I reload the pots with cowhide, cow hocks, and fish heads.

An hour after dawn, Kim decides to head farther out to sea, and the horrible bucking and swelling begins again. The waves come at us sideways, rolling us up and back, up and back. For the first time in my life I realize how horrible it must be to get seasick. There's no surprise element; just the unending roll of the sea, wave upon wave, with no relief in sight.

For the first time in my life I realize I am going to be seasick. A strange, involuntary moan begins somewhere deep inside my throat. "Unhhhhh." Another wave hits. "Unhhhhhhhhhhhhh." I feel as if someone's put me on one of those carnival rides that go round and round and round, and no one's there to turn the machine off. "Unhhhhhhhhhhhh." I can smell the cow hocks and fish heads smeared on my shirtfront. I can feel the beer I drank last night, sloshing around in my stomach. I can hear Gary coming up behind me to offer some advice.

"You look awful, mate," he says, leaning close so he can see just how awful I look. "Eat some bread. Then at least you'll have something solid to spew." He smiles. "Do you want me to get Earl on the line?"

A huge wave shoves us both against the starboard rail. I've got my head over the side and a voice in my belly gives the order: Let go. The next wave carries us portside. Let go. I am letting go over the rail, inside the rail, on the rail. The boat's lurching and I'm letting go again, all over myself this time. I am collapsing in a heap now, wondering what will possibly be left of me by the end of the day.

The engine shuts off and the fishermen go about their fishy business without me. I crawl to the center of the boat, where the swell's not so strong, and just lie there on my side, trying to keep my stomach down. All I can see down here at sea level is bare feet sprinting past, with the occasional cray scampering by as well. Then the engine starts up, we move to the next set of buoys, and I roll over to call Earl again.

By mid-morning Kim and company have filled only one bag. The tense excitement at reeling in the first pot has turned to outright despair. I hear the crackle of a radio as Kim tries to tune in his brother a little farther up the reef.

"This is Kim, mate. Bugger all down here. What about you?"

"Bugger all. But Jimbo hauled in four bags yesterday at 21,22. Must be a good patch up there." Kim checks the coordinates on a nautical map. Apparently, it's open slather on the cray beds; the boats spy on one another and if somebody gets lucky, the others are sure to follow.

Kim spins the boat around and I stagger from floor to rail. Please, God, not again. I am sucking in sea air and thinking of solid, neutral things. Brick. Linoleum. Gravel. Wood. Plaster . . . Plaster of Paris. Clay. Mud. Mudcakes . . . Fishcakes. Fish heads. Cowhides. Cow hocks. Calling Earl. Calling ERRRRRRRL! ERRRRRRRRRL!

My trips to the rail become buoys marking our progress along the reef. "Bill's Lump." "Cleo Reef." "Ground 240." I mark them all. Then, finally, I have nothing more to call Earl about. Just an open mouth and nothing at all coming out.

Gary's impressed.

"Good thing we're not on a hot patch today," he says. "Anyone could trail us by just following the yellow brick road. Good effort, mate. Really."

At point 21,22, there is already a cluster of boats. My companions manage to bag 180 crays, worth about eleven hundred dollars, before heading for shore. Kim and Justin go below for another nap. I make a few more trips to the rail, then slump on the floor to endure Gary's jokes for another two hours.

"And so one bloke says to another, 'put it up my butt, willya.' And then the other bloke, he says, 'How can I get it in your butt hole when you're talking?' So the other bloke, he says—"

"Gary," I moan, "put a lid on it. Please."

He smiles. "Didn't I tell you what to do if you're feeling crook? Stick one finger down your throat, and the other one up your bum." I want to hear the punch line again about as much as I want to feel the next wave.

As soon as we reach shore I lunge out of the boat and flop onto the wooden pier like a lump of seaweed. Off with the trousers, sea-soaked, spew-soaked. Off with the shirt, which is even worse. There is nothing like illness to make a man unself-conscious and unashamed. All I can do is lie here half-naked on the dock, kissing terra firma while Kim and Gary and Justin unload their catch.

"Nice-looking snapper you got there, Kim." I open one eye and look straight at the toe of a fisherman's gumboot. Then the boot starts nudging me gently in the ribs. "Want me to head it and gut it for tea?"

I want to tell the man that there's no head and guts left. But I seem to have coughed up my vocal cords as well. No matter. I have an official spokesman.

"We'll keep him for bait," Gary says. "Bloody crays will eat anything. Stick your dick in a lobster pot and they'll eat that too."

I am feeling better already. Not the conversation, just the firm ground. In fact, the sickness is passing almost as quickly as it came on. I can even stand up, get dressed, and unload a bag or two—about the first useful thing I've done all day. Kim is good-natured about it, even flattered. Nothing like a rookie getting sick to provide a little entertainment, and to make you feel like a veteran salt again.

We all shake hands. "Great day, Justin . . ." "Anytime I can help you out, Kim, anytime . . ." "Gary, I'd like you to meet my sister." Then I stagger into town, weak but more or less well. The sun is setting on the ocean behind me. It has been the longest day of my life, not to mention the most revolting. I check into the first pub I come to, wash up, and walk past a half-dozen seafood restaurants until I find a place with chopsticks and phony Chinese lettering on the window.

The waitress is uncomprehending when I don't order seafood. "Snapper, scallops, they very special in this town," she says, even pointing them out on the menu. No, thanks. Just rice, plain and boiled, please. Enough for a small Cantonese village.

The world is still rolling and swaying when I close my eyes. But the bilge pump holds.

20
NOR'WEST
TIME

No one's exactly sure where the "Nor'west" of Western Australia begins. Looking at a map, the Tropic of Capricorn seems a logical border, slicing off the sultry head of Western Australia from the temperate torso of the state (the navel, of course, being Perth). But it seems more accurate to treat Nor'west as an imprecise term, like "the bush" or "outback"—denoting a state of mind rather than a geographical fact. And given that, it makes no sense to try and locate the place at all. To do so would violate the essential character of the Nor'west, which is a vagueness and lassitude of lobotomized proportions.

Agriculturally at least, the tropical Nor'west begins in Carnarvon, a half-day's drive north of Geraldton. The town is a miniature banana republic, subsisting on fish and prawns and plantations of pineapple, mango, banana. Carnarvon has local honchos to match. This is the home of the parliamentarian Wilson "Ironbar" Tuckey, who earned his middle name by clubbing an Aborigine at the pub he ran before going to Canberra. In fact, he didn't use an iron bar at all, just a rubber truncheon. Whether this distortion was intentional—to enhance Tuckey's reputation for toughness—or simply the result of sloppy reporting, remains, like everything else in the Nor'west, a bit unclear.

But it is the sense of time—or lack of it—that is the distinguishing characteristic of the region.

"There's Eastern Standard time, Central, Western, and then Nor'west time," explains a traveling salesman as we drive past the banana plantations that separate Carnarvon from the arid interior. "Might as well set your watch back a couple of hours."

"Haven't got a watch."

"Even better. You'll fit in just fine." He glances at his wrists. "In Perth four o'clock means four o'clock. Here, you make an appointment for four and no one's fussed if you don't front up until five-thirty."

This carefree attitude meshes well with Nor'west drinking. Some years ago the Western Australian government struck a curious compromise between wowsers and boozers. Pubs were allowed to open on Sundays, but only in five-hour "sessions." The idea, apparently, was to let people drink while still leaving time for church, a Sunday roast, and the other decent, God-fearing activities that get washed away by beer during the rest of the week.

The practical effect, in the Nor'west at least, has been entirely different. Carnarvon's three pubs simply reached a gentleman's agreement to stagger their sessions. The Port Hotel opens from midday until late afternoon; the Gascoyne, or "Gassy," picks up the afternoon crowd and carries it into the evening; and the Carnarvon Hotel splits its session in two, with a few hours in the morning and a few more at night, after the Gassy closes. The hours, of course, are a little fluid but that is the basic schedule. And the result is an enforced pub crawl from the Carnarvon to the Port to the Gassy and back to the Carny again, with the appropriate "pig swill" of a few quick beers as each one closes. People like to so much that Sunday is now the biggest drinking day of the week.

Carnarvon has three thousand inhabitants, plus or minus a few thousand, and when I arrive late Sunday afternoon, fully half of them are attending the afternoon session at the Gassy. The ramshackle pub is so crowded that the street outside has become an extended beer garden, with drinkers sprawled across the grass and footpath on both sides. Inside, a mass of hot, moist bodies jostle to get a glimpse of three men sweating through their pearl-studded shirts as they pluck American country and western songs. "Now this little song made my good buddy Johnny Cash a rich and famous man," the lead singer says, in an ocker

imitation of a Tennessee drawl. He tips back his ten-gallon hat and
wails:

> *I hear that train a-coming, it's rolling round the bend,*
> *And I ain't seen the sunshine since I don't know when,*
> *I'm stuck in Folsom Prison, and time keeps dragging on . . .*

The image of a sunless Southern prison has about as much relevance
to the Nor'west as a digital watch, but no one seems sober enough to
take notice. Except perhaps the kids, who join their parents in barbecuing steaks near the bandstand. Roughneck fishermen crowd the bar,
and a third group, somewhat outside the mainstream, gathers in the
beer garden: young, shaggy and colorfully clad—the women in sarongs,
the men in tropical shirts with earrings and bandannas.

Sweaty and sunburned and carrying a rucksack, my place is clearly
with the Untouchables in the beer garden. Before I can so much as
squeeze in at one of the picnic tables, a beer, a home-rolled cigarette,
and five different conversations have been thrust in my direction.

"You're a Yank? I thought you were German. Lot of Germans seem
to hitch through here."

"Get this man a beer—two beers. He's come all the way from America
to see us."

"You want one too, Snow, or you still drinking water?"

"Dunno."

"Cummon, Snow. Easy question. Easy answer."

"Aw right. Too much water makes you rust."

Then, to me again: "You passing through for long?"

In any other place, "passing through for long" would be a contradiction
in terms. But here, that's simply the way it goes. People wander in
from Perth or Adelaide, or even Melbourne, plan on beachcombing
for a few weeks, and then the rot sets in. Before long they're working
part-time at the prawn factory, line-fishing for snapper, cutting banana
on a plantation. Or just hanging out at the Gassy.

"I came here for six months," says a Melbourne woman named Jessie.
"That was six years ago." Her smile reveals a tiny star-shaped filling set
in the middle of her front tooth. "Nor'west time."

And time to move on to the Carnarvon Hotel for the evening session. I climb in the back of Jessie's ute and am joined, en route, by half a dozen stragglers weaving the few miles or so from the Gassy to the Carny. The journey has the air of a Napoleonic retreat, with half the army falling by the wayside as the others press on to the next pub.

The Carny's society is more clearly delineated than the Gassy's. Middle-aged men hold sway in the smoky public bar while the under-thirty crowd gravitates to a discotheque at the back, where they are instantly blinded by flashing colored bulbs laid into the dance floor. With only two hours until closing, and already well-oiled from stops at the Port and the Gassy, a few dozen people begin a languid sort of dancing.

My "passing through" compatriots take up their place on the fringes again, rolling cigarettes and gazing listlessly at the scene. None of the sarong set wants to dance, so I ask a black woman at the next table. Her eyes widen with surprise, and I wonder if I've violated an unwritten law against the races commingling on the dance floor. Not that I care, so long as we don't provoke a race riot.

Sure enough, as soon as we reach the floor, I feel a few hundred eyes upon us. But the attention is only indirectly related to the color of our skin.

"You must not be from around here," my partner shouts over the music." White fellas around here don't dance." She's right. There is only one other man—a black—among the thirty women on the dance floor.

"Why not?"

She laughs and dances us over to two white girlfriends who are doing drunken twirls. "Hey, this guy wants to know why the blokes don't dance."

"Dancing's not macho," one of them answers, raising her arm to let the other pass underneath.

"They're scared they'll spew," adds her partner. "If you'd been drinking for the past eight hours, you would be too." Then they collapse on the floor, giggling.

I go for a beer after a few songs, leaving my partner twirling with her friends to the grinding beat of a band called Cold Chisel.

Two amiable-looking men are splayed out against the bar. Some fair comment is called for; I tell them what the women said, and ask for their rebuttal.

"The problem's not spewing, it's staggering," the first says without hesitation. "If most blokes got up there now, they'd stumble into some-one else's sheila and start a brawl without even trying."

His mate sees it in aesthetic terms. "I like watching the girls better. Why would I ruin the show by getting up there?"

The two men unbolt themselves from the bar to claim a partner as the dance floor empties. It's last call at the last pub of the day, so if propositions are to be made, it's now or never. I reclaim my pack from Jessie's ute and wander down the wide main street of Carnarvon. According to my tourist guide, the street was designed at the beginning of the century to be wide enough for camel trains to turn around in it. The camels are gone but the street's girth has found a modern function: to contain the legions of drunk citizens who would otherwise collapse in front yards or doorsteps on their way home from the pub.

A group of three men throw their arms over one another's shoulders and do a sort of slow, exaggerated Nor'west shuffle through the door of a takeaway. It seems some of the blokes can dance after all.

At dawn I begin a journey north that promises to rate about an eight on the dullness scale (with the Rock checking in at one and the Nullarbor representing the Tropic of Boredom, at ten). There's nothing on the map except roadhouses, dry riverbeds, and a vermin fence. The traveling salesman I rode with yesterday advertised this stretch as "about as exciting as watching a fly crawl across the windscreen." After a thousand or so trips he should know.

Not that anyone in Carnarvon is in any rush to give me a tour. There's traffic, plenty of it. Smiles, plenty of those too—even a sandwich handed through the passenger window. "My mum saw you standing there sweating," the driver says. "It's one of her chicken specials." He also hands me a Sunday newspaper with a front-page story of yet another driver being bashed by hitchhikers. Inside, an editorial warns against showing any charity to roadside strays.

Three hours of waiting confirms that the story has been widely read. It seems I may join Jessie and company "just passing through"—and staying forever. I scrawl my name on a roadside post ("M.L. from Edmonton" holds the record with a five-hour wait on 26-3-86), then settle in by a plantation to watch baby bananas grow to cereal bowl-hood.

It is well past the muesli hour when I finally decide to abandon my position and begin a slow, forced march to a truck stop at the other end of town. Hitching rides with truckies has always been a last resort for me. Contrary to popular belief, truckies don't often stop to pick you up. Most trucking companies forbid passengers, and anyway, stopping a road train at short notice is dangerous and petrol-consuming. So I usually don't bother sticking my finger out as trucks approach; it makes more sense to scramble off the road and turn your back against the shower of gravel the seventy wheels inevitably kick up.

The only sure way to catch rides with truckies is to frequent my least favorite of places: the highway truck stop, full of sullen men sipping overpriced coffee and chatting up waitresses who have been chatted up a thousand times before.

Truckies have always seemed like hard men to me—as hard and lonely as the bitumen they spend their lives traversing. Trucks, tires, and transmissions are the stuff of which their dreams are woven. Nor are they travelers in the true sense of the word. "The truckers cruise over the surface of the nation without being a part of it," John Steinbeck writes in *Travels With Charley*. "Except for the truck stops they had no contact with it."

But prejudices are made to be broken down; that is, after all, what hitchhiking is all about. The first man to set me straight is Jim Duff, whom I find changing a tire outside the Carnarvon truck stop. I flash him my cardboard sign ("Pilbara Pls") and the plaintive smile of a man who has just hiked five miles through midday heat to catch a ride. He flashes me the plaintive smile of a man who has spent too much of his working life at roadhouses like this, pulling off truck tires and putting them on again.

"I can get you there," he says, straightening his back with a pained wince, then crouching again to struggle with the tire. "But as you can see, I'm not breaking any speed records."

Nor am I. We take turns yanking at the tire jack, then climb aboard, sweaty and exhausted, for the long slow drive to the Pilbara. Jim's load is seismographic gear for an oil-drilling company on the North-west

Shelf, but his chariot is strictly low-tech: a ten-year-old rig rolling down the road at 40 miles an hour on fourteen bald or receding tires. It is said that dog owners come to resemble their pets. The same might be said of truckies and their trucks. Jim is a forty-seven-year-old workhorse with a spare tire strapped around his waist and a few too many miles clocked under the bonnet. He also has the deeply tanned right arm of all truckies, who spend most of their working lives with one hand on the wheel and the other one hanging out the window.

"Big trucks means big commitments," Jim yells over the grinding engine. He has to use both hands to move the gearstick, which is vibrating like a jackhammer in the space between us. "This truck works for me, I don't work for it."

Jim aligns himself with the old school of truckies—the ones who drive small rigs and keep their runs to a manageable distance and frequency. He leaves the big trucks to a new and younger breed who lease huge rigs—sometimes costing a quarter of a million dollars—and make "hot shots," or emergency runs, to earn extra dollars. A lot of them go broke or just burn out from the pressure.

They also pop pills and sip a spiked drink called "rocket fuel" to stay awake. Jim used to do the same. "But the pills blow your bloody brains out," he says. "Slow and steady wins the race." It occurs to me that maybe hot shots and rocket fuel had something to do with the truck collision I passed in the Nullarbor. I'm safe with Jim, though: all he stokes himself with is Coca-Cola and hand-rolled cigarettes.

Jim also avoids the legendary refuge of lonely truckies: roadhouse waitresses who moonlight as call girls. "This guy was telling me over the CB radio yesterday that he went fifth and ninth with some bird up at the Fortescue Roadhouse," he says, chuckling. "I told him he'd better bloody well watch who went first, second, third, fourth, sixth, seventh and eighth. I reckon AIDS will make an honest man out of a lot of those blokes. That'd be a hell of a thing to bring home to the missus."

All Jim's brought home for twenty-seven years is "tucker money"—enough to raise three children he rarely saw. "Most of the time I'd be yelling at them to keep quiet so I could catch some sleep before my next run," he says. "Now I wish I'd taken a little more time to get to know them."

Instead, Jim has got to know the same dull stretch of bitumen, from

Perth to Carnarvon to Port Hedland and back to Perth again. There isn't much to do but keep one eye on the road and one on the scrub. A moment's inattention and a cow may wander onto the road to smash the truck's grillework or send the cab rolling.

To add to the monotony, a few hours north of Perth the radio can't pick up anything except the offshore crackle of Indonesian fishermen. Jim twiddles the dial impatiently, then breaks into a high-pitched parody of Asian chatter. "Hoy hien hee hoy hi hee ho hoy. Bloody lot of good that does me. Hi hee hoy hien hi hee ho. They could be talking about me for all I know." He hits the radio off and rolls another cigarette.

The logistics of getting from here to there form the skeleton of each journey north. But Jim fleshes the trip out by working and reworking the homespun philosophy he's developed over twenty-seven years of solitary travel. On work: "Lonely, that's all. Got to bring the tucker money home." On world affairs: "We're all buggered in the long run. If the Yanks and Russians don't blow us up, the bloody Indonesians will." On Destiny: "Planned, isn't it? I hope so, 'cause I could have done something better than this."

There's little to contradict his cynical world view on the lonely stretch of highway north of Carnarvon. There are no towns to speak of, just flat, empty scrub and a chain of roadhouses that resemble the cookie-cut Howard Johnson way stations that dot American interstates. Called "Swagman," they are so sterile in their air-conditioned comfort that no self-respecting swagman would be seen dead in one. So when Jim decides to call it quits at twilight—"What's the rush? When I get to Hedland all I'll do is turn around"—I try my luck with a truckie pumping diesel fuel into his three-trailer road train. He waves me aboard.

If Jim Duff is a philosopher of sorts, this truckie is strictly a dreamer. As soon as I'm on board, the fantasy begins unrolling, as if from a psychiatrist's couch.

"You know what I want to do? You know what I really want to do?" He pauses, as if thinking about it hard enough will make the dream come true. "Ditch this truck in Karratha, drive it right into the bloody sea, and go home to Perth to start my own takeaway restaurant."

This man has the same problem as Jim; he's provided for a wife and four kids well enough, but now, pushing forty, he feels as if he barely knows them. Twenty-eight days out of every thirty, he's on the road, to Karratha or Hedland or Broome. The other two days he's at home, paying bills and catching up with his children.

"My oldest boy, he's into computers, outer space, that sort of thing, at least he was the last time I was home. And you know, the other three, I couldn't even tell you what they're into."

The best he can do is provide. And now that his kids are in high school, he wants to be a kind of Catcher in the Rye—to shield them from the world by setting up a business where they can stay together, in a tight, protected circle. That's where the takeaway comes in.

"I don't know the first thing about cooking and my missus isn't too crash-hot either," he says. "But a takeaway? I reckon anyone can fry a bag of chips."

He has the scheme mapped out to the very last spud. The corner in Perth where he'd like to set up shop. Two kids up front with him. The other two in the kitchen with the missus. And all of them together, one big, happy family, serving up spring rolls and fish sticks for the rest of their days.

A modest dream, really. I ask him why he doesn't go after it.

"Any business is a gamble," he says. "If I was free like you, I'd do it tomorrow. But you can't gamble with a family on board."

Problem is, he gambles every day to bring the dream closer. The load we're carrying is frozen fruit and vegetables. But in Karratha he'll pick up his usual cargo—flammable chemicals. The risk earns him an extra $1.60 an hour. "On my last run, guys came out in spacesuits to unload the stuff," he says. "Made me wonder what it was I had back there." But the truck payments, repairs, and insurance keep piling up, so the chemical runs continue—and so does the dreaming.

"You can sort of think a fantasy through on these empty roads. Then think it through the other way. Then you load the truck again and think it all through again."

We reach the turn-off to Karratha around midnight. I thank the truckie and wander off to find a camping spot. And as I walk down the moonlit highway I can hear him, jack iron in hand, testing for flats with a tap on each tire—all seventy-two of them. Somehow, the dull thwap of metal against rubber, seventy-two times, is an apt anthem to the loneliness and monotony of the truckie's life.

21
THE GHOST OF COSSACK

Some travelers can't drive past a pub. Others never miss a scenic turn-off. I'm the sort who skids onto the gravel whenever a row of weathered gravestones pokes up from the roadside. It's not a morbid thing, just a fascination with the long dead and gone.

Making gravestone rubbings was about the only hobby for which I showed any aptitude as a child. One summer I transformed a family beach cottage into a kind of mausoleum, with charcoal rubbings hanging from every wall. My favorite was the terse inscription above the grave of a one-year-old child swept away in the 1800s by a fever in Charleston, South Carolina:

> SOON BORN.
> SOON DEAD.
> SOON ROTTEN.
> BUT NOT FORGOTTEN.

Maybe I was a bit morbid after all.

Anyway, when I wake up near Karratha and see a dot on the map ahead marked "Ghost Town," my mission for the day is set. Except that the dot, labeled Cossack, sits at the dead end of a small road well off the highway. Hitching to a ghost town strikes me as a rather more ambitious effort than most.

But I have allowed the tyranny of the Main Road to squash my sightseeing too many times already: except for Ayers Rock, Pink Lake, and a few lesser attractions, I've been an utter failure as a tourist. In fact, much of my expedition has been like Ernest Giles's wretched tour of central Australia, distinguished by the discovery of vast stretches of territory to be avoided.

So I hitch a ride to the Cossack turn-off, hide my pack in a bit of roadside brush and start hiking the 3 miles of dirt track into ghost land. Of course, I've got my camera and a notebook, just in case there are a few good headstones poking out of the spinifex.

The hike is hot and dusty, but very promising in a desolate sort of way. A tight formation of pink galahs flutters overhead. Kingfishers hop along a baked mudflat. Bats squawk and flutter above an island of mangrove trees. The only hint of human life is an iron signpost with no sign, standing like a gallows beside the road.

Then, just over a small rise, there's a rail car on wooden tracks that disappear into the tall grass. A bit farther on loom the skeletons of ancient stone buildings, set against a backdrop of open water that is so turquoise as to seem phony—like the Mediterranean in bad Italian prints on the walls of pizzerias. One building, a post office apparently, has a well-preserved mail slot set in its crumbling façade. Peering inside, all I can see is a hollow shell with no roof and no windows.

"No one home, mate."

The voice is behind me. I turn around—jump, really—and find myself about 50 yards from two Aboriginal men in green work clothes, painting a fence in front of another stone building.

"You live here?" I ask.

"No way, mate. We're prisoners."

"You're joking."

"Wish I was. We're maximum-security, mate. Big prison just up the road."

I half expect Rod Serling to step out of the scrub and announce that I've entered the Twilight Zone. Instead, a truck pulls up with more black prisoners and a white guard with a beer gut and reflector sunglasses. Now the Twilight Zone looks a bit like Georgia, circa 1935. Until the guard opens his mouth.

"Cripes, what in fuckin' hell are you are doing here?"

I gesture at my camera. "Just having a look around."

"Fuck all to take pictures of here, unless you get a fuckin' rise out of old stone buildings."

As a matter of fact, I do. But it's gravestones I'm really after.

"Is there a cemetery anywhere nearby?" I try to say it nonchalantly, as if I'm inquiring about the nearest gas pump. But the guard already has me pegged. Weirdo.

"Cripes. Not any fuckin' sight to write home about. But if you want a ride, hop in."

Hitching a ride with a chain gang wasn't part of the day's plan. But I climb inside and climb out a mile farther on, beside a dozen headstones staring out to sea from behind clumps of spinifex. Very promising indeed. I hop over a rusted iron fence and walk among the headstones like a child in a toy store. There's one to the memory of William Shakespeare Hall, of Shakespeare Manor, England, and another In Loving Memory of ZB Erikson, his wife Minnie, and their child, Pearl. Drowned in the Foam Passage, Jan 10 1894. And beside them lie Little Alex and Our Baby Eric, God's Will Be Done.

Except for the drowned Erikson family, none of the headstones explain exactly how God's Will Was Done. But whatever the scourge, it felled the town young; most of Cossack's ghosts are four-month-old babies and thirty-year-old mums. An adjoining graveyard is even more mysterious. Instead of rounded headstones, it contains pointed obelisks with vertical Asian script. Only one has horizontal writing as well: "In memory of S. Murmats." That's it.

As graveyards go, these two don't offer many clues. A baby named Pearl and a family drowned at sea—some definite possibilities there. But Shakespeare? And S. Murmats? A kamikaze attack, perhaps? And how do Cossacks fit into the picture? And why are there prisoners painting fences?

The guard can answer that. He stops for me again as I trudge back toward the stone buildings. "Some fuckin' idiot thinks this place can be a fuckin' tourist attraction. So they hire us for some cheap fuckin' labor. That's all I know."

I hop in the back with the prisoners this time, but don't know exactly what to say when I disembark. Have a nice day? Or stop in and see me if you're out Sydney way?

"Thanks for the ride, I—"

"Got a car anywhere close by?" The prisoner is speaking quickly, through lips that don't seem to move at all. I'm not sure if he's joking or not, but I don't stick around to find out.

There is a car—unlocked—sitting beside a well-preserved building labeled "art studio," so I knock at the open door. A middle-aged woman comes to the screen as if she's been expecting me all morning.

"I'm the crazy artist you heard about," she says. In fact, I hadn't. "You're just in time for a fresh pot of tea," she adds, opening the screen. I am past the point of being surprised, so I follow her inside.

Kathy Van Raak and her husband, Geoff, are the caretakers of Cossack and the first permanent residents the town has had in half a century. She's a sculptor who specializes in "emotive human studies" (in a ghost town) and looks after Cossack's restoration in her spare time. He works as an architect in Karratha.

"We came here ten years ago from Perth to get a little money together and get out. But things didn't work out that way and well, you know—"

"I know. Nor'west time."

Kathy laughs. "Yeah. Except that Cossack's different. It's out of time altogether."

She has the dreamy expression I imagine crosses my own face when I stare at gravestones. I have found the proper guide for Cossack and she is only too willing to oblige.

We begin at the wharf, because that's where Cossack began in the 1860s. It was called Tien Tsin in those days and founded as the principal port in the North-west, supplying inland towns like Marble Bar and Roebume. The harbor filled with Malaysian and Timorese schooners and the mudflats outside town became a camping ground for the Afghan camel drivers who carried goods from the port to the interior.

"What a motley crowd was there to receive us as we stepped ashore," Kathy says theatrically, reciting the impression of a visitor named Charles Edward Flinders who landed here in 1887. There were "colored people" in sarongs, "wiley Japanese," and Malays, "black hair plastered with coconut oil."

But the sight that most impressed Flinders was the dock itself—a land wharf that permitted boats to pull right up to the shoreside buildings, one of which happened to be a tavern. This gave Flinders what must have been the dream of every Australian traveler in the hot North-west: "the novel experience of being on a steamer which anchored almost at the door of the pub."

The pub is gone now, though there was supposed to be another. Prefabricated in England, the timber building was on a ship that blew off course in the late 1880s and landed farther east, where the hotel still stands, at a place called Whim Creek. All that's left of Cossack's wharf are a few stone steps descending into the Indian Ocean.

By the time Flinders arrived, Tien Tsin had been renamed Cossack (after the boat that carried a West Australian governor here in 1871). And its inhabitants had done enough beachcombing to discover that the region was rich with pearl shell. By the 1890s, the town's population had swelled to several thousand, many of them Japanese pearl divers like the mysterious S. Murmats I met in the graveyard. Scottish stone-masons were imported to cut the local diorite rock into solid civic structures to match the seaport's growing wealth and influence: a jail, a bond store, a customs house, a courthouse, a tidemaster's residence—even a Turkish bath.

The buildings were cyclone-proof but Cossack's fortunes were not. Several "big blows" in the 1890s silted the harbor, as well as filling the graves outside town. Port Sampson built a bigger wharf with better access to the interior; farther east, Broome took over the pearling trade. By World War I, Cossack was doomed. With the pearlers gone, there were only the sandflies, the mudflats, the fruit bats. Better left to ghosts, and so it was. Until Kathy Van Raak and her husband came along.

"There aren't many places like this, where you can live in a time warp," Kathy says, poking her head into a solitary confinement cell at the old jail. When she and Geoff inquired about restoring the police barracks as a home, officials from the nearby town of Roebourne saw a chance to rebuild Cossack as a museum. And so a prisoner-led recovery began.

Then last year, after several structures were returned to their original grandeur, a new visitor washed up at Cossack's beach: *Mastotermes darwiniensis*, alias Darwinian termite. The insect set about accomplishing what successive cyclones had failed to do—knock down the town, from the inside out. Kathy's art studio has been condemned and now the whole restoration of Cossack is in doubt. But the artist remains philosophical.

"Maybe people never belonged here," she says, shrugging. We are standing on Nanny Goat Hill, overlooking what remains of the town. From this vantage, the half-ruined buildings are but a pimple on the mudflats and mangrove swamps that stretch inland from the sea. Squinting, it looks to me the way Australia must have appeared to early European settlers. A harsh and hot and threatening land, to be settled tentatively and plundered for whatever riches could be easily gathered. No more than a beachhead, really. "Australia is a weird, big country," D. H. Lawrence wrote to his sister-in-law in 1922, soon after landing in Australia. "It feels so empty and untrodden . . . as if life here really had never entered in, as if it were just sprinkled over and the land lay untouched." Cossack is one of the places where life never really entered in.

"Come back in ten years," Kathy says, dropping me by the highway. "Maybe then we'll have a museum, a son et lumière show—the works. Then again, maybe the termites and the ghosts will win." She gives me a loopy grin and drives back to the abandoned place she calls home.

My reentry into twentieth-century Australia is abrupt and unpleasant. Max—"Mad Max" to his fellow bikies—is just the sort of character who stalks the nightmares of every hitchhiker's mother. His black car looks like a hearse, except that the back wheels are jacked way up, shoving the nose of the car into the bitumen. Max himself appears dressed for a funeral. He wears a black leather vest over a black T-shirt, with a black headband to match his black sunglasses, long black hair, and stringy black beard. He is even listening to Black Sabbath on a ghetto blaster set against the dashboard, just beneath a bumper sticker that reads "Screw Helmet Laws." The only mystery about Max is why he's in a car instead of on a bike.

"Left the Harley with me missus in Perth," he explains, flipping the tape. "Port Hedland's a shitty town for bikes."

"What takes you to Hedland?"

"Work."

"What in?"

"Don't know. Whatever I find when I get there."

"So why'd you pick Hedland?"

"Felt like taking a ride."

He turns up the music. Our conversation proceeds in fitful bursts between songs.

"You from Perth originally?" I ask.

"Melbourne."

"Do you still have family back East?"

"Yeah."

"Why'd you leave?"

"To get away from them."

Black Sabbath for another ten minutes. Then the cassette runs out. For some perverse reason I resume our awkward conversation.

"What's your missus do?"

"Looks after the kid."

"Yeah? How old's the kid?"

"Six weeks."

"Really! What's it like to be a dad?"

"It's not mine. The old man killed himself when the baby was born. The missus and me have only been going out since then."

I flip the tape. Max turns up the volume. And Black Sabbath serenades us through the burnt orange plains of the Pilbara.

In Port Hedland the color scheme changes from orange to rust. The iron ore town is the Cleveland of Australia: a bloated Queen Bee of industry bordered by rust-colored rail cars on one side, and rust-colored ore boats on the other. Dust from the open heaps of iron ore blow through the streets and paint the buildings in a grimy, purplish wash. Even the sky seems rusted over.

But the economy is booming—more like Alaska, really, than the American Midwest. Or like Mintabie in the opal fields of South Australia; a place geared around the fast buck and the fast exit. High pay, high rents, and hordes of single men searching vainly for single women. Single white women, that is.

"Any blond sheilas back in the kitchen?" a brawny man asks an Oriental waitress at the Chinese restaurant. She manages a smile and a quick shake of the head before retreating to the kitchen. The man and his six mates return to their beer and chop suey.

"Did you see Kev's sheila?"

"Which one?"

"The bitch with the harelip."

"Oh my fucking godfather. I wouldn't take that fucking sheila to the shithouse."

"You don't bang faces, mate. Just put a bag over her head and keep going."

"Two bags."

"Whaddya mean?"

"One for her, and one for you, in case hers tears open."

Laughter. More beer. More chop suey. The men of the Pilbara, like the mines in which they labor, display all the sensitivity of a gang bang. Their rapaciousness will be equally short-lived. But unlike Cossack, Port Hedland doesn't sit so lightly on the land. When the minerals play out and the people drift away, their ghosts will linger in the pitted earth and the rusted tangle of smokestacks.

22

GOING TROPPO

For the twentieth consecutive morning, I awake in an unfamiliar town. Pub beds, however, are becoming depressingly familiar. My lumpy mattress is within an arm's length of an electric jug, just like the jug I reached for in Geraldton and Fremantle and Esperance and Coober Pedy and anywhere else I've stayed at a pub. The complimentary biscuits are stale. I eat them anyway; my acceptance of all things free has become instinctive. I stir one packet of instant coffee into hot water, and then another, and then another. But my nervous system refuses to wake. My toes can't find their thongs. Even my finger wants to chuck a sickie.

A cardboard sign—BROOME PLEASE!—leans against my pack, mocking me. I have taken to scrawling signs at night, like a child saying his bedtime prayers. Only once have I failed to reach the appointed destination. The props are in order. I know the way through 3 miles of dust-choked streets to the main highway east. All that remains is for me to get up off this lumpy bed.

I reach for a newspaper on the floor instead, and feel the same melancholic twinge as I did yesterday when I noticed the date on the front-page banner. The Jewish festival of Passover, which commemorates the biblical escape from slavery in Egypt, is about to begin. The occasion is traditionally celebrated en famille, with a drunken feast called "seder." I am an atheist: as my nonatheist father puts it, a "spiritual pygmy." Or, as my mother prefers, a "nonbeliever." But I'm a great believer in family feasts. And Passover is really more of a cultural than a religious celebration; prayer takes a backseat to singing and eating and drinking sweet Kosher wine, at least in my family. Also, it's about liberation, which is an okay thing to celebrate, religious or not. The thought of spending seder night over a pub meal in the Pilbara makes me feel more than a little despondent.

Once in America I found myself in a similar fix while working as a labor organizer in rural Mississippi. The holiday was Yom Kippur—when Jews fast instead of feast—and I had one Jewish friend for company. But there was the same odd sense of longing for a tradition that had meant little to me at home; Yom Kippur was like an old schoolmate to whom I had never felt attached—until he moved away. So a few hours before sunset, when all Jewish observances begin, my friend and I set about the seemingly hopeless task of locating fellow Jews in the phone book of Meridian, Mississippi.

Not only did we find one—Sammy Somethingstein, I can't remember his last name—but also a small congregation just two short of a "minyan," which is the number of adult males (ten) required to make a prayer service, according to Jewish law. So we "made minyan" that Yom Kippur in a small wooden synagogue in Meridian, Mississippi, and were asked afterward to make minyan at a card game as well. On every Sabbath after that, as Rich and I settled in for a beer in the makeshift wooden shack that was our home, the phone would ring and on would come a curious mix of Southern and Jewish intonation.

"Tony, this is Sammy. Can y'all make minyan over at the church tonight?" Church was what they called synagogue in the backwoods of revivalist Mississippi. "There might be a card game after prayers. . . ."

I reach for the Port Hedland phone book. Who am I kidding? I've got as much chance of locating a Jew in the Pilbara as I have of finding manna in the desert. I check the Yellow Pages. No synagogue, predictably, nor anything called church that might be a Jewish temple in disguise. Catholic, Methodist, Latter Day Saints. I flip to the white pages and start searching for Semitic names . . . Bernstein . . . Cohen . . . Goldberg . . . Goldstein . . . nothing. Even if I did find one, what would I do? Call them up at dawn and say, "I was just wondering if you're Jewish"? Levy . . . Rosenberg . . . Steinberg . . . Weiner. . . .

Not a thing. Not even a German-sounding surname that might actually be Jewish. Just an Anglo-Saxon litany of Browns and Harrises and Smiths.

I look out the window at the reddish-brown buildings and the reddish-brown streets. Just as well, I guess. Twelve hours in Port Hedland and already I feel the rust setting in. If I stay here another night, I'll be as roadworthy as an abandoned car.

Half an hour later, on the street outside, a car limps past and grinds to a halt 30 yards farther on. Not for me, I assume; I'm not interested in local traffic and didn't bother to stick out a finger. And the way this guy's climbing out of the car—as slowly as life emerging from the primordial slime—suggests either mechanical trouble or a wicked hangover.

"Where ya headed?" he calls to me. Even his words seem to limp out of his vocal cords.

"Broome. How about you?"

"Broome, eventually. If you're not in a hurry, I can get you there."

Normally, I am suspicious of unsolicited rides. Sort of like candy from a stranger or, more typically, the preamble to a homosexual proposition. But there are no other cars on the road and I'm not exactly zapping with energy, so I climb aboard.

Dave is sluggish, even by Nor'west standards. It takes him twenty minutes to swallow the Coke he's just purchased in Hedland. Sipping it slows him down to 25 miles an hour; when he's done, we reach our cruising speed of 40. This gives me time to take in the full breadth of Hedland's ugliness, in slow motion. A huge salt plant with massive white dunes slides onto the surrounding plain. Railroad cars filled with iron ore stretch in a line toward the horizon, going on forever. In the opposite direction, gray-faced men in reddish-brown cars drive to another day in the industrial hive. Then we reach bare, hard scrub again, stretching ahead of us for several hundred miles.

Two hours after picking me up and still less than 60 miles out of Hedland, Dave pulls in for a sausage roll at a mining town called Goldsworthy. Twenty minutes later we are still parked in the shade while Dave munches meditatively on the crumbs. I feel as if I'm watching a Death Row inmate finish off his last supper. So I wander off to see the sights of Goldsworthy, which consist of a water tank imprisoned inside a locked cage and a sign warning that anyone who pilfers from an adjoining ice supply is subject to prosecution. Not much of an oasis.

We water instead 120 miles farther on, at a roadhouse called Sandfire. It is well named, sitting as it does in the middle of a burning semidesert. And it is well placed, like the pubs in the Northern Territory, to scoop up thirsty cars and drivers coming from either direction; as a sign near the roadhouse announces, there's no more petrol for 170 miles.

The Sandfire Roadhouse also shares the Territory's penchant for outback whimsy. There's no bush bank here, just a curious repository called the Sandfire Sleazey Sleeveless Shirt Club. To join, the traveler need only pay two dollars and cut off his own shirtsleeve. The money goes to the Flying Doctors and the sleeve is pinned to the ceiling, which looks like a laundry line after a storm: shredded bits of unmatched cloth, dropping almost onto the heads of drinkers.

Shearing off a sleeve and pinning it to the rafters occupies five minutes or so; drinking a beer consumes another ten. But Dave is still only midway through his eating. So I kill another ten minutes studying the Broome phone listings. No synagogues again. No -witzes, -steins, or -bergs even. Just me. The only Jew for thousands of miles, wandering in the desert as my heathen captor munches on sausage rolls.

Dave is on an Exodus of his own, which he tells me about during the hot, dull drive after Sandfire. He left a factory job in Melbourne six months ago to find some other work, some other place to settle down. "I grew up on a farm, which was hard yakka," he says. "But you only shoveled shit until the shit was gone, then you knocked off. In the factory, you'd spend all day doing half a day's work. I couldn't hack it."

Now, after several months of travel, Dave's money is running out. He reckons he's only got enough for six more days of petrol and sausage rolls. "Someplace around Darwin, I'll just pull off the road and take whatever work I can get," he says. I push away thoughts of my own impending return to the office.

Late in the day we reach a roadhouse on the outskirts of Broome. It has taken us eleven hours to cover a distance of 360 miles. "What a car," Dave says, puttering over for another ration of sausage roll. "If it was a woman, I'd marry it."

I sue for a quick divorce and begin hiking briskly toward town. If Dave finishes eating before I get there, well, I can always propose again. A hundred feet from the roadhouse, my pace slows from a full gallop to a canter. A hundred feet farther on, the canter becomes a trot, then a slow amble. My shirt is soaked. Somewhere beneath me, ten toes are swimming in their thongs. Even my eyes are sweating. I spy a bench across the road and stagger over to collapse on it.

The climate has switched on me again. Inland Western Australia is baked and arid, but the sea is bordered by sultry mangrove swamps. Cossack gave me a taste of humidity. Now Broome's giving me the full show.

I hadn't expected the tropics to surprise me this way. After all, I was raised in a city that is built on a swamp. Every summer in Washington, D.C., there's a kind of boggy revenge, when the air doesn't move and the heat and humidity seep up through the concrete. Even the government grinds to a halt.

But Washington's mugginess is minor league compared to Broome's. I feel like someone's trying to smother me with one of those hot, wet towels they give you at Japanese restaurants. At least the scenery is refreshing after so many days of uninterrupted scrub. There are palm trees lining the street and black-skinned natives in bright clothes lolling past: Aborigines of course, in what looks like cast-off clothing from St. Vincent de Paul's. But if I squint hard enough it could be a travel poster for Fiji or Jamaica.

There's architecture to match my tropical fantasy. Across the street is a raised, one-story wooden house with a 360-degree veranda. It looks like a jerry-built parody of a plantation in Louisiana; the kind of home where you expect to see a planter in a white suit and a wide Panama hat, sipping mint juleps while the slaves hoe quietly in the fields.

I catch my breath (sort of grab for its tail, really) and continue in a slow shuffle down the wide, hot street. A mile farther on, there's still no sign of a pub, but there is a sprawling house with cyclone shutters and a roof that spreads like a wide-brimmed hat, casting a cool shadow all the way around. Better still, there's the hum of an air-conditioner in one window, and a sign that says public library. I stagger inside, drop my pack, and sprawl on the floor beside it.

A middle-aged woman smiles at me from behind a pile of filing cards. Apparently, it's acceptable behavior in Broome to collapse in a sweaty heap at the first public building you come to. Smiling back at her, it occurs to me that I've never met a mean librarian.

"This is nothing," she says cheerily. "You should have been here a month ago. Talk about hot!"

I have heard this line, or something similar, about six dozen times since leaving Sydney. It seems I've been trailing the worst heatwave in Australian history, by just a few days, all the way across the continent.

"Hot enough for me, thanks."

"In the wet season," she continues, "in the Wet, people just go troppo. Completely crazy. There's nothing to do but wait out the rain at the pub."

The Wet sounds rather soothing at the moment. So does the pub. I ask her for directions.

"The Continental sells more beer than any hotel in Australia," she says. "But everyone goes to the Roebuck." I nod. Nor'west economics.

She walks me over to a picture of the Roebuck on a wall in the next room. It is an old black-and-white photo of publican Bill "Possum" Ward posing in front of a colonial-style wooden building. He has his arms crossed over his chest, a proud, almost defiant smile on his face, and two flappers in bathing suits standing to either side. The photo is dated 1920.

"The prettiest girls are always at the Roebuck," she says. It is an odd comment, coming from a schoolmarmish librarian. The wink is even odder. Not knowing what else to do, I wink back, then pull on my pack and head for the pub.

The Roebuck looks as if it hasn't changed too much since Possum's day. Low-slung and a bit ramshackle, it is the collection point for all the Continental Drift that washes up at Broome. A group of well-tanned men—fishermen or sailors, it seems—sip rum and Cokes by the door. Most of them have tattoos; all of them have earrings. They're watching a woman in a sleeveless cotton dress who is playing pool with another woman in an orange sarong. In the corner, two hippies dance slowly to a blues song on the jukebox. There is not an unhandsome person in the bar. Taken together, the crowd has a shabby, tropical sort of style, like a Club Med weekend gone to seed.

Disguised beneath the earrings and sarongs is a racial mix unlike any

I've ever seen. The Aboriginal blood is obvious, but there's also an Asian influence, or several strains of Asian, and a touch of Spanish as well. What's most striking, though, is that no one appears to belong to just one ethnic group. Each face is a mix of two or three flavors, like a well-spiced Indian curry. There are mocha-colored men with delicate Asian features, and women with Oriental coloring but broad Aboriginal noses or startling blue eyes.

It's all to do with the pearls, of course. Malays and Japanese and Filipinos and Chinese and Koepangers (Timorese of Portuguese descent, which accounts for the Spanish look) and Thursday Islanders and, finally, a few Europeans—all came here at the end of the nineteenth century to dive for mother-of-pearl. After 1901 immigration policy took a racist turn, and White Australia laws forbade Asians bringing their families along, so the melting pot was stirred a little more. And even before the pearlers came, there were longboats swooping down from Malaysia to ply these shores for a delicacy called sea slug or "bêche-de-mer." This history is recorded in the Asiatic features of many Aborigines hereabouts and also in the local cuisine. Some Aboriginal clans around Broome still cook their turtles Indonesian style, with chili and garlic.

But somehow I imagined that Broome, like so many other places on my journey, would fall short of its advance billing; surely, the town's history and color would be buried by development. The Roebuck tells me my cynicism was misplaced.

I order a beer and ask the barmaid whether the pearling fleet is in or out.

"In," she says. "In here." She points at the brawny, bronzed mob I'd spotted near the door. Apparently this is all that remains of what was once the biggest pearling fleet in the world. "Guy with the towel's the best diver in Broome," she says. "The one he's talking to is a dealer."

I sidle up to the diver. The towel, which is wrapped around his bare, bulging pectorals, gives him the look of a prizefighter, except that he has a complete set of gleaming teeth and a long, unbroken nose.

"Lost tourist here," I say to him, smiling. "Can I shout you a beer?"

He shrugs. So I buy a round and begin quizzing him about pearling.

"Our boat's out for ten days, in for one, then out for ten again." He taps the side of his beer glass. "Never really lose our sea legs." He downs his beer in one swig and heads for the toilet. Apparently one round doesn't buy very much information in Broome.

I have a go at his companion, a tall, swarthy man with a droopy moustache, jet-black hair, and two gold loops hanging from one ear. His appearance, like the diver's, begs for a tourist question.

"Where are you from?" I ask him. "I mean, where's your family from before Broome?" It comes out a bit awkward but he doesn't seem to mind.

"Koepanger, way back," he says. "That bloke you were just talking to is from Thursday Island." It is the kind of answer a tourist to Broome likes to hear. What's curious, though, is that despite their exotic appearance, the men have broad ocker accents. The melting pot has had some time on the fire in Broome.

I forge ahead: "You're a dealer, right?" The Koepanger's face goes blank, but I continue. "How does it work? Do you buy from them or do the divers come to you?"

He turns away, as if to talk to the back of a man on the next stool. Then he turns to face me again, with an expression that is quizzical, almost hostile. "You serious, mate? Or you some kind of pig?"

Pig? This conversation has taken a wrong turn somewhere.

"I'm nosey, if that's what you mean." His face doesn't change. "Sorry," I continue. "It's just that the barmaid said he was a diver and you were a dealer, so I thought I'd learn a little bit about pearling. That's all."

The man studies my face for a few seconds, then laughs. "You got it all wrong, mate, I deal hemp, not pearls. But I'm lying low right now, because the town is crawling with narcs." He points at a man across the bar with a red bandanna and wire-rimmed glasses. "Try that bloke over there."

It seems like a polite exit from an awkward conversation. So I wander across the bar, which is suddenly crowded with evening traffic. Wire Rims gives me an amiable smile as I approach. What does he deal, I wonder, pearls or grass?

He's wondering the same thing about me. As I slide onto the next stool, he says out of the side of his mouth: "Buying or selling?"

"Neither, sorry."

"Shit. I saw you talking to The Man and thought maybe you were on to some dope." We sit silently for a moment. "Anyway, I'm Mark. This is Gavin. Join the bloody club."

Mark doesn't seem to be a club member. Short and balding and a bit anxious, he reminds me of overworked graduate students I knew at college. But Gavin is as laid-back and handsome as everyone else at the Roebuck: tall and blue-eyed, with a well-trimmed goatee and thin moustache that are so blond that they seem to be painted onto his deeply tanned face.

In fact, Mark and Gavin aren't regulars at all. The Roebuck is just a stopover between isolated cattle properties, where the two men do odd jobs for a traveling contractor. They get these breaks about once a month, for a few days at the most. And this one is due to end at midnight, when their boss arrives to carry them off to the next remote station. No wonder, then, that Mark and Gavin are drinking like prisoners on parole.

"One for the road!" Mark yells at the barmaid. Then, giggling, "Two for the road!"

Gavin joins the chorus. "Ten for the road—"

"Twenty—"

"Twenty thousand!"

The barmaid smiles tolerantly. "They've been going on like this since yesterday afternoon," she says to me in a stage whisper. "You'd think they were drunk."

Getting drunk was originally a secondary mission. Mark wanted to score some grass for the long nights out in the scrub. Gavin just wanted some female companionship.

"I've been out of circulation for six months," he says. "It's depressing." Unfortunately, he hasn't had any more luck than Mark.

"Empty-handed," he says. "Until tomorrow night. Then I'll have you-know-what in my hand again."

Mark laughs. "If I wank anymore, my dong will fall off."

The barmaid returns with three beers. "My shout," she says.

"I'd like to shout you something," Gavin says, leaning over the bar. It is as well rehearsed as a movie script—for both of them. "What's wrong, is it me or my face?"

"Face is fine," she says. "Too desperate, that's all." She turns and sashays down the bar, leaving Gavin with his face on his arms, moaning.

Mark checks his watch. "Three hours to go, mate. This is looking serious."

"Back to work."

"Back to the bush."

"No girls."

"No dope."

"No nothing."

They collapse against the bar and I can't tell if they're giggling or whimpering. Probably both.

I ask them why they don't quit their jobs. Mark tells me that he will as soon as he's saved enough money to go back to Melbourne. "I had this delusion that I'd make my fortune swinging a pickaxe somewhere out West." Gavin suffered from a different delusion. His catering business in Perth went bust, then his marriage did the same. He figured a few months of hard labor in the bush would "set the boat straight again."

At the moment, though, he's about as straight as a plumber's snake. And things aren't going to get any clearer. Mark has just caught the eyes of "The Man"; it seems some dope deal may transpire after all. Mark follows him out of the bar.

Gavin perks up; maybe his own chances will improve. He spots a slim Asian woman in a short skirt who is bent over the jukebox, studying the list of songs. Gavin finishes off his beer and tucks in his singlet. "Wish me luck, mate." Then, just as he slides off his stool, a man comes up to the jukebox and wraps his arms around the woman's waist. The man begins nibbling at her neck. She flings her head over one shoulder and sticks her tongue out. He takes it in his mouth and they begin kissing, slowly and passionately.

"Jesus fucking Christ, will ya look at that?" Gavin cries. He has lost his earlier calm and appears on the verge of tears. "Jesus fucking Christ. He's licking her tonsils." We watch the couple smooch for a minute, then Gavin shouts across the bar.

"For Chrissake's, mate! Haven't you ever heard of the privacy of your own fucking home?" No one at the bar even turns a head. The couple keeps kissing. Gavin buries his face in his arms again.

A few minutes later Mark returns. He hasn't had any luck either. "That dickhead's been jerking me off all night." He checks his watch. "Two hours and counting, mate. This is looking serious."

I leave Mark and Gavin at the Roebuck, looking serious, and head out into the tropical night. Now that the stifling heat is gone there is something very agreeable about Broome. Maybe it's all the beer. Maybe I'll lay up for a few days, like the pearl boats. Patch a sail or two, fix a leak, untangle my halyards.

"Why is this night different from all other nights?"

"On all other nights we eat either sitting up straight, or reclining. On this night we recline."

As the youngest child I had to ask that question in Hebrew—chant it in fact—at Passover after Passover. It's part of the tradition. My father always got to do the reclining.

I count my money. Enough for a short stay in a decent bed if I recline on the ground on all other nights. I hike to a quiet motel, order a room-service dinner, and don't make a sign before going to bed.

23
PEARLS BEFORE MATZO BALLS

Overnight the heat breaks and the great "king" tide of Broome washes in. Boats that appeared stranded on the mudflats last night are floating now by a wooden jetty a few blocks from the Roebuck Bay Hotel. An island of mangrove a little way offshore is swamped altogether.

It is this remarkable shifting water—up to 30 feet change in depth between high and low tide—that allowed William Dampier's ship, the *Cygnet*, to drift ashore near here in 1688. "We hal'd our Ship into a small sandy Cove, at a Spring-tide, as far as she would float; and at low Water she was left dry and the Sand dry without us near half a Mile," the English sailor wrote. "We had therefore time enough to clean our Ships bottom, which we did very well." The sailors also hunted turtle and dugong in Broome, though it seems Dampier had little success in encouraging his crew to do other labor. "While we lay here, I did endeavour to persuade our Men to go to some English Factory; but was threatened to be turned ashore and left here for it." Even then, men went troppo as soon as they hit the sun and sand of Broome.

Three centuries later, sailors still use these tides to bring their pearling luggers close to shore. And in the morning when I wander down to the docks, there is much Factory going on. Half a dozen men are off-loading crates of pearl shell and on-loading gas and food before the ebbing tide leaves them high and dry again.

I recognize some of the faces from last night. By daylight, stripped to the waist, they form a rainbow of races stretching down the pier. The crates pass from Chinese hands to Koepanger to black to Japanese to Malay and then to Chinese again. And then to a pair of Caucasian hands—my own. Stepping onto the narrow pier to chat with one of the men, I have a crate thrust into my arms, and so join the human chain. Turn right, receive crate, turn left, hand crate on, turn right, receive crate, and so on down the line. When the crates are off, we change direction to load on food. After so many mornings on the road it feels good to be part of some useful labor.

The boats are as colorful as their crews: two-masted wooden schooners, resembling Chinese junks, with buoys and nets and clothing draped from the halyards. If the boats were not so worn, they would seem almost too quaint, like museum pieces. As it is, tied up at the shaky wooden pier, they give our labor the air of another time and place: colonial Singapore, say, or a whaling port in Massachusetts.

"Pearling's still an eighteenth-century operation," the man to my left says, pausing as the dead weight of another crate hits him in the chest. "Great for the tourists. Tough on us."

He is Malaysian, I think; a big, bronzed oak of a man with thighs like tree trunks and arms as strong as low-lying limbs. I ask him all the questions I'd wanted answers to last night, and in between crates he fills me in.

On "the bends," for one. The paralysis is caused by the pressure change of rising too fast from the ocean floor. In the old days, before modern equipment and modern medicine, divers died by the dozens— if not from the bends, then from shark attacks or cyclones. A big blow in the 1880s swept away more than 20 boats and 140 men; another cyclone killed the same number in 1935. Some of them are buried in group graves at a Japanese cemetery outside town. For many years after, descendants filled small bottles with rice wine and set them beside the gravestones for the spirits to drink.

In the 1920s, Broome had 4,000 divers and the town produced something like 80 percent of the world's mother-of-pearl. But plastic buttons undermined the pearl market. And when World War II broke out, many of the luggers were requisitioned and their Japanese divers interned. Only the development of cultured pearls saved the Broome fleet from extinction, though no more than half a dozen boats survive.

"At least no one gets the bends anymore," the pearler tells me. "Unless they come up too fast from the bottom of a beer glass at the Roebuck."

When the crates are loaded on, I wander off through "China Town," a few wide streets bordered by makeshift shanties of tin and wood. At the beginning of the century this was the heart of Broome's pearling community and the meeting point for its curious mix of races. "Satay men" worked the footpath with poles slung over their shoulders, balanced like seesaws with strips of beef at one end and charcoal braziers at the other. China Town also had brothels and gaming houses, as well as a movie house, the Sun Picture Cinema, which still operates in a corrugated iron building.

It was during a silent movie at the Sun, in a 1920 heatwave, that the so-called Broome riots began. Several hundred Koepangers took knife and club against the Japanese, who were then the lords of the pearling fleet. Two hundred whites were hastily deputized to control the rioting, but four Japanese and Koepangers died before the fighting was done. It is the only recorded instance of public violence between the many races of Broome.

Today, most of the buildings in China Town have been taken over by tourist shops, or by "mung beans," as the hippies of Broome are called. It is now the sort of place where people can duck into a shady café, munch on vegetarian snacks, and read an alternative paper called the *Broome News*, which has a columnist named "Fettuccine Ferret."

I am halfway through a whole-meal enchilada and a poem called "Ode to Troppo" when Mark, my drinking companion from last night, wanders in.

"What are you doing here? I thought you and Gavin were headed out bush."

"We were." He slumps into the seat across from me and wipes his forehead with the bandanna he wore last night. The wire-rimmed glasses are gone.

"Where's Gavin?"

"Dunno. He disappeared with the barmaid not long after you left." Mark smiles. "Then I got lucky too." He reaches into his pocket and pulls out a small plastic bag of marijuana. "Forgot all about the boss at midnight. Anyway, Gavin wasn't around. No bloody way I was going back out there alone." He looks up as a waitress in a loose cotton frock swishes by. "I've seen worse places to go AWOL for a while."

Two more pieces of driftwood for the beaches of Broome.

After lunch I decide to resume my own small quest. I rent a bicycle—from the same place that sells the Mexican food—and pedal to the shire offices at the other side of town. There isn't too much happening on a Thursday afternoon in Broome, so the shire clerk is only too happy to show me inside. We chat about Broome and then I explain Passover to him.

Australians often seem uncomfortable when the subject of Judaism is raised. It's not prejudice, just ignorance about all things Semitic; knowing nothing of Judaism, they're frightened of saying the wrong thing. But the shire clerk in Broome is perfectly at ease; he has obviously had some practice at dealing with other people's customs.

Unfortunately, my people's customs are among the few species he's never encountered.

"Mr. Horwitz, we've got all types in Broome—and I mean all types." He starts counting them on his fingers: white men, black men, yellow men, Malay men, Manila men. "There's even a whole cemetery full of Japs at the end of town. But I've lived here my whole life and you're the first Jew I've ever come across. I'm sorry."

He gives me an armful of tourist brochures and shows me to the door. Then he has a parting thought.

"See that house over there, the one on stilts? Go in there and ask for a chap named Father Mack. He might be able to help."

I thank him. It is a common sort of misconception, particularly in secular Australia. If there's no rabbi about, well, try a priest. One religious ratbag is as good as another.

Then again, I've got nowhere else to go (except the Japanese cemetery), so I wander across to the stilt house. Inside a screen door is a small room where a man is waiting to see Father Mack. He is of such unusual beauty—coppery brown skin, wide lips, straight black hair falling almost to his shoulders—that I find myself blurting out the same awkward question I tossed at the Koepanger last night.

"Where are you from? Your family, I mean."

He shows no offense at the question. "Malay, and Filipino on my father's side, Maori on my mother's." He smiles, a white flash of a smile, and takes off his sunglasses to reveal hazel-colored eyes. "With a dash of Irish in there. I didn't have much say in the matter." He studies my face for a moment. "How about you?"

"I'm from Sydney. Well, not really. America, originally. My family went there from Russia, except that they were Jewish, so they weren't really from Russia at all. Kind of in transit."

"All mixed up," he says. "Like me."

Father Mack—actually, Father Michael McMahon—is a different sort of jumble. He is a Catholic priest, but also manages a trucking company, an undertaking service, and a few other businesses, all of them associated with Broome's Aboriginal community. Father Mack is the sort of one-person social-service agency that you only find in small, isolated towns. Just the sort who would know if there are any stray Semites in Broome, which is why the shire clerk pointed me this way.

"There's a doctor named Wronski who works at the Aboriginal Health Centre," he says. "I'm pretty sure he's Jewish, but then again, I have no idea if he observes anything." Father Mack pauses. "If he doesn't, stop by here tonight. We can patch something together, or talk about it at least." Religion, like everything else in Broome, is open house.

Pedaling slowly to the Aboriginal clinic, it dawns on me that I have no idea what I'll say to Dr. Wronski; up to now, just finding a Jew seemed improbable enough. But the randomness of it all excites me, like hitchhiking. There's a part in the Passover service that honors the wandering prophet, Elijah. A big glass of wine is poured—Elijah's cup, it's called—and midway through the seder the door is opened, just in case Elijah or some other homeless seeker happens to be wandering about. As a child, I always raced to open the door, hoping that a stranger would actually appear and tramp across my mother's oriental rug to claim his glass of wine and bowl of matzo ball soup. He never did, of course, and my brother and I would end up splitting Elijah's cup on the sly.

Now I may have a chance to change roles and wander in to surprise some child in the Wronski household.

I leave my bike leaning against the porch of the clinic, wipe the sweat off my face, and walk inside. There's no one at the desk so I wander down the hallway to an open door. Inside, a small man with thick dark hair is scribbling notes at his desk. He is the image of the bush doctor: tanned and bearded, dressed in khaki shorts and a khaki shirt.

"Dr. Wronski?" I feel like adding "I presume," but don't.

"Uh huh." He doesn't look up from his notes. "Just a minute." He keeps scribbling, then closes his notebook and extends a hand. "Ian Wronski. What can I do for you?"

Firm grip. Purposeful. This man is not on Nor'west time. "I'm Tony Horwitz. This is kind of odd, but I'm traveling through Broome, and, well, it's Passover—"

"And somebody told you that Wronski was the only Jew in town."

"Well, yeah. And I was wondering—"

"If we celebrate Passover, and if you could celebrate with us."

I nod. Wronski's gaze travels from my thongs to my slouch hat, as if in preparation for a physical exam. Then he breaks into a toothy smile. "So you want to come to seder already?" he says, parodying the accent of a Jewish clothes merchant on the Lower East Side of New York. He scratches his beard. "I think maybe we can find room for a wandering Jew."

Then Ian escorts me out of the clinic and to his home a few blocks away, where his wife, Maggie, is preparing Passover dinner. As we walk into the kitchen, I'm hit with a familiar, though long-forgotten, smell— chicken broth and matzo balls. Maggie is at the table, making gefilte fish. She puts a spoonful in Ian's mouth.

"Whaddya think?" she says. "Is it the real thing or what?"

Ian smiles. "My grandmother would be proud." He moves to the stove and ladles a matzo ball into his mouth. "Did you get the menorah out of the bank?"

It is not a conversation I had imagined overhearing in Broome, Western Australia.

The Wronskis are as lapsed in their Judaism as myself—so lapsed, in fact, that they didn't realize it was seder night until Ian's mother called from Melbourne. "We got the dates mixed up," Ian tells me at sunset, when I return for dinner. Everything about the evening is improvised: the odd collection at the dinner table (Ian, Maggie, their four-year-old son Zip, myself, and a visiting Jewish doctor from Melbourne named Theresa), the sunhat I am offered as a ceremonial skullcap, and the gefilte fish, which has been fashioned from the catch available that day at a local market—a mix of salmon and bluebone and barramundi.

In my own home, we make a rather cursory tour of the high points of Passover—lighting candles, blessing the symbolic foods on the seder plate, retelling the story of Exodus—before getting down to the serious business of eating and drinking. My father leads the service, prompted by my grandmother, who bangs her cane at intervals and orders him to "skip that bit!" or "keep it moving!" Somehow, the ritual becomes more abbreviated each year, and the many-coursed feast begins soon after sunset.

The Wronskis' Passover is considerably more truncated than that. Family, after all, is what Passover is about, and in this family there's a noisy, hungry child who has little patience for symbolic stories and Hebrew blessings.

"Why is this night different from all other nights?" Ian asks, translating the first of the "four questions" about the meaning of the celebration.

"On all other nights," we answer in unison, "we can eat bread or matzo, but on this night only unleavened bread."

"When?" Zip asks.

Ian raises a wineglass and continues: "Blessed is He our Lord, King of the Universe, who createth the fruit of the vine."

"I don't like that stuff!" Zip pipes in. "Where's my juice?"

And so it goes for half an hour, before we abandon the prayer book and hoe into the food. But not before we've reached what was always my favorite part of the Passover service—the recitation of the plagues God will visit upon the Egyptians:

"Blood."

"Frogs."

"Lice."

After each, we spoon a bit of wine onto our plates, symbolic of spilt blood.

"Wild beasts."

"Boils."

"Hail."

"Locusts."

"Darkness."

We put our spoons down and finish off the cup of wine. "I always liked that part too," Theresa confides with a wicked grin.

Such is the nature of religious training. You throw a bunch of Hebrew prayers and moral tenets at a kid, like so much spaghetti at the wall, and most of what sticks is the bits that appeal to a child's gory imagination.

From plagues and Exodus we turn to our own tales of wandering. This is the Wronskis' first Passover in Broome: in previous years they've celebrated with Ian's family in Melbourne. Not that Melbourne had been home for long; Ian's parents made their way to Australia via Poland, Iran, and Israel. Theresa's family migrated across Russia and spent some years in Siberian labor camps before coming to Australia after the war.

Listening to them, my own path to Broome doesn't seem quite so circuitous. But they are as intrigued by my travels as I am by theirs, and as the wine flows, so does the tale of my trip across the continent. I listen to myself replay the journey for the first time: stumbling on an Aboriginal circumcision at Tennant Creek, running off the road near Alice, hopping a freighter in Elleker, "calling Earl" aboard the Geraldton lobster boat. The journey seems suddenly rather remarkable to me, and this dinner is yet another remarkable moment in it.

Maggie waits for me to finish, then shakes her head. "You're game," she says.

Somewhere deep inside, I smile. A part of me has been wanting to hear those two words for 6,000 miles.

We are well into the second or third bottle of sweet Israeli wine when an Aboriginal neighbor pokes her head inside the door. She sees the candles and seems to understand that something ceremonial is in progress. Ian asks her to join us but she declines: "I'll let you do your thing," she says respectfully, "and maybe stop by later."

Ian says he has spent more time discussing Judaism with Aborigines than he ever did with non-Jewish friends in Melbourne. "Blacks see parallels with the Holocaust, and disenfranchisement," he says. "Plus the whole bit about people wandering in the desert."

I think back to my conversation at Ayers Rock with the Pitjantjatjara man named Tjamiwa. At the time I was struck by the rootedness of his heritage, which is etched in a giant rock. Now I realize how portable my own culture is. Aboriginal belief has endured 40,000 years through its close tie to a sacred patch of ground. Judaism has survived—albeit a much shorter time than that—because its adherents have been able to break bivouac at a moment's notice and set up shop in alien lands.

"When we lived in Melbourne, I felt like that was the center of the world," Ian says. His skullcap fell away hours ago and Zip sleeps soundlessly in his lap. "Now I feel that way about Broome. I'm not sure what's home anymore."

It is after midnight. The warm tropical air wafts in through the open door, reminding me of the sultry summer nights in Sydney when the idea of hitching across the continent first took form. I set off more out of compulsion than desire, feeling my restlessness nagging at me like an adolescent virus for which a hitchhiking adventure would be the final cure.

Now I see it differently. Rootlessness is too deep in my blood to ever be so easily washed away.

Perhaps a belief system suffers from constant movement; our fleeting attention to the seder ritual is evidence of that. But I'm not sure it matters. It is the being together of five people, some of us strangers to one another and to Broome, that makes this night different from all other nights.

24
SHE'LL BE RIGHT

At sunrise there is another ceremony to attend. Twenty middle-aged men have gathered at a park by the water, waiting for the first rays of dawn. One carries a bugle, another has a flag under his arm, and a third is setting up a record player in the back of his station wagon. The others mill around in the still-cool dark, smoking cigarettes and talking quietly among themselves.

The sun filters through the trees and a scratchy, martial tune begins playing on the record player. The men right-wheel and left-wheel across the grass to the sound of *Bridge on the River Kwai*. Slowly, a crowd gathers and a troop of Brownies joins the march. Then four soldiers plant their bayonets in the dirt, and the bugler blows out a breathy Last Post.

At the going down of the sun and in the morning we will remember.

A gun goes off, wreaths are laid, and the Anzac Day parade disperses before the sun has lifted itself 10 degrees off the tropical horizon.

"You can't dawdle in this heat," explains Les Davis, a World War II infantryman. Behind him, the Brownies hike up their dresses to let cool water from a tap run across their ankles. "Broome by mid-morning can be as grueling as Tobruk."

It is not my ceremony—not my country, even—but somehow the brief remembrance feels more genuine than Memorial Day in the U.S.

There is nothing in American history to match the unredeemed slaughter at Gallipoli; only Vietnam, which is being gradually recast as a defeat grasped from the jaws of victory. And for many Americans, mourning of the war dead is mixed with the celebration of continued military might.

In Australia there is only the mourning.

"The whole war thing is bullshit," Les Davis tells me as the marchers drift from the park to the Catholic church, where Father Mack will conduct a brief memorial service. "I'm here to remember me mates, not all the throats I cut. The army, the saluting, the whole lot of it makes me bloody bitter."

Not many American veterans of World War II talk that way—particularly not veterans like Davis, whose chest is covered with stars and crosses from Egypt and France and Southeast Asia.

Anzac Day has an added poignancy in Broome, where so many of the citizens are of Japanese descent. When the internment order came through at the beginning of the war, a local pearlmaster declared: "It's hard to hate a particular fellow who's been a good shipmate, even if he is Japanese." In the jingoistic fever of wartime, such a statement was tantamount to treason.

Now the races are united again and peppered across the pews listening to Father Mack.

"I was visited by a Jewish traveler yesterday," he tells them soon after I wander in and take a seat. "It was Passover, the day when Jewish slavery is remembered, and he wanted to find a Jewish family to remember with. It made me think about our own ceremony, here, today. Of how we gather together, to remember. That's what collective memory, what Anzac Day, is all about."

I am happy to repay Father Mack for his help, and pleased to hear myself listed as an exotic new ingredient in the racial ratatouille of Broome.

Anzac Day resembles Passover in another way: the remembrance is quickly softened by drink. Until a few years ago, the veterans of Broome marched straight from the park to the nearby Continental Hotel for a few rounds on the house. But a new owner at the pub discontinued the early opening, fearing that the whole thirsty town of Broome would crowd in for a freebie at dawn. So now, after the service at the Catholic church, the men retire to a liquid breakfast at an army barracks instead.

"AttenSHUN!" shouts the local Returned Services League president, raising his tinnie for a 7 A.M. toast.

"To the Queen!"

"Hear! Hear!" (*All drink.*)

"To those we left behind, at Gallipoli, at Tobruk, in New Guinea!" (*All drink.*)

"To me 'Nam mate, Michael, who got killed in a car prang last week." (*All drink.*)

A stooped Digger fills a large glass of beer and places it in the corner as a sort of Elijah's cup for all the ones that didn't make it home. "To absent friends," he croaks. All drink again. And then another Digger, an ex-submariner, starts the singing.

> *This is my story*
> *This is my song*
> *I've been in the Navy too bloody long.*

And so it goes, all drinking, all singing, into the heat of the day. The party moves from the barracks to a tin-and-wood RSL building back in town. By midday the men have descended into stuporous mateship, slinging arms over one another's shoulders and slurring out toasts to everyone they have ever heard of.

"To George Franklin's birthday!"

"Hear! Hear!"

"Who the bloody hell is George Franklin?"

"Me next-door neighbor."

"Hear! Hear!"

I slump on the floor beside a middle-aged woman named Marian Choice. She is chaperoning her uncle, a World War II veteran named Tassie, the only male in her family to return from the front lines in one piece. More or less.

"He's got radiation burns from being in a prisoner of war camp in Japan," she says. "But otherwise he's fine."

Marian's father fought at Gallipoli and returned with shrapnel in his forehead ("didn't bother him much"). Her father's brother was killed in a trench somewhere in France, and Marian's own brother died in

New Guinea nine days before World War II ended. He was a few weeks short of his twenty-first birthday.

"All three of my sons went to Vietnam," she says. "They came out okay, physically, that is. It shook 'em all up mentally." She goes quiet for a moment. "It doesn't seem fair that the old men start the wars and the boys got to fight them."

Man and boy, veteran and private, are fighting a losing battle now to keep from falling on the floor. They are saved by an Aboriginal veteran who steps outside, rolls a tarpaulin over a patch of dusty ground, and bangs two empty tinnies together to get everyone's attention.

"Mates, it's two-up time." And the building empties out into the yard.

"Five dollars on the heads!"

"I'll take it." A few crumpled bills exchange hands.

"Ten to make guts! Ten to match the spinner!"

"Guts made!"

"Come in, spinner!"

I have read about two-up, which supposedly originated in the trenches of France. But I've never seen the living, breathing game. And what strikes me is the simplicity of it all—a game of chance so crude as to be absolutely captivating. Two old-style pennies, with a Queen on one side and a kangaroo on the other, are balanced on a wooden "kip" of wood. Then they're flipped into the air, with two Queens a victory for the heads, two kangaroos a win for the tails, and one of each a throw that doesn't count at all.

"Tail 'em up! Tail 'em up!" shout the tails bidders.

"Head 'em, ya bastard, head 'em!" yell the heads bidders.

And then the "Come in, spinner!" beckoning each man in turn to take his place in the circle to flip the coins.

"Foul toss!" the men yell, as my turn as spinner sends the coins rolling into the dust. "Send the Yank home!"

The jest is light-hearted, though. I get another chance, and then another, as I hit a run of heads. I feel like a child at ring-around-the-rosie, the center of attention as twenty drunken Diggers wait for my wrist to flick two old pennies into the air.

"Tails, ya bastard! You've tailed out, mate!" The five-dollar bills at my feet disappear and someone else takes the kip. My second turn at spinning is a tails on the first toss. And in between, I lose twenty dollars making side bets on other people's spins.

If I had a line of credit handy, I'd borrow money and gamble on. But I know no one, except for Father Mack, who watches the illegal game with a bemused smile from the shade of a nearby tree. A policeman, meanwhile, joins in, "just to keep the game clean," he says.

So I climb my bike again and pedal off, wondering that the Germans didn't win the war while the Aussie spinners came on in.

I awake in a park some hours later, sweaty and hung over, to the realization that I have been too long in Broome. It's not that I've overstayed my welcome—far from it. Ever since that first friendly wink from the librarian, two long days ago, Broome has been nothing if not welcoming. The Wronskis invited me to visit again, as did Father Mack and several of my two-up companions. And Mark and Gavin are still wandering about, ready to shout me another beer—or a joint. If I wanted to, I could bludge my way through a year or two in Broome.

It's my own itinerary that's the problem. There's a plane leaving Darwin for Sydney on Tuesday morning, three days from now. I negotiated a month away from Sydney with the promise that I'd be on that plane—and back at the office the following day. My employer's goodwill was stretched to the limit allowing me that much leave, and I don't like to consider my chances of stretching it any further.

The only problem is, I don't like my chances of making it either. It's Friday evening and I'm still a 1,200-mile drive from Darwin. Much of the road is unpaved, and most of the rest is unpopulated. If I'd left Broome yesterday morning, as originally planned, there wouldn't have been any problem. But now I'll need some luck and a lot of stamina to make it through in three days.

Nor am I the only person who wants to linger in Broome. Just before sunset, I return the bicycle and catch a ride to a gas station at the main highway, 12 miles south of town. My plan is to find a truckie or long-distance driver to travel with through the night. But the only traffic at the station is a squadron of sandflies and mosquitoes, pulling in to pump my blood before heading on into the night.

The handiwork of other stranded hitchhikers isn't very encouraging, either.

"Is five hours here too long?" says the top scratch on the back of a road sign.

"No."

"Pat stuck 3 days. Christmas 85."

"Wayne, the same. Get into Jim Beam."

Then, at the bottom, a half-quoted lyric from the rock band Talking Heads.

> *You may find yourself . . .*

Nice song. Nice thought. I scratch out a stanza to pass the time.

> *You may find yourself*
> *In another part of the world.*
> *You may find yourself*
> *Behind the wheel of a large automobile.*

You may find yourself . . . a short way into the scrub. In a not-very-large sleeping bag. Wondering, well, how did I get here?

Saturday morning finds me still in search of a large automobile. The sun is high and hot in the sky before a car finally pulls over to pick me up. It's about twenty minutes after that when the same car, driven by an Aboriginal couple, pulls off the road with a flat. The driver takes a pair of pliers out of the glove box, uses them to roll down his window, and opens the door from the outside. Then he passes the pliers over his shoulder so I can do the same. Outside, we struggle with a broken old jack until it collapses under the weight of the station wagon. Not that it matters. The spare tire doesn't fit.

I've hitched half a dozen rides with Aborigines since leaving Sydney and all but one has ended something like this.

I catch a ride to the next roadhouse, give the mechanic five dollars to drive back and rescue the couple, then seek out a swifter steed to carry me on. A brawny man in a sleeveless jean jacket is pumping gas, and when I ask him for a ride, he waves me into his station wagon. Strangely, the other passengers—a teenaged woman and two babies— are in the backseat, so I climb into the front for the 210-mile trip to Fitzroy Crossing.

The mangrove swamps that hug the shore give way almost immediately to a flat and barren plain, much like the flat and barren plain I've been crossing since Perth. After half an hour, lush and sultry Broome seems unreal; sealed off from the world, like a pearl, by the hard red crust of outback Australia.

"Whole bloody town was crawling with gins, wogs, and slit-eyes," Bruce says when I tell him I've just come from Broome. Unlike me, he couldn't get out of the place fast enough. In fact, he cut short his three days of company-paid R and R, spent the rest of his stipend on a few cases of beer, and loaded his family into the station wagon for an early drive home.

"I couldn't leave the motel without bumping into some kind of weirdo," he tells me, draining a beer and reaching a hand over his shoulder so his wife, Tish, can hand him a fresh tinnie. "At least they aren't taking any white jobs. As far as I could see, no one in that bloody town works."

Bruce's own work is laying down bitumen on the rough stretch of highway between Fitzroy Crossing and Hall's Creek. He hates it, but he doesn't have any choice. Last year he was laid off from a job cutting cane stalks in his native town of Bundaberg, Queensland. Tish was pregnant with their second child, and they'd just moved into a new house.

"The dole wouldn't have made a scratch in the bills I had to pay," he says. So he hitchhiked west until he found road work, then saved enough to send for Tish and the kids. Ever since, their home has been Nowhere, Western Australia—a caravan beside whatever patch of highway the road crew is paving over.

I ask Tish what there is to do while Bruce is at work.

"Nothing," she says. "Except looking after the kids and turning the air-conditioner from high cool to low cool."

She hands me a beer and passes another over Bruce's shoulder, which he plops into the Styrofoam stubbie cooler with a loud thunk. He opens it, drains it, then reaches over his shoulder for another.

"You know something?" he says. "I missed being junior fishing champion of Victoria by three months." Then he launches into a long and rambling story of how he traveled to Victoria with some Bundaberg mates, hit a big patch of salmon, and came in first at the contest's weigh-in. But he was disqualified because the age limit for the junior division was six months younger than in Queensland; the award went to someone else. "I gave fishing away after that," he says.

I'm not sure if he tells me the story out of pride, or to illustrate the basic unfairness of a life that finds him now, at the age of twenty-three, driving a dozer in the Western Australian desert to support a wife and two children.

The conversation lags after that, but the beer-drinking continues at a fierce pace. If the alcohol is affecting Bruce's driving, I don't want to know about it; after a few beers, I'm too tired and apathetic to muster my usual passenger-seat panic. So I pull a T-shirt over my head and doze through the afternoon, listening to one mortar after another being loaded into the stubbie cooler, then opened and drained. Thunk. Pffft. Swerp. Reload. Thunk. Pfffft. Swerp. . . . When Bruce nudges me awake at Fitzroy Crossing, tinnies lie scattered around the car like spent shells.

The battlefield outside is even more impressive. A dense carpet of tinnies surrounds the Fitzroy pub, shimmering in the late afternoon light. It looks like an aluminum reproduction of the salt lakes I saw in South Australia.

"Welcome to the Fitzroy snowfields," Bruce says humorlessly. "Watch out for the gins." With that he roars off to the caravan that is his home in the desert.

Ian Wronski told me a little of Fitzroy Crossing's history. The town was no more than a roadhouse until about twenty years ago. Then the government ruled in favor of equal wages for all workers, white or black. The law was liberal-minded in intent but disastrous in practice, at least for poorly paid blacks on cattle stations in the Nor'west. Rather than pay the award wage, most property owners simply let their Aboriginal workers go. So hundreds of black families were left to drift into towns like Fitzroy Crossing, to collect their government assistance, and to live in fibro government homes. They have been there ever since.

Each Aboriginal community I've encountered has been locked in some form of battle with the enemy Grog. At Mutitjulu, near Ayers Rock, opposition to alcohol is so intense that booze is barred from the community altogether. In other places, such as the Beagle Bay Mission north of Broome, a truce has been worked out. Alcohol is permitted in designated quantities at designated times. Someone might drive into Broome and pick up a few cases of beer for a Friday-night celebration, but anything more than that is *verboten*.

Fitzroy Crossing appears to have fought the same battle and retreated in abject surrender. Even the elderly women I pass in the street are red-eyed and wobbly. And the area around the petrol station, where I stand watch for another ride, resembles a downtown street at 2 A.M. on Saturday. Dozens of drinkers mill around with no apparent activity or destination, on the verge of collapse.

Standing alone by the road, I become a natural target for their stumbling, imperfect English.

"Hey, mate. Hey. Where you going, mate?"

"Hey, mate, got a smoke, mate?"

"Mate, got me a dollar, mate?"

I empty my pockets of change then pull the insides out, to show that I have nothing left. But conversation is difficult. The men aren't unfriendly or aggressive, just out of it. One man urinates in full view of a busload of kids at the gas station. Another lies down for a snooze a few yards from where I stand. And as the heat and glare drain from the sky, the abandoned tinnies go from white to orange to red in the fading sun.

I am about to look for a camping spot when a truckie pulls in at the gas station and offers me a ride to Hall's Creek, 185 miles to the east. "You're lucky," he says, driving off quickly. "Most people avoid stopping at Fitzroy altogether, unless they run out of petrol. It gives them the creeps."

An hour out of Fitzroy, the bitumen turns to gravel and the driving becomes slow and silent, so slow that it is after midnight when I climb out at a camping ground on the edge of Hall's Creek. It's drizzling, so I crawl under my tarp for what promises to be another brief and uncomfortable sleep. Shining my torch at the map, I calculate how far I've come: 450 miles since Broome, about 7,000 since Sydney. Only 750 or so to go. I make a sign to the next town—"Kununurra Pls!"—and return to the same lullaby I hummed last night.

You may find yourself
In a beautiful house.
With a beautiful wife.
You may ask yourself,
Well, how did I get here?

Sunday morning I don't even make it out to the road. I am seated on my pack at dawn, trying to muster the energy to roll my swag, when a voice beckons from the morning mist.

"Where ya headed, mate?"

I turn around to face the picture of campground self-satisfaction. He is elderly but trim and fit, with a wide-brimmed Akubra pushed back on his brow. There's a bit of egg still lingering on his lip, staining the side of the day's first cigarette. The man squints a bit as he inhales, smiling, as if he's never tasted anything so good in his life.

"Where ya headed?" he asks again, exhaling. Actually, I was headed to the toilet block, but I flash him my Kununurra sign instead.

"It's your lucky day, mate. That's where I'm headed. Let me know when you're ready and we'll ship out."

I am momentarily suspicious. "How'd you know I was hitching?"

He smiles and takes another long pull at his cigarette. "When you've been at this game as long as I have, you develop an eye for these things."

The game is nonstop travel, and Jack Pearton is a professional at it. For starters, he's got professional equipment: a spanking new station wagon hauling the latest and finest in caravan technology.

"Hydraulic," he says, pressing a button that makes the trailer rise up like a loaf of bread. He presses the button and the trailer goes flat again. "Here, give it a try yourself." Up and down, up and down, like an accordion. "Amazing, eh?"

The inside of the caravan looks like a department store display of recreational gear. Fishing poles, deck chairs, eskies with power points, eskies without power points, a television, wires, hoses, a magnum .22 repeater rifle, tents, hunting knives. Jack picks up each article, recites its price, place of origin and utility, then returns it with military precision to the exact spot. Apparently, every item in the trailer has a well-defined place and purpose in furthering the grand strategy of the road trip.

The same discipline reigns in the control room, up front. An enamel St. Christopher, patron saint of travel, stares down from the dashboard. A line of hats covers the backseat for Jack to choose from, depending on what state he's traveling through: a Stetson for Queensland, a leather bushman's hat for the Northern Territory, the flat-brimmed Akubra he wears in Western Australia, and a fishing cap for "general travel."

Jack orders me to open the glove box as soon as we're underway. "Check the log, mate," he says officiously, pilot to copilot. The log is a thick spiral notebook, stuffed with receipts and penciled notes on every detail of the voyage. One column lists where Jack has stayed each night; another tells where he stopped for gas, how much it cost him, and how many miles he averaged per gallon since the last stop. There's even an estimate of how much gas he has lost by driving into a headwind since Broome: "Sixty dollars in three days."

"You lose as much again if you don't take the curves right," he says, demonstrating how to steer straight through a bend so as to minimize the distance covered. "Simple geometry."

Another column in the log book lists Jack's tea breaks, every ninety minutes, with "cigarettes" in parentheses beside alternating stops. Then, in the back pages under "Notes," Jack records his impressions of the places he's traveled through, and brief footnotes for future journeys. "Adelaide to Melb. much better than Melb. to Adelaide, because cliff's on the left, the water's on the right, so it's easier to look at scenery while driving."

Jack lets me browse for a while, then nudges my shoulder.

"I haven't been to the middle of the Simpson Desert yet, but I reckon I'll get there," he says. "Two hundred and forty thousand kilometers"—140,000 miles—"in six years. Not bad for an old-timer, eh?"

Just last night I was congratulating myself on having covered 7,000 miles of Australian roads. It is a mere sprint compared to Jack's marathon tour.

Jack Pearton's life story is as precise and well ordered as his log books. "When I was twelve, I decided to make a list of my priorities and read it every day," he says. "I stray, but eventually I always get back on course." His list included joining the navy, which he did at fourteen ("lied to buggery, of course"), which promotions he wanted and when ("started at fifteen cents a week and made it to lieutenant commander"), and getting his kids along in life ("six of 'em, all well established").

Since retiring six years ago, he's mapped out his travels just as carefully, navigating rambles through places he's never seen or wants to see
again. Route 1 from Tasmania to northern Queensland and back again.
A fishing trip to the Gulf of Carpentaria. A visit to a friend in Exmouth
at the northwest tip of Australia.

He's done this trip through the Nor'west before, but the timing is
important; his departure coincided precisely with the arrival of in-laws
at his "home" in Perth.

"My wife doesn't like traveling quite as much as me," he says. "So
when I get itchy feet—which is most of the year—I hit the road and
she meets up with me somewhere along the way." It is an odd model
for retirement and an even odder model for a marriage. But then, Jack
is obviously content with the arrangement; perhaps his wife is too.

"Eventually, when my reflexes go, I'll have to take myself off the
road," he says dispassionately, as if inspecting the wear on a tire tread.
"But I reckon I've got some miles left." I suspect he's written down
exactly how many somewhere in his log.

Jack keeps me so busy checking mileage markers, comparing them
to the log, and making new entries, that it is some hours before I notice
the scenery. And scenery there is, for the first time since leaving Broome.
The land rolls and heaves in rocky outcroppings, dark brown and lay-
ered, like a chocolate cake. They are the first real mountains I've passed
through since Alice. To the east lies the Bungle Bungle range, hidden
away from all but the most intrepid of bushwalkers. To the west are
the mountains and high plateau country of the Kimberleys. And in the
foreground loom giant anthills, interspersed with bloated boab trees that
stand by the road, like black women reaching out their arms for a bear
hug. They are even fatter than the bottle trees I saw in Queensland.

"One boab in Derby is so big that it was used as a jail," Jack tells
me. He can see from my smile that I'm not convinced. "Fair dinkum.
Check the log."

Sure enough, an entry marked "Derby: sightseeing" and a short note
beside it: "hollow boab with metal grille, once used to house prisoners
overnight. Remarkable."

Every ninety minutes, on the dot, we pull off the road and have a
drink of sugary tea from Jack's Thermos. The only movements that Jack
doesn't regulate are his trips to the toilet; apparently, old age has made
chaos of that. "I've leaked all over this country," he says, running to

pee behind a boab tree between tea stops. "Fair dinkum. Check the log." This time he is joking.

The lectures and log entries make for slow driving, which is fine as far as Jack is concerned: "Better mileage that way," he says, "and anyway, what's the rush?" But I use my own haste as an excuse for declining his invitation to drink a beer when we finally reach Kununurra.

"I always have one beer, same time every day," he tells me, checking his watch. Then he slaps his forehead; it seems he's made a rare miscalculation. "Oh my God, I forgot it's Sunday. I have no idea what pub session we're up to."

Nor does anyone else in Kununurra. It is a town that launches Nor'west time into a whole new dimension of vagueness. After Jack drops me off, I wander down a commercial street to find some food and a fresh piece of cardboard before hitching into the Northern Territory. One shop is closed, despite a sign on the front saying "open." The next store lists its hours as 9–12 on Sundays, but it's still open at mid-afternoon. At a takeaway (which lists no hours at all), I chat with a truckie headed to Katherine, 300 miles east. He offers me a ride, if I don't mind waiting while he meets a mate for a quick one at the pub. When he hasn't returned an hour later, I wander over to the pub as well.

"Sorry, mate," he slurs, still at the bar. "How 'bout tomorrow?"

I hike back out to the highway through ugly, suburban-style subdivisions, pausing every five minutes to keep from overheating in the afternoon sun. It is so hot and muggy that my body feels like a bouillon cube melting in a mug of boiling water. Incredibly, this is the Nor'west's temperate time, just after the end of the wet season. But the thermometer at a gas station registers 105 degrees. The humidity makes it feel twice that.

Sometimes it gets so hot in Kununurra that a local plant, called the kerosene tree, spontaneously bursts into flames. At least that's what the woman at the gas station says (I'd like to have Jack's log to check on it). What needs little confirmation, though, is that the Wet in Kununurra, from October to February, is so oppressive that locals call it the "suicide season."

"The people that don't suicide just hole up at home by the air-conditioner," she says. "They might as well be dead."

No one comes to Kununurra for the weather, of course, though it could be said, as Humphrey Bogart did of Casablanca, that they come for the waters. The damming of the Ord River and the dream of a rich irrigation valley brought farmers here in the 1960s. Many of the farms failed, but Kununurra grew nonetheless: an artificial town perched by an artificial lake, servicing the farms and the Argyle diamond mines. Tourists started using Kununurra as a jumping-off point for the Kimberley and Lake Argyle. And then it became a public service center as well: an outpost for young bureaucrats to cut their teeth on before moving up the ladder to Perth.

It's also a place where hitchhikers can swelter for a few days before escaping east to Darwin or west to Broome. A small party is already there to greet me when I finally make it to the eastern edge of town. First in line is a young couple from Paris, standing at rigid attention, like French Legionnaires in the North African desert. Huge sweat stains spread across their backs and under their arms.

"Combien de temps ici?" I ask in broken French, wanting to know how long they've been there.

"Deux jours," the man says wearily.

"Trois," his girlfriend interjects.

"Deux ou trois. Trop long."

They bicker over whether it's been two days or three as I make my way to the end of the queue. Nor'west time is apparently an infectious disease, even for foreigners.

The next two places in line are occupied by ragged-looking men on their way to Darwin. They are too hot and tired to mumble more than a few words. Apparently, 90 percent of the road traffic is made up of locals going back and forth to the lake. The other 10 percent is parked at a pub down the street. "One bloke got so tired of waiting that he started walking," hitchhiker number three informs me. He gestures vaguely down the road toward the Northern Territory, as if he'll be forced to do the same in a few hours.

I hike a mile out of town, hoping that maybe some driver will reach the first line of hitchhikers, and, fearful that they'll all try to cram inside, drive past and stop for me instead. It is wishful thinking. Four hours later I am still sitting by the road, holding my cardboard sign—"Katherine Pls!"—as a visor against the setting sun. I hike back toward town to find the French couple standing just where I left them, and the other two prone beside their rucksacks. It has the look of a terminal occupation.

I sit on my pack and study the map. Almost 300 miles of road to Katherine, and another 200 to Darwin. The highway looks good, but even so, that's ten to twelve hours of driving. Assuming I can find a driver. And there's only fourteen hours or so of daylight between now and when my plane leaves from Darwin. If I weren't sitting in a windless desert, a day's drive from the sea, I'd call that "sailing close to the wind."

Clearly, I'll have to travel through the dark. But the gas station is closed and there's no truck stop in sight. Slowly, as I hike to the pub through the twilight, I ponder a contingency I have dreaded, and thus far avoided: catching a bus.

It is a disgrace I have faced only once in an otherwise blessed hitching career. One summer at university, I hitched across Europe and was stranded for two days by a road in Salzburg, Austria. The weather was clear, the highway uncluttered by other hitchhikers, but all I could coax from drivers were unfriendly stares. Apparently, Austrians believe in walking. I caught a coach instead and escaped across the border to a German autobahn.

Kununurra calls for a similar sort of compromise. If there's a bus tonight, I'll take it as far as Katherine and hitch the last leg to Darwin. If there's no bus until tomorrow, and I still haven't caught a ride by then, I'll hide my face in shame and ride it straight through to the Top End. If there's no bus at all, I'll just have to hijack a car.

The good news when I go inside the pub is that there is a bus; in fact, it stops in front of an adjoining restaurant later tonight. The bad news is that no one can tell me when it arrives. A schedule on the wall says eight-thirty, the publican says it comes at ten, and a drinker at the bar swears that it never pulls out of Kununurra before eleven. "Unless she's hit a kangaroo or something between here and Broome," he says. "Then maybe she won't get out till morning."

Exasperated, I finally lose my patience with Nor'west time.

"Goddammit!" I hear myself shouting. "What the fuck's wrong with this place?"

The bar goes silent. Then the publican flashes me a smile that I recognize from my first few months in Australia, when I lost my patience frequently. Before he speaks, I can hear the words like the rumble of incoming artillery.

"She'll be right, mate," he says, in a laconic rendition of the Australian national anthem. "Settle down and have a drink."

I order a beer and slump in the corner of the pub, which is still open three hours after its session was supposed to have ended.

Two hours later, at nine o'clock, the pub's still open but there's no sign of a bus. The schedule on the wall, which I'd judged the most reliable of my three sources, is now proven wrong. I pace the street outside, always staying within eyeshot of the supposed depot in front of the restaurant ("I didn't think the bus came at all on Sunday," was the intelligence I received there).

Then, just after ten, the bus to Darwin pulls in. Twenty people pile out of the bus and go straight into the pub. I follow them, find the driver eating a meat pie at the bar, and pay him for a ticket to Katherine. It is another hour before the coach sets off again.

Just as the man at the bar said: Never leaves before eleven. I make a quick logistical calculation: Katherine by dawn, on the road again soon after, and, with any luck, into Darwin with six hours of sunlight to spare.

She will, in fact, be right.

25
ONE FOR
THE ROAD

There is a gentle apartheid on buses separating the sleeps from the sleepnots.

A lucky few—the same lucky few who can sleep on New York subways or in battlefield trenches—fall immediately into deep unconsciousness, as if struck over the head. The rest toss and turn in the vain hope of achieving so much as a doze. This gives them plenty of time to contemplate the unique engineering that makes coach seats sleepproof.

Consider the options:

1. Slump straight back or slightly to one side, with the knees crammed against the seat in front, and the head pushed forward upon the chest, as if in preparation for the executioner's axe.
2. Curl up in a pained fetal position, with the head shoved against the armrest and the feet pushing off against the wall of the bus, compressing the knees upward into the chin.
3. If the seat beside is empty: Recline across two seats, trying to curl around the armrest, the point of which inevitably lodges like a tomahawk between the shoulder blades. Alternately, roll over and take the hatchet directly in the chest.

Sleep-nots on coaches are among the truly wretched of the earth. I am among them, of course, which is one reason I always avoid traveling by bus.

After an hour of fidgeting, Misery sits up and searches the bus for Company. Most of the seats in the back are occupied by flaked-out mothers and children, sound asleep. But up front an American voice, a doesn't-want-to-sleep, is quizzing the driver as we race through the night.

"Sir," says the woman's voice, "what would we be seeing if it weren't dark?"

"Bugger all. Empty scrub."

"What'd he say?" It is a male voice, tired and irritable. A sleep-not.

"He says 'not much,' dear. Like what we saw between Perth and Broome."

"Oh."

Back to fidgeting—and wondering, perhaps, about the acrobatic nature of buggery: the word, that is. It can be a verb, as in "bugger it"; an adjective, as in "buggered"; a noun, "bugger all"; a place, "out to buggery"; and an insult: "bugger yourself," "get buggered," or the less offensive "bug off." You can even be "buggered," which means worn out, with none of the homosexual overtones it carries in America.

Sort of like "crook," another word that means everything in Australian except what it means in American, or better yet, the ever-flexible "knock": to knock (criticize), knockerism (the art of criticizing), knocked up (pregnant). Alternatively, to knock back (say no to, or to drink, as in knock back a beer).

Inventive buggers, these Aussies.

But as buggered, knocked around, and crook as I feel, sleep is still an impossibility. Across the aisle from me, a young woman opens her eyes and reaches blearily for a cigarette. We make sympathetic eye contact, like neighbors in a hospital ward.

"Where ya headed?" she asks.

"Katherine. Darwin eventually. How about you?"

"Darwin," she says. "If I don't go nuts and climb off before then. I can't even remember how long it's been since we left Perth."

I ask her what she does back home.

"Been waitressing for three years, and just got fed up with it," she says. "Reckon I needed to take a break and head off somewhere."

"So why'd you pick Darwin?"

"A mate told me there's a great pub at some suburb called Humpty Doo. That's where they have the World Championship Darwin stubbie drinking contest."

"What's that?"

"A race to see who can drink fastest. You get a two-liter stubbie and a plastic garbage bin, and the crowd stands around yelling 'Spew! Spew! Spew!' " She pauses. "I reckon Humpty Doo will be a good place to start."

She stubs out her cigarette and closes her eyes, leaving me to wonder what it is she's about to start. A new life? A pub crawl? Is there a difference in Darwin?

It is my first reminder that the Top End is only a six-pack away. The second reminder comes an hour later, when the bus pulls in at a roadhouse called Timber Creek. I gaze out the bus window and through the open door of a pub, which is crowded with drinkers. A clock above the bar says 2:30 A.M. No Sunday session I know of goes on that long.

"We're in the Northern Territory, mate," the driver explains. "This isn't kiddie land anymore."

Indeed it isn't. When the driver climbs out to unload some luggage for a departing passenger, a drunken man weaves aboard.

"Zis is a stick-up," he slurs, patting his hand against a lump beneath his shirt. It could be a few stubbies in a brown bag. Then again, it could be a gun. "Zis is a stick-up," he says again. "Sheilas, take off your jewelry. Blokes, hand over the wallets."

No one moves. Suddenly even the sleep-nots seem to have achieved deep and untroubled slumber. "For Chrissake's!" he shouts. "Izza stick up!" Still no one moves. Then the driver returns and shoulders the drunk out of the bus. "Get outta here!" the driver yells, vaguely irritated, as if he often deals with drunken highwaymen at this particular stop.

It is still two hours before sunrise when we arrive in Katherine. My plan, as much as I have one, is to hang out at the bus depot until morning, then try to hitch a ride from there. That way, if no rides materialize, I'll be able to hop onto the next bus to Darwin. A half day by the road in Kununurra has shot my confidence in ever catching a ride again.

But five minutes at the station forces me to change my plan. Katherine's bus depot is like bus depots everywhere: dank and depressing, and smelling as if its floors have been swabbed with some evil mix of urine, stale coffee, and cigarette butts. It is a bus passenger's purgatory, a place to suffer before the greater hell of the bus itself. No place for a hitchhiker.

So once again I make the Long March from downtown to out of town. How many times have I done this, I wonder, hiking past a mile or two of silent shopfronts? Orange, Dubbo, Cloncurry, Tennant Creek, Kimba . . . I know the face of commerce in every outback town . . . Norseman, Albany, Geraldton, Carnarvon, Kununurra. And everywhere the same as this: an endless stretch of angle parking and footpaths shadowed by awnings.

There is a Greenwich of the soul to which our internal clocks are set. My own is winding down quickly. I have just enough strength to carry me to the end of this town, just enough energy to scrawl one more sign, and just enough patience to wait for one last ride. If the road is suddenly washed out, causing me to take a 100-mile detour, I may have to be carried off the battlefield on my cardboard shield.

Across a bridge, and finally out of town. I can dimly make out a grassy field on the left—a park maybe—and beyond it the empty road to Darwin. Wrapping myself in a blanket, I lie on the ground to wait out the night.

At first light it becomes apparent that this is quite a popular park. There are Aboriginal men everywhere, wrapped in blankets and strewn across the grass like Nubian mummies. No sleep-nots in this crowd. I make an imaginary entry in Jack Pearton's log book, in a column labeled "Strange places I've spent the night": in a ditch during a cyclone, in an abandoned bus in the Nullarbor, at a pub with no publican in Rocky Gully, and now in a makeshift Aboriginal camp.

Slowly, as the sun lifts its gaze across the park, the men come awake and wander off toward town. Then the truck traffic begins: huge, three-trailered road trains, strafing me with gravel and sending up clouds of dust as they shoot through to Darwin. An hour after that—rush hour in Katherine—the local traffic begins, headed toward an industrial park around the next bend. Brawny men in dusty four-wheel drives with Monday-morning faces: unsmiling, haggard, hung over. Then the housewives, headed in the opposite direction, to drop the kids off at school or to do some shopping. Then the housewives returning from town, with grocery bags in the passenger seat instead of kids. I know the face of commuter traffic in every outback town.

Nonetheless, I make the hopeless gesture of standing there with my finger out, grinning like a maniac. No one's headed to Darwin, obviously, and even if they are, they aren't about to let me into the family sedan.

By mid-morning I feel spent, which is how I've felt for the last few days, except now it's acute: not just a bankruptcy but a full-blown debt crisis. When the heat arrives in another hour or so I'll just disappear into the dust, melting like a stick of butter that slipped out of one of the housewives' grocery bags. Even the hike back to the bus depot seems beyond me, though the shame I feel about bus travel has long since departed. I'll crawl to Darwin on my hands and knees if that's what's required.

I wander into the park to piss behind a tree, leaving my "Darwin Pls!!" propped against my pack, facing the northbound traffic. As soon as I unzip my fly, I hear the sound of rubber hitting gravel. Great, now I've not only been abandoned in Katherine, but I'm about to be ripped off as well. While taking a leak.

"Don't rush yourself, mate," the driver calls out, as I come running from behind the tree with the pained expression of pissus interruptus. "I've got to pee too," he says.

It is the first ride I've ever caught by sticking out my dick instead of my finger.

My fellow pisser is a sympatico driver named Trevor. The fraternal recognition is instant, at least for me. He is middle-aged, wearing stubbies, a T-shirt, and thongs. But a crumpled suit is falling off a coat hanger in the back. Beside it are half-folded shirts, a toiletries bag, and other signs of a man who makes his living on the road. Plus a stack of cheaply mimeographed fliers, some handmade posters, and a pile of small cards labeled "membership application." Having once been a member of Trevor's trade, I know what club it is he's hawking.

"I did some labor organizing myself," I tell him as we drive off toward

Darwin. "A union of timber workers in a place called Meridian, Mississippi."

Trevor laughs. "Mate, welcome to the Mississippi of Australia."

Trevor is an abattoir slaughterman when he's not organizing for the Meatworkers Union. And for the first hour of our drive, he educates me about boning buffalo and bargaining with the boss. The Northern Territory, like America's Deep South, is hostile turf for union men.

"Talk to ten men—"

"And you're lucky to convince one," I finish for him. He smiles. Then we exchange our union "rap." About how you don't get anything if you don't demand it—and then fight for it if they don't give it to you. The employers are together, they have trade associations, why can't we? Your union dues, well, we need the money, but really they're just a token of your commitment to the cause.

"Same as my speech," Trevor says when I'm done. "Except my men cut beef, not timber." And for the umpteenth time on this journey I am struck by how the globe, for all its girth, is in many ways no bigger than an India rubber ball.

Trevor continues his union rap, but somewhere between Katherine and Darwin I fall asleep, as woodcutters in Mississippi so often did when I stood up to give a speech. I stir awake as we pass through a monotonous expanse of crowded freeways and suburban subdivisions. It is Darwin but it could be anywhere in urban Australia: arcades, highrises, traffic.

I take Trevor's card and step out into the blinding light of a Top End afternoon. At first glance, Darwin resembles an oversized Alice Springs, hiding its face behind concrete-and-glass buildings and acres of suburban sprawl. Of course, Cyclone Tracy blew away most of the original town in 1974, so at least Darwin has an excuse.

I don't need a tourist guide to find the real Darwin. In a place that drinks more beer per capita than any other on earth, there's little mystery about that. But I am not ready for the pubs, not yet.

Holding my cardboard sign overhead to ward off the sun, I hoist my pack and go in search of a bed on which to lay my turtle self down. Five minutes and fifteen dollars later, I'm rewarded with a rabbit hole just off the bitumen: a chamber that is stark naked except for a bed, a drippy air-conditioner, and a broken refrigerator. Standing by the bed,

I can almost reach out and touch all four walls. I open the fridge in the vain hope of finding something cold to drink. There is nothing but a cool pool of water on the bottom shelf.

I collapse on the motel bed with my pack still on, like a shell-shocked soldier falling into a foxhole. It has been about a month since I left Sydney, plus two weeks of travel from the city to the center, way back in January. Not a long time for a journey, really.

But hitchhiking time should be measured like the years of a dog's life. Each day must be multiplied by a factor of seven to account for the intensity of climbing into strange cars with strange people headed to strange places. And there's always the chance of encountering a homicidal maniac to stretch each moment by a few more factors than that.

My supply of small talk and my energy for new faces is depleted. I feel as I sometimes do at the end of a long week of newspaper reporting, when all I want to do is stop extracting information from people I've never met and will probably never speak to again.

Physically, I'm even more burned out. My legs and arms are covered in lumps; some from bug bites, some from scrambling through the scrub in the dark, some from the gravel lodged in my flesh by passing road trains. My head aches from sunburn, glare, and lack of sleep. And my stomach has become a Sargasso Sea of meat pies and beer. Another few weeks on a roadhouse diet and I'd succumb to scurvy, cirrhosis of the liver, or worse.

Did I feel this wrecked at seventeen, coming off the road after two months of hitching across America? If I did, I don't remember.

I am lying on the motel bed in Darwin, listening to the air-conditioner drip at 2 P.M. on a Monday afternoon, when the recognition comes. It is a thought that has played at the fringes of my consciousness for the past seventy-two hours; now, with my defenses down, it congeals into a simple declarative sentence.

My career as a hitchhiker has come to an end.

Someday there may be the stray itch between the first and second joint of my forefinger—like the longing for a cigarette, resurfacing years after kicking the habit. And certainly there will be other travels, other adventures. But setting off alone, with a swag and only my finger to move me along—those days are done.

I greet this insight with wistful relief; like the winter's dawn at college six years ago, when I shoved an overdue thesis under a professor's door, knowing the instant it disappeared that my days as a scholar were over. As at university, I've exhausted the discipline, or it has exhausted me. Hitchhiking was something I held in reserve; something I could return to without fear of disappointment. However unpredictable the adventure might be, it was sure to be that—an adventure.

But now, the thrill of the road is becoming overripe. Hopping freight trains, hitching on lobster boats—I feel myself reaching out for something a bit more extreme, a bit more self-conscious and contrived. I've become jaded. Sated. Oversated. Another few weeks and I'll be looking for a Grand Prix to hitch at, or pointing my finger toward a border skirmish somewhere.

The world has changed with me, of course. When I started hitching in the mid-seventies, it was an article of faith among young people that a hitchhiker should not be passed; a van or Volkswagen on the horizon was as good as a bus ticket. Added to that were middle-aged parents with children of their own on the road, plus ex-Okies, ex-servicemen, ex-beatniks and anyone else who had traveled by thumb or forefinger at some point in the past. All together, that gave you a fair slice of the population to rely on for rides.

But gradually the old brotherhood of the road is disappearing. Maybe it's just that the Volkswagen drivers of the seventies have moved onto Volvos and BMWs, sealed off from the world of the roadside traveler. Or maybe it doesn't take much for people's natural suspicion to re-emerge. A few Sons of Sam, the occasional Midnight Rambler, and Edna starts nudging Norm to keep on driving.

A bit of eye contact and conversation is enough to dispel the distrust, which explains why I've been lucky getting rides at roadhouses and gas pumps. But if those same drivers passed me standing by the road, with only my forefinger and smile as a character reference, they weren't likely to stop.

I lie on the bed for several hours, just listening to the air-conditioner drip. It is an appropriate tomb, this Darwin fleapit. Not Jon Hamilton's flophouse in New Orleans, but close enough. A deep interior grave opens up, my thumb and forefinger jump in, and an RIP sprouts overhead.

> *I grow old . . . I grow old . . .*
> *I shall wear the bottoms of my trousers rolled . . .*

I shall give up on T. S. Eliot too, I think. Seven thousand miles and I've memorized only a dozen stanzas of "The Love Song of J. Alfred Prufrock." At that rate I'll have to orbit the earth a few times to get through the whole poem.

But there will be time, Eliot writes (in about the third stanza). Time yet for a hundred indecisions and revisions. Time for you, and time for me—to hitchhike through the pubs of Darwin before the taking of toast and tea.

I force myself off the bed and out to the motel pool, a brackish moat with water the temperature of unpoured pig iron. There is a single sunbather lying supine on the concrete. He is well tanned, but he has the drawn, hollow look of a man at the tail end of a bender. A fountain, no doubt, of pub-touring advice.

"I've seen the sun rise for the past three days," he confesses, rising on one arm to light a cigarette. Me too, I realize wearily. Four, in fact. He sucks at the cigarette like a baby at a bottle of milk. "One more night and I'm history."

Doug is twenty-five; I would have guessed thirty-five at least. He came from Sydney six months ago and has been living at the motel ever since, working at one of the bars at the Diamond Beach Casino —an establishment known locally as the "shearing shed" or the "chip factory." Unfortunately, Doug moans, "they don't pass the proceeds along." But they are generous with the drinks, which is what gets Doug into trouble. His shift ends at 2 A.M. but he typically "kicks on" for several hours.

"Too bad you weren't here yesterday," he says. "Depraved, mate. Really wild."

Apparently, as in the Nor'west, Sunday is *the* drinking day in Darwin. The action peaks in late afternoon at "the Rage in the Cage." That's when half of adult Darwin crowds into Lim's Rapid Creek Hotel, a prisonlike pub with a concrete floor and wire mesh for walls. "The cage keeps the action in but lets the spew out," Doug explains. "Also makes it easier for them to hose the place down the morning after."

Charles Darwin would be struck by the devolution of the species that has occurred at the Top End since the *Beagle* landed here in 1839.

I ask Doug what my chances are of finding some action tonight.

"Monday's kind of quiet," he says. He pulls at his cigarette. Again, the smoke seems to give him some deep, primal nourishment. "But I think we can find you a rage at a few local venues."

Quiet by Darwin standards is a sonic boom by the lights of any other town. Doug's itinerary runs as follows: The Nightcliff for an apéritif ("leave early, before the fights start"), the Victoria Hotel to hear music ("group called Scrap Metal on tonight"), and Fannie's Disco to kick on until 4 A.M. ("local joke about it: 'go to Fannie's for a stabbing' ").

"There's a gay disco on at the Settler's pub if you're into that," he says finally. "Otherwise, just the casino and the usual run of a dozen or so pubs."

Like he said, kind of quiet.

I invite Doug to give me a personalized tour. But he has to work until two. "Anyway, I'm getting too old for this. Three nights running is all I can take anymore."

I wash a few clothes in the pool and bake them in the late afternoon sun. It is a futile attempt at achieving respectability—and a misguided one. At the Nightcliff, where I arrive around sunset, a drinker is over-dressed if his stubbies are the same color as the plastic on his thongs. It is also the sort of pub where a man feels naked without a tattoo on his arm.

The pub is plain and smoky, and chock-a-block with bikies. It has the look of a locker room after a brutal rugby match. Human limbs not encased in casts have the pale, shriveled look of having just been liberated from plaster. But it's hard to see much flesh beneath the tapestry of tattoos. Most of the bikies are covered in both plaster and india ink—plus keys, studs, rings, chains, and maces. Every time one of them moves toward the bar it's like a knight in armor clunking across a castle floor.

Beneath all the hardware is a racial mix reminiscent of Broome:

whites, blacks, Chinese, Malays, and one man who has rendered his race indeterminate with tattoos. I can't help staring at a particularly vivid scorpion on his upper arm, peeking beneath his T-shirt sleeve at the plaster cast that begins just above the elbow. The man looks Chinese, maybe Indonesian.

"What ya staring at?" he yells. I was wrong. Genus ocker, species aggro.

"Just your, uh, decorations." Genus Americanus, scared shitless. "Could you pull up your sleeve so I can see the full show?"

"I'd have to pull my pants down to do that, mate." He's glaring at me now. "What's so funny? Hunh? What youse smiling about?"

An involuntary grin always crosses my face in tense situations. I wipe it off and assume the mien of an undertaker.

The bikie isn't impressed. "Do you want the full show, mate? Hunh?"

The imp in me wants to call his bluff. Body tans yes, but a body tattoo? I'd like to see it. Then again, I can live without seeing it, and I probably won't live through the mayhem that could follow a bikie stripping at center stage of the Nightcliff Hotel.

Before I can answer, a hand grips my elbow and begins leading me outside. The arm above it has no plaster and no tattoos, nor is there any hint of violence in the voice that accompanies it.

"Steer clear of the feral natives," it says with a smile. "We're a bit tamer out in the beer garden."

A moment later I am seated at a picnic table with a curious collection of drinkers. My savior is a man named Lloyd, who is passing through Darwin with a theater group. He likes coming to the Nightcliff to "soak up some local color." His companions include a long-haired hospital orderly, a dissipated young actress, and a mammoth, shirtless Maori who doesn't state his occupation. But he whittles deftly at a wooden spoon, then promptly sells it to another drinker for a few dollars before carving another.

The others amuse themselves by counting ambulances, which scream down the adjoining highway at regular intervals—like every minute and a half.

"Usually the ambulances are coming here," the hospital worker says.

"They were too late the other night, though. Bloke chucked in his cards before they got here."

Chucked in his cards? This isn't the casino. "What do you mean?" I ask.

"He croaked, mate," the Maori says, running the penknife across his throat and grimacing. "Went out of here a stiff."

The death was nothing special; after all, the Northern Territory has a murder rate five times the national average. But a bikie having his throat cut led to a radical reform at the Nightcliff: a large sign announcing that children are no longer allowed in the pub.

"Killing's one thing," the Maori says, returning to his whittling. "But kids getting killed would be serious shit."

Apparently, most of the fights are started by "gin jockeys," which the unabridged Darwin dictionary defines as "white males who get black women drunk, fuck them, and then beat them up." The man I spoke with at the bar is one of this charming breed. When the gin jockeys ride in, usually on motorbikes, most of the black drinkers retreat rather than resist. But Aborigines hold sway in the public bar, where whites are unwelcome. Even gin jockeys respect the color bar.

As the evening wears on, a few theories are floated as to why there are no fights tonight. The orderly argues that everyone is "too stoned" on a crop of joints that circulates openly in the pub. The Maori thinks everyone's still a bit hung over after the serious Sunday drinking. And the actress blames the quiet on an end-of-month cash shortage.

"It's easy to be sober when you're broke," she hypothesizes. I search the bar in vain for signs of sobriety. "Wednesday's the first of the month," she continues. "Things will be back to normal by then."

At nine o'clock a few of the ambulatory drinkers kick on—or limp, rather—to the Victoria Hotel. The "Vic" is a tame-looking place in a downtown pedestrian mall: hanging plants, brick walls, and a huge ceiling fan that sweeps the sultry air one way and then another. Nor are there any bikies in evidence, but every other group in the world is represented: Rastafarians, rednecks, mung beans, American tourists, women in tight red dresses, Aboriginal men, white-haired hippies, a man with a bicycle. The place is a kind of Noah's Ark of all the curious species that collect at the Top End.

The band hasn't started playing yet, but already half the bar is dancing. A shaggy-haired jackeroo clad in stubbies, singlet, and a grubby stockman's hat is doing "the bump" with an Aboriginal man. They knock hips for a few minutes, embrace, and slap each other's palms in a drunken "high five." Then they return to their dates.

Another two men perform a roughneck go-go routine from atop bar stools, waving their arms over their heads like caged girls at the back of a TV dance show. One of them falls onto the floor, taking his beer with him. No one seems to notice.

Meanwhile, three men in black leather pants—Scrap Metal, apparently—are going through a seemingly endless succession of sound tests. "Testing. One, two, three. Testing." Pause, haul in two more speakers, haul out two others. Plug in three hundred more leads. "Testing, one, two, three. . . ." They go about their business like electricians, littering the entire bar with wires and speakers and discarded fuses. When the music finally starts up, close to midnight, it is almost indistinguishable from the feedback that the speakers have been coughing out for the past two hours.

I move on to Fannie's Disco, which is only a few blocks down the mall. Thankfully, it doesn't live up to its reputation for quickly drawn blades, at least not tonight. All I see is a blinding strobe light and a mass of dancers who are either blatantly underage or way overage. Two girls, who look not a day over ten, are teaching a gray-haired man in a safari suit how to dance. He holds their hands for a few minutes, then drifts off on his own, shuffling his feet from side to side and moving his arms backward and forward in a repetitive motion, as if opening and closing a pair of French doors. He appears very pleased with himself.

The girls, meanwhile, face each other and bounce up and down, as if they're jumping rope, which is what they probably do when they're not hanging around Darwin pubs at 1 A.M. on a Monday night.

The week may be just beginning in Darwin, but time is running out for me. I can barely lift my beer glass, much less try to jump rope or open French doors. I make my way to the toilet and splash cold water in my face. The urinal is full of broken glass. Time to move on.

The Diamond Club Casino is still doing a brisk business at 1:30. Apparently, the high rollers—fatcats from Singapore, Saudi sheiks, drug smugglers—are ushered into a back room for the privilege of tossing away their millions in private. I don't qualify. So I crowd in at a roulette table with the masses, clutching chips and watching a little metal ball spin around a giant, brightly colored wheel. I make short work of the roulette table; or, rather, it makes short work of me. By two o'clock the last of my loot has vanished beneath the croupier's ugly little chip sweeper.

There are still a few coins in my pocket so I hand them over to the one-armed bandits: obese poker machines with appetites to match and names like Winners Circle, Aristocrat, Dollar King, and all the other things people could be if they stopped giving all their money to pokies. I feed my last dollar coin to a monster named Dreams and listen to the rumble of money traveling through the pokie's gut on its way to the casino bank.

Busted. Finis. Done like a dinner. I look up at the man beside me, who seems to be having better luck. His face glows with the machine's reflected light, and his eyes roll like apples and oranges on the pay line. Better to lose quickly than to turn into a zombie.

I consider finding Doug for a free drink at the bar, but think better of it. I have no intention of seeing another dawn. The party's over and I'm glad to see it done.

No one else shares my fatigue. Outside, the street is still busy with drinkers and gamblers, stepping from cabs or stretch limousines. I seem to be the first person to call it a night—at 2 A.M.

Except for one couple, reclining on a wall by a fountain, back to back, fingers intertwined, murmuring to each other over their shoulders. They are well dressed but somewhat disheveled, as if, like me, they've just crapped out at the casino. His tie is undone, her high-heeled shoes are off and dangling loosely from one finger.

They murmur for a moment more, kiss once, and climb off the wall. Then he bends over and claps his hands. She jumps onto his back, as if mounting a horse, and they trot off down the street, going clippety-clop into the tropical night.

It is a pleasing, connubial image. In a few hours, when the morning breaks, I too will be headed home, no longer alone.

In a beautiful house
With a beautiful wife

She will come with me next time. We'll be restless together.

A taxi pulls out of the casino and I leap off the footpath to hail it. The last mile and a half of this odyssey will be done in style. Except that I don't have a penny left to pay the fare.

"Got room for a hitchhiker?" I ask, flashing the driver my best roadside smile.

"Get stuffed."

He roars off before I have a chance to return the compliment. My luck, it seems, is finally spent. I fall in behind the couple traveling piggyback and begin the long journey home on foot.

GLOSSARY

I haven't explained certain oddities of Australian word usage, such as pubs being called "hotels," or the fact that "tea" usually refers to dinner. Also, hitchhiking in Australia is done with the index finger of the left hand rather than with the thumb of the right.

In alphabetical order, with American equivalents:

Abo: short for "Aborigine," usually used in a derogatory manner.

aggro: unpleasantly aggressive.

Akubra: a brand of hat, stiff and broad-brimmed, worn in the outback.

Anzac Day: a day of remembrance. Anzacs were WWI soldiers from Australia and New Zealand, many of whom died on this day at Gallipoli.

Baygon: the brand name of a strong insect repellent.

bitumen: road surface, tar.

bonnet: the hood of a car.

boot: the trunk of a car.

bottle shop: a liquor store.

bowser: a pump.

bush balladeers: a group of poets who wrote about rural Australia.

bush tucker: berries, roots, and other foods gathered in the outback.

bustard: a turkey.

chuck a sickie: take a sick day.

cockie: slang phrase for "farmer."

corroboree: celebratory gathering of Aborigines.

cot: a colloquialism for "bed."

crook: sick, spoiled, broken.

dag end: the grubby bit of wool around a sheep's butt. *Daggy* is also used to describe an unfashionable person.

damper: a cakelike bread, traditionally cooked in campfire ash.

Digger: slang for "veteran," or, sometimes, simply an Australian.

dingo: a wild dog.

Do the Right Thing: advertising phrase used to discourage littering.

dole: welfare. *Dole-bludgers* are welfare cheats.

drover: a person who herds and moves stock, feeding it along the way.

dunny: slang for "outhouse" or "toilet."

egg nishner: rhyming slang for "air-conditioner."

emu: a flightless, ostrichlike bird.

fair dinkum: genuine, "tru-blu" Australian.

fibro: cheap housing material.

Fourex, or XXXX: a beer brand common in Queensland.

gins: short for "Aborigines"; derogatory.

geek: freak or hayseed.

goanna: an Australian lizard.

Grace Brothers: a chain of department stores.

greenies: slang for "environmentalists."

Hawke, Bob: Australian prime minister, from left-leaning Labor party.

Holden: a line of large Australian cars.

humpie: a lean-to or shack in Aboriginal communities.

Kelly, Ned: an antihero bankrobber of the nineteenth century, like Jesse James.

kip: a nap.

Kombi Van: a large recreational vehicle.

lolly: candy.

Lucky Country: a famous phrase, often used ironically, that refers to Australia's plentiful minerals and other assets.

Maori: the native people of New Zealand, Polynesian in appearance.

middy: a small glass of beer.

muesli: a breakfast cereal like granola.

mug: a fool or sucker.

mulga: a low shrub common in the outback.

new, old: light and dark types of beer.

ocker: an unsophisticated or redneck Australian; noun or adjective.

pad (as in cattle pad): cowpie or manure.

piss: slang for "beer" or "alcohol." *Pissed as a newt* means to be very drunk.

plonk: alcohol, usually cheap stuff.

pokies: slot machines.

quid: slang for "dollar" or "money."

ratbag: a ranter, dogmatist, proponent of unpopular causes.

road train: a long-distance truck, often with three trailers.

RSL: Returned Services League, a veterans organization.

sandpit: a sandbox. *Sandshoes* are sneakers.

schooner: a large glass of beer.

scrum: a huddlelike formation in rugby.

Sheep's back: a phrase denoting Australia's traditional dependence on wool, as in "Australia is a country that rides on the sheep's back."

sheila: a sexist word for a woman, like "bird" or "chick."

she'll be jake, or *she'll be right:* nothing to worry about. Stay cool.

shout, shouting: buy a round, usually beer, as in "It's my shout." Traditionally, if several people go to a pub together, each shouts a round.

singlet: a sleeveless T-shirt.

slog: a strenuous activity or walk, i.e., "a hard slog."

spinifex: spiky grass common in the outback.

station: a large grazing property or farm.

stinker: an extremely hot day.

stubbies: small bottles of beer; also, men's shorts.

subeditor: a copy editor.

swagman: a tramp or itinerant laborer. *Swag* is a bedroll.

ta: an abbreviation for "thank you."

TAB: the equivalent of off-track betting parlor.

Tasman, Abel: a Dutch explorer, the first to circumnavigate Australia, in 1644, and the man for whom Tasmania is named.

Tasmanian tiger: a doglike marsupial, believed to be extinct.

thongs: flip-flops.

tinnie: a can of beer.

Tobruk: a grueling WWII battle in North Africa.

Tooth's Old: a brand of dark beer.

Top End: the top of the Northern Territory, taking in Darwin.

troppo: short for "tropical." It usually refers to the lassitude of Australia's hot north, or to going crazy or becoming lazy from the heat, as in "go troppo."

tucker: food.

two-up: a gambling game in which two coins are flipped, popularized by WWI veterans. Now illegal, but widely played on Anzac Day.

ute: short for "utility truck," such as a pickup truck.

windscreen: a windshield.

wirly-wirly: small, tornadolike gusts of wind.

wogs: immigrants, usually Italian; derogatory.

wombat: large, low-slung marsupial, like a very fat, grounded koala.

wowser: a teetotaler, sometimes aggressively so.

yakka: work, as in "hard yakka."

yarn: a tale.

yonks: a long time.

ACKNOWLEDGMENTS

The author wishes to acknowledge the following sources from which material has been reprinted:

"Folsom Prison Blues" by Johnny Cash.

"The Biggest Disappointment" and "Camooweal" by Slim Dusty.

"The Waste Land" and "The Love Song of J. Alfred Prufrock" from *Collected Poems 1909–1962* by T. S. Eliot. Copyright © 1963, 1964 by T. S. Eliot.

"Take It Easy" by Jackson Browne and Glen Frey. Copyright © by Swallow Turn Music.

"Once in a Lifetime." Copyright © 1980, 1981 by Bleu Disque Music Co., Inc., Index Music Inc., and E. G. Music Ltd. All rights reserved.

Tony Horwitz was born in Washington, D.C., in 1958. He was educated at Brown University and Columbia University's Graduate School of Journalism, and has worked as a teacher, a labor organizer in Mississippi, and a newspaper reporter in America and Australia. He now writes on the Middle East from Cairo, where he lives with his wife, Geraldine Brooks.